no spirit/matter divide
spirit found in matter
p. 135
Stars fall into world.

An American Jungian

Marie-Louise von Franz, Honorary Patron

**Studies in Jungian Psychology
by Jungian Analysts**

Daryl Sharp, General Editor

An American Jungian

In Honor of
Edward F. Edinger

Edited by George R. Elder and Dianne D. Cordic

Library and Archives Canada Cataloguing in Publication

An American Jungian: in honor of Edward F. Edinger/
    Edited by George R. Elder and Dianne D. Cordic.

(Studies in Jungian psychology by Jungian analysts; 125)

Includes bibliographical references and index.

ISBN 978-1-894574-26-6

1. Edinger, Edward F. (Edward Ferdinand), 1922-1998.
2. Jungian psychology. 3. Psychoanalysis.
I. Edinger, Edward F. (Edward Ferdinand), 1922-1998.
II. Cordic, Dianne D., 1933-. III. Elder, George R., 1942-
IV. Series: Studies in Jungian psychology by Jungian analysts; 125.

```
BF109.E35A43 2009     150.19'54     C2009-901102-6
```

INNER CITY BOOKS
Box 1271, Station Q, Toronto, ON M4T 2P4, Canada.
Telephone (416) 927-0355 / Fax (416) 924-1814

Toll-free (Canada and U.S.): Tel. 1-888-927-0355 / Fax 1-888-924-1814

Web site: www.innercitybooks.net / E-mail: booksales@innercitybooks.net

Honorary Patron: Marie-Louise von Franz.
Publisher and General Editor: Daryl Sharp.
Senior Editor: Victoria B. Cowan.
Office Manager: Scott Milligen.

INNER CITY BOOKS was founded in 1980 to promote the
understanding and practical application of the work of C.G. Jung.

Cover: Edward F. Edinger (1985).

Index by George R. Elder.

Printed and bound in Canada by Thistle Printing Company Ltd.

CONTENTS

VIII. MORE TRIBUTES 261

See final pages for descriptions of other Inner City titles

List of Illustrations

Editors' Preface

This volume commemorates the life and work of the Jungian analyst Edward F. Edinger. At his death just over ten years ago, he was widely considered the "dean" of Analytical psychology in the United States, a status of high regard. It was bequeathed to him, one might say, by Esther Harding—Edinger's own analyst—who worked with Jung and whom he called, upon her death, the dean of American Jungian analysts. He had also written upon the death of Marie-Louise von Franz, the well-known Swiss analyst, that she was "a true spiritual daughter of Jung." She died exactly five months before Dr. Edinger, and it seemed to many of us that we had just lost a "true spiritual son" of Jung—a sibling of equal psychological footing. The pages that follow, the editors hope, will help to justify this lineage and estimation since most of the words are Edinger's own. It is also true—as Edinger taught—that a person's greatest achievement is by nature an invisible one, a level of consciousness that moves civilization ahead. In that regard, Edward Edinger's achievement is inestimable.

Nearly all the contents of this book have been published before, but none of it has been readily available. The essays and interviews have existed—one is tempted to say, languished—in journals, in newsletters, or in taped form. Now they are available to everyone; and nothing that one can already find in a book by Edinger has been duplicated here. Given the nature of a collection, however, the reader will hear certain themes repeated; but it is our hope this will not be taken as a weakness so much as a clue to what is really important. Toward the end of this book, there are items of a more personal kind befitting a commemoration.

PART I contains, first of all, a bibliography of Edward Edinger's books. They have been organized somewhat artificially into categories, but the arrangement should make it easier to see where the author's interests lay and also easier for the reader to find just what might interest him or her. Although a bibliography usually includes a writer's independent essays, we have refrained from listing these dozens of journal entries since nearly all of them are now incorporated into book-length titles. We have indicated, however, what electronic materials are currently available to the public.

It seems fitting to include, as well, a bibliographical essay by Robin Robertson written shortly after Edinger's death. Although the essay could not cover all of the author's works—some of which were published posthumously—its assessment provides a fitting introduction to Dr. Edinger's oeuvre.

The editors have dispensed with the usual biographical chronology since the main turning points in Edinger's personal life are mentioned at several points in the book. Some of them are described by Edinger himself, and one comes away with a feeling and not just a date and a place. Still, the reader might feel the lack of something more visible, with a bit more flesh, and so there are several photographs to ponder.

PART II features a long interview in three parts entitled, "An American Jungian"—whence the title of this commemorative volume. The interview was conducted in 1990 by the late Jungian analyst Lawrence W. Jaffe who had already written of Edinger's influence. Ranging over many topics, the conversation provides a sense of "Ed" the person. Indeed, the tapes have sold rather well among the Jungian community; and there have been several showings in a public setting. But this conversation has not been available in written form, except for a portion published in 1991 in the journal, *Psychological Perspectives.* It has been edited in full and printed here for the first time.

The title of this interview and this book, "An American Jungian," was suggested by a child. When Lawrence Jaffe mentioned to his son that he was about to ask some questions of an important Jungian analyst living in Los Angeles, the child pranced about shouting, "An American, an American!" It seems he thought all Jungians of note lived in Europe.

PART III is entitled "Jung Distilled" since it opens with Edinger's enduring article, "An Outline of Analytical Psychology." He wrote this terse and lucid piece for the first issue of the journal *Quadrant* in 1968. Ed was pleased with the "Outline" and its position in the journal's history because it really says all that one needs to say to be "Jungian." To put it differently, the intellect can think of much, much more to write about—and others, including Edinger, have done so. But if the reader chews on each tight sentence and absorbs the meaning—a process that takes time and insight—then one's psychological belly will be filled. The essay has been available until now only in pamphlet form as a reprint from the journal *Quadrant*. We have left it virtually unedited with its bite-sized paragraphs that Dr. Edinger apparently intended to aid assimilation.

The following two early and relatively obscure essays were intended for the psychiatric community. Edinger was, after all, a medically trained psychiatrist; and he thought he was obliged—as he himself was developing psychologically—to speak to that group about the Jungian point of view. He was not comfortable doing so. The reader may be surprised by the passive voice in these essays, the frequency of "perhaps," and the use of the lower case rather than capitals in naming archetypes—all of which would disappear in Edinger's mature style. Following one of his lectures at this period in his life, a physician in the audience complained, "You speak as if the symbol were alive!" Edinger answered—"It is!"—but knew, then, that he was not authentically obliged to the medical world.

PART IV includes nine pieces on persons the editors conceive to be Dr. Edinger's "Soul Mates", that is, persons with whom he had a particular psychological rapport:

1) A discussion of Paracelsus whom Edinger recognized as "one of the great-souled ones of history" and as someone important to Jung. Like Paracelsus, Edinger was himself something of an "alchemist," the meaning of which will become clear in the personal materials at the end of this volume. We have included here Maurice Krasnow's introduction to the lecture, "Paracelsus," presented in New York City, 1994.

2) A study of Ralph Waldo Emerson whose introverted—and religious—temperament was so much akin to that of Edward Edinger. In a sense, they were both "American Jungians," and we are especially pleased to make this important essay readily accessible.

3) Edinger's review of James Jarrett's edition, in two volumes, of Jung's seminar on Nietzsche's *Zarathustra*. Edinger's kinship here is

with Nietzsche as well as with Jung who, Edinger explains, could not have performed his life's task if Nietzsche had not preceded him. Edinger calls Nietzsche "the first depth psychologist" and evaluates Jung's seminar accordingly.

4) A review of Jung's *Psychology and Alchemy*, volume 12 in the *Collected Works*.

5) A review of the publication of Jung's *Mysterium Coniunctionis*, volume 14 in the *Collected Works*.

6) A review of Marie-Louise von Franz's biography, *C. G. Jung: His Myth in Our Time*. Here we are privy to Edinger's deep regard for both von Franz and Jung.

7) Memorial remarks upon the death of Eleanor Bertine who was Dr. Edinger's training analyst. She authored *Human Relationships* (1958), subsequently re-edited and published as *Close Relationships: Family, Friendship, Marriage* (Toronto: Inner City Books, 1992). This is an important work for which Edinger provided a foreword.

8) Memorial remarks upon the death of M. Esther Harding, Edinger's personal analyst and author of many works on Jungian psychology.

9) And, finally, thoughts upon the death of Marie-Louise von Franz.

PART V contains essays on the life of the psyche from two different angles, "The Individual and Society." The first essay is entitled "Individuation: A Myth for Modern Man" delivered initially as a lecture in San Diego in 1988. And, then, as his last public lecture—delivered in New York in 1995—Edinger helps us think through "The Question of a Jungian Community." He spoke at the time to a community of Jungians beginning to fracture, and what he concludes here should be required reading by all groups who consider themselves Jungian in some way. Although not entirely obvious, Edinger is feeling his way toward defining a genuine Jungian training organization: it should be at once "functional" (training analysts) and "sacred" (true to its individual members' experience of the psyche's numinous depths).

PART VI. Although this book contains an extended interview already as PART II, this section includes two more interviews that are shorter and have already been published in written form. They bear the same virtues as interviews with Jung: more personal, colloquial, somewhat outspoken, with nuggets of wisdom scattered about. The reader will find Edinger's view of the political scene, as early as 1983, precocious and not a little disturbing.

PART VII is very personal. It is a record of the Memorial Service on the occasion of Ed's death. On July 26, 1998, a group of invited guests gathered to speak of this man. And with his coffin present, we listened to the music and the poetry that he himself had requested. We were even surprised by a short tape of his "last words" that included gratitude for our being there. Reading the heartfelt comments from friends and family in this section helps to put "flesh" on Edward Edinger if one did not know him personally. But, then, he would say that knowing him psychologically is more important.

PART VIII continues these tributes to Dr. Edinger of a more personal nature. They were written by those who knew him and those who did not, by analysts and others, yet all with the same sense that this man was rare. Several of these reflections appeared in the journal *Harvest*, published by the C.G. Jung Club of London. They open with acknowledgment that Edward Edinger was not well known in Europe, a regrettable fact not likely to persist as the world becomes increasingly in need of wisdom. Indeed, we hope this book may help in that regard.

Perhaps a note on this book's style is appropriate. The editors have not always reproduced exactly what has been published. Because the sources are many and the styles varied, we have had to make minor changes for consistency: regularizing punctuation, capitalization, and format. We have also made corrections but apologize in advance for any errors that remain.

We wish to express our heartfelt gratitude to Daryl Sharp, editor and publisher of Inner City Books, for accepting this work enthusiastically and for seeing to its speedy publication. Our book is no exception, however, since Daryl's dedication to Jungian wisdom extends now to well over a hundred titles. We like to think that Dr. Edinger himself is grateful for this latest offering from the "Inner City."

The Editors

George R. Elder, Ph.D., is a Jungian analyst residing in Ocean Ridge, Florida. He has written *The Body: An Encyclopedia of Archetypal Symbolism*, in collaboration with ARAS (The Archive for Research in Archetypal Symbolism) and edited Dr. Edinger's *Archetype of the Apocalypse*.
.

Dianne D. Cordic is a Jungian analyst practicing in Santa Monica, California. She is a founding member of the C. G. Jung Study Center of Southern California.

Publisher's Note

I am extremely grateful to George Elder and Dianne Cordic for gathering this material together from disparate sources and offering it to me to publish. It is a long-overdue tribute to a great man, whose work, together with that of Marie-Louise von Franz, has constituted the bedrock of my publishing enterprise for thirty years.

Edward F. Edinger was such a significant presence in the worldwide Jungian community that this volume—although it reveals his essence—can only begin to assess his value as an interpreter of Jung's work and his dedication to the importance of Analytical psychology. His many contributions to the psychological well-being of individuals and the collective—only exceeded by his personal modesty—will resonate for many years.

We all miss him, but he is with us as we rejoice in these reminders of his worth.

Daryl Sharp
Toronto, 2009

Figure 1. Edinger in Garden (1985).

PART I

INTRODUCTION

BIBLIOGRAPHY OF BOOKS AND ELECTRONIC MEDIA

PSYCHOTHERAPY

Ego and Archetype: Individuation and the Religious Function of the Psyche. New York: G. P. Putnam's Sons for the C. G. Jung Foundation for Analytical Psychology, 1972.

The Living Psyche: A Jungian Analysis in Pictures. Wilmette: Chiron Publications, 1990.

Science of the Soul: A Jungian Perspective. Ed. Daryl Sharp and J. Gary Sparks. Toronto: Inner City Books, 2002.

JUNG'S WORK

Transformation of Libido: A Seminar on C.G. Jung's "Symbols of Transformation." Ed. Dianne D. Cordic. Los Angeles: C. G. Jung Bookstore of Los Angeles, 1994.

Transformation of the God-Image: An Elucidation of Jung's "Answer to Job." Ed. Lawrence W. Jaffe. Toronto: Inner City Books, 1992.

The Aion Lectures: Exploring the Self in C.G. Jung's "Aion." Ed. Deborah A. Wesley. Toronto: Inner City Books, 1996.

The Mysterium Lectures: A Journey through C.G. Jung's "Mysterium Coniunctionis." Ed. Joan Dexter Blackmer. Toronto: Inner City Books, 1995.

The Mystery of the Coniunctio: Alchemical Image of Individuation. Ed. Joan Dexter Blackmer. Toronto: Inner City Books, 1994.

Anatomy of the Psyche: Alchemical Symbolism in Psychotherapy. La Salle, IL: Open Court, 1985.

16

The New God-Image: A Study of Jung's Key Letters Concerning the Evolution of the Western God-Image. Ed. Dianne D. Cordic and Charles Yates. Wilmette, IL: Chiron Publications, 1996.

The Creation of Consciousness: Jung's Myth for Modern Man. Toronto: Inner City Books, 1984.

THE ANCIENT WORLD

The Eternal Drama: The Inner Meaning of Greek Mythology. Ed. Deborah A. Wesley. Boston: Shambhala, 1994.

The Psyche in Antiquity. Book One: Early Greek Philosophy, from Thales to Plotinus. Ed. Deborah A. Wesley. Toronto: Inner City Books, 1999.

_____. *Book Two: Gnosticism and Early Christianity.* Ed. Deborah A. Wesley. Toronto: Inner City Books, 1999.

THE BIBLE

The Bible and the Psyche: Individuation Symbolism in the Old Testament. Toronto: Inner City Books, 1986.

Ego and Self: The Old Testament Prophets, from Isaiah to Malachi. Ed. J. Gary Sparks. Toronto: Inner City Books, 2000.

The Sacred Psyche: A Psychological Approach to the Psalms. Ed. Joan Dexter Blackmer. Toronto: Inner City Books, 2004.

Encounter with the Self: A Jungian Commentary on William Blake's "Illustrations of the Book of Job." Toronto: Inner City Books, 1986.

The Christian Archetype: A Jungian Commentary on the Life of Christ. Toronto: Inner City Books, 1987.

Archetype of the Apocalypse: A Jungian Study of the Book of Revelation. Ed. George R. Elder. Chicago: Open Court, 1999. (The paperback has a different subtitle: "Divine Vengeance, Terrorism, and the End of the World.")

DRAMA AND LITERATURE

The Psyche on Stage: Individuation Motifs In Shakespeare and Sophocles. Ed. Sheila Dickman Zarrow. Toronto: Inner City Books, 2001.

Goethe's "Faust": Notes for a Jungian Commentary. Toronto: Inner City Books, 1990.

Melville's "Moby-Dick": An American Nekyia. New York: New Directions, 1978. (Reprinted with index, Toronto: Inner City Books, 1995.)

ELECTRONIC MEDIA

Currently, the following lectures are available on CDs from the C. G. Jung Bookstore of the C. G. Jung Institute of Los Angeles (www.junginla.org/bookstore):

"Aion"

"Apocalypse Archetype"

"Commentary on Jung's *Answer to Job*"

"Gnosticism and Early Christianity"

"Greek Philosophers"

"Mysterium Coniunctionis"

"The New God-Image"

"A Psychological Approach to the Old Testament"

A GUIDE TO THE WRITINGS OF EDWARD F. EDINGER
Robin Robertson[1]

Too soon after the death of Marie-Louise von Franz, Jungian psychology has lost a second great creative force: Edward F. Edinger. Both have left behind rich collections of their writings and lectures to which we can still turn for their wisdom. As I did in discussing von Franz's work, I am restricting myself to Edinger's published books.[2] Again, as with von Franz, a number of Edinger's books have been transcribed from lectures or assembled from previously published articles.

---

[1] Robin Robertson, Ph.D., is a Jungian-oriented clinical psychologist in and professor in Alhambra, California. This essay first appeared in *Psychological Perspectives* 39 (Summer 1999), pp. 47ff.—Eds.

[2] See Robin Robertson, "A Guide to the Writings of Marie-Louise von Franz," *Psychological Perspectives* 38 (Winter 1998-1999), pp.70ff.

Individuation and a New Image of God

I'm going to discuss Edinger's books in chronological order, using the dates of the original lectures or articles in the case of the compiled books. But occasionally I'll take a jump in time, when one book seems to demand mention of another. I want to begin with one of his later books, the *New God-Image: A Study of Jung's Key Letters* (Chiron, 1996), which was compiled from lectures given at the C. G. Jung Institute of Los Angeles in the fall of 1991.

Edinger begins this book with a sentence that could be seen as a summary of his oeuvre: "The history of Western man can be viewed as a history of its God-images, the primary formulations of how mankind orients itself to the basic questions of life, its mysteries" (xiii). Later in the same paragraph, he says that "we are right on the verge of witnessing the birth of a new God-image as a result of Jung's work." What does Edinger (and Jung) mean by "God-image"? Here is a selection of Edinger's thoughts from the same book (xivf):

> The God-image is virtually a synonym for the Self in Jungian terms. The term God-image should not be confused with the term *God*.

> More specifically, the term God-image is synonymous with a particular aspect of the Self—what would be called the collective Self. In other words, it is a transpersonal center shared by a whole body of humanity. . . . we can understand all manifestations of the God-image as descriptive stages of humanity's experience of the autonomous aspect of the psyche.

Edinger identifies six major stages in the evolution of the Western God-image: animism, matriarchy, hierarchical polytheism, tribal monotheism, universal monotheism, and individuation. If Edinger is correct, then the recognition and articulation of the emergence of a new God-image through the process of individuation is, indeed, not only the most significant contribution of Jungian psychology but marks the next evolutionary stage of human consciousness. This idea is examined and amplified in one way or another throughout Edinger's work.

The Ego-Self Relationship

His first and perhaps greatest book, *Ego and Archetype: Individuation and the Religious Function of the Psyche* (Shambhala, 1992), was originally published in 1972. It begins with a paraphrase by Jung of a statement by Ignatius Loyola:

> Man's consciousness was created to the end that it may (1) recognize its descent from a higher unity; (2) pay due and careful regard to this source; (3) execute its commands intelligently and responsibly and (4) thereby afford the psyche as a whole the optimum degree of life and development. (xv)

One could not better define the essence of Edinger's view of Jungian psychology. *Ego and Archetype* is a rich and complex work that has often offered me, and I'm sure others, comfort from the suffering which is everyone's companion on the journey of individuation. Suffering becomes holy when it has a purpose. In Edinger's words, "It is impossible for the ego to experience the Self as something separate as long as the ego is unconsciously identified with the Self. This explains the need for the alienation experience as a prelude to the religious experience." (52)

In *Ego and Archetype*, Edinger first introduced his famed diagram of the ego-Self axis (Figure 2, opposite), which depicts the stages of development of the individuated ego. The first stage pictured is described this way: "In the early stages of psychological development, God is hidden—in the cleverest hiding place of all—in identification with oneself, one's own ego." (102)

During the following stages, the ego gradually emerges from its identification with the Self yet keeps the connection intact. This is largely done through the removal of projections in our relationships with the people and things of the outer world. "We must exclude all merely apparent relationship which is actually based on projection and unconscious identification." (170) At the endpoint of this process:

> But to the extent that we are related to our individuality as a whole and its essence, we come into objective and compassionate relation to others. To put it concisely, we might say that the ego is windowless, but the Self is a window on other worlds of being.

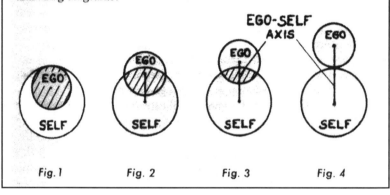

The process of alternation between ego-Self union and ego-Self separation seems to occur repeatedly throughout the life of the individual both in childhood and in maturity. Indeed, this cyclic (or better, spiral) formula seems to express the basic process of psychological development from birth to death.

According to this view the relation between the ego and Self at different stages of development could be represented by the following diagrams:

Figure 2. The Ego-Self Relationship
(adapted from Edinger, *Ego and Archetype,* figs. 1-4).

The Great White Whale

Melville's Moby-Dick: An American Nekyia (Inner City, 1995), Edinger's next book, was originally published by New Directions in 1978.

This slight volume, which combines two of my least favorite genres—a psychobiographical study of Melville with a psychological study of literature (Melville's masterpiece *Moby-Dick*)—is, nevertheless, a small masterpiece. Jung suggested the Greek word *nekyia* for the journey into the unconscious. Edinger recognized that "Melville was writing out of the universal, archetypal theme of the night sea journey, or descent into the underworld" (27). As Edinger carefully takes us through the psychological significance of both Ishmael's voyage with Ahab and its parallels in Melville's life, great literature for once is not reduced to simpleminded pathology, as is usual in such studies.

Moby-Dick opens with "Call me Ishmael," which ranks with Hamlet's "to be or not to be" as the greatest overt expression of alienation. It closes with Ishmael floating on Queequeg's coffin-lifebuoy: "both the container of death and the womb of rebirth." Perhaps after the grand scale of *Ego and Archetype*, Edinger turned to a study of literature because only literature can capture the great and eternal themes within the lives of individuals like you and me—and Ishmael.

Edinger wrote only one other psychological study of literature: *Goethe's Faust: Notes for a Jungian Commentary* (Inner City, 1990). All of the themes we encounter in *Moby-Dick* are also in *Faust*; the only exception is the absence of an anima figure in *Moby-Dick*, where hatred serves instead to turn the anima fascination on its head. Edinger himself said that "*Moby-Dick* could be called the American *Faust*." The basic themes that run throughout *Faust* are: descent to the underworld (*nekyia*); love in all its aspects (libido); the opposites; the quaternity; and the *coniunctio*. These are also the central motifs of both the process of individuation—which runs through all Edinger's works—and alchemy, which Edinger will study more directly in later books.

The Gods Within

The Eternal Drama: The Inner Meaning of Greek Mythology (Shambhala, 1994) was assembled from two series of lectures Edinger gave in the 1970s, one in New York City and one in California. This is an extended examination of the third stage of development of the God-image: "hierarchical polytheism." The important thing to remember is that each of the stages is still alive inside the psyche. We have to be equally able to connect to the most primitive as well as the most advanced. Edinger notes that, "As we consider the basic images of Greek mythology, we should ask what the particular images could mean in our own individual lives." If we make an attempt to understand how these myths relate to our own lives, "we will start to build a personal connection to the myth;

particular myths, at least, will be living themselves out in one's own life. Asking these questions will be rewarded every now and then by a shock of recognition that says: 'This is my myth. This is myself I am seeing here' " (3).

To mention a single example, consider the myth of Dionysus who, while playing with a mirror soon after being born, was torn apart and devoured by the Titans. But his heart survived; and from it, Dionysus was reborn. This man of the heart was beloved by women, and he happily led them in ecstatic celebrations. The fifth-century Neoplatonist philosopher Proclus "expressed the idea that Dionysus represented original unity, which sees its image in the mirror of matter, and out of the desire to be incarnated . . . submits itself to multiplicity, to being broken up into specific parts in time and space." (146) Artists are especially prone to the danger of losing their identity in the process of projecting themselves into their creations. Edinger warns:

> So people who are intoxicated by some creative effort should be warned that the only safe creativity is that which makes one feel uncomfortable. If one feels burdened down with every sentence one writes or every brush stroke comes with an effort, then one is safe and not in danger of falling, one is already down. But otherwise, to identify with Dionysus has the opposite danger, and Nietzsche is an appalling example of this. (149)

Our Relationship to God

Edinger continued his examination of the stages of development of the God-image in a series of lectures in the late 1970s and early 1980s that were collected in *The Creation of Consciousness: Jung's Myth for Modern Man* (Inner City, 1984). In "The New Myth" he develops a theme which, for many of us readers, is more problematic: the explicit connection between Jung's groundbreaking new ideas and Jung's personal life. "Jung is an epochal man. I mean by this a man whose life inaugurates a new age in cultural history." (12)

It is quite possible to accept that Jung was the first to realize that "the essential new idea is that *the purpose of human life is the creation of consciousness*" (17)—without wholly accepting Jung's life as an exemplar of the individuated life. In another essay from this collection, "Depth

Psychology as the New Dispensation: Reflections on Jung's *Answer to Job*," Edinger continues an examination he began in *Ego and Archetype*, which he extends in more detail in two later books: *Encounter with the Self: A Jungian Commentary on William Blake's "Illustrations of the Book of Job"* (Inner City, 1986), and *Transformation of the God-Image: An Elucidation of Jung's "Answer to Job"* (Inner City, 1992). The latter is a transcription of lectures given at the C. G. Jung Institute of Los Angeles in the fall of 1989. Ideally, all three should be studied together, along with Jung's *Answer to Job* and the actual Book of Job from the Bible. I'll move back and forth between Edinger's three books in the discussion that follows.

In *Transformation of the God-Image*, Edinger explains how Jung came to write *Answer to Job*:

> Jung's letters give us a picture of how he came to write *Answer to Job* in the spring of 1951. It wasn't the result of a rational decision. He was seventy-five years old and in the midst of a febrile illness. It was virtually dictated to him from the unconscious and as soon as it was completed, the illness was over. (17)

Edinger adds that "Esther Harding told me that during his illness a figure sat on his bedpost and dictated *Answer to Job* to him." He tells us Jung's own estimate of the work: "In his old age, Jung remarked that he wished he could rewrite all of his books except this one. With this book he was completely satisfied," (*Creation of Consciousness*, 60)

As *Answer to Job* was significant for Jung, Blake's study of Job's story in twenty-one pictures was his last completed major work. Edinger tells us: "Blake's rendering of the Job Story shows us the effect of this archetypal image on the unconscious of a modern, or almost modern man. . . . In these pictures the objective psyche speaks directly to us" (12). Let us briefly recall the story of Job in relation to Blake's first few pictures. Job was God's most beloved servant, a man of prosperity and contentment. In Blake's first picture, Job and his family "are gathered together under the tree of life in a state of prayer." (17) At their feet sleep their animals, while their musical instruments hang from the tree. Edinger sharply notes that "both instinctual and spiritual cultural energies are not functioning." In Blake's second picture, Satan appears in a "stream of fire" to tempt God. Edinger notes that "Satan represents the return of banished energy and desire." (20f) Satan argues that Job would not love God so much if things were less rosy for him in his life. That is all it takes for Yahweh to subject Job to a series of increasing deprivations, including the destruction of his children and their families. In Blake's picture, Job and his family are totally engulfed by Satan's fiery energy. "Psychologically, this might correspond to the onset of bad dreams and neurotic symptoms in an individual." (23)

Job's situation matches that experienced by any of us when something terrible happens in life. We ask ourselves: "Why did this happen to me? Why did God permit this terrible thing to happen?" Edinger presents five different ways to answer that question in *Transformation of the God-Image* (40f):

1. "God has punished me for my sins." [Job's friends and neighbors try to force this conclusion on him, but he won't accept it.]

2. "I'm the victim of Satan, the Evil one, who is responsible." [Job refuses to believe that God would allow Satan to persecute him, since he has always honored God and obeys his will.]

3. "This catastrophe is actually good for me in some higher way I can't understand."

4. "God doesn't exist, or if he does exist, he doesn't concern himself with man."

5. "God is an antinomy who isn't conscious of what he is doing." [That's Job's reaction, as interpreted by Jung.]

At any time earlier in the history of consciousness as reflected in the Bible, someone in Job's position would have accepted either conclusions 1 or 2; 3 and 4 are modern alternatives that would never have occurred to Job or his predecessors. Instead, Job turns to God himself for relief from God, thus inaugurating a new stage of consciousness:

Since Job did not fall victim to the proposition that all good is from God and all bad from man, he was able to *see* God and recognize his behavior to be "of an unconscious being who cannot be judged morally. Yahweh is a *phenomenon* and, as Job says, 'not a man.' " (*Creation of*

Consciousness, 69)

Edinger relates Job's situation directly to Jung's life: "Jung was appalled by the way Yahweh treated Job, just as he must have been appalled at the torture which he, Jung, had to endure in his encounter with the unconscious." (ibid.) Jung was thus forced to the surprising but eminently logical conclusion that the Book of Job records the beginning of a change in the God-image, in which an unconscious Yahweh, the stern patriarch of the Old Testament, is forced to turn to humanity, in the person of Job, in order to advance his own consciousness. This is the first step that leads ineluctably toward God's incarnation in Christ. As Jung says, "Yahweh must become man precisely because he has done man a wrong."

Alchemical Symbolism in the Psyche

Throughout the late 1970s and 1980s, Edinger wrote a series of seminal articles on seven alchemical processes; the articles were later collected into a single volume, *Anatomy of the Psyche: Alchemical Symbolism in Psychotherapy* (Open Court, 1985). If *Ego and Archetype* isn't Edinger's greatest single volume, then *Anatomy of the Psyche* is. It is hard to imagine anyone working either with one's own dreams or the dreams of a patient who would not find this an invaluable reference. How can something as arcane as alchemy be useful in dealing with the psychology of the unconscious? Here is Edinger's answer:

> Each of these operations is found to be the center of an elaborate symbol system. These central symbols of transformation make up the major content of all culture-products. They provide basic categories by which to understand the life of the psyche, and they illustrate almost the full range of experiences that constitute individuation. (15)

Edinger devotes a chapter to each operation and is kind enough to include with each operation "a chart indicating the major symbolic connections that cluster around the core image. The charts are an important part of my method because I want to emphasize the structural nature of each symbol system." (ibid.)

These charts are unique study tools for anyone interested in the psyche. Time and again, I've taken an element of a dream, looked it up in the index of *Anatomy of the Psyche*, then read what Edinger had to say about it in the context of the alchemical process or processes in which it figures. Then, I look it up in the appropriate chart or charts [e.g., See Figure 3, next page]. By doing so, I can usually define not only what alchemical—hence, what psychological—stage is being addressed, but what will come next. This is because you can follow the progression of symbols between alchemical operations. This is as close to a true "dream book" as it is possible to have, given the complexity of the psyche. If readers new to Edinger read only this book, they will have gained a great deal of insight into the psyche.

Throughout the 1980s, Edinger gave several series of lectures on Jung's alchemical works. These were collected into three books:

The Mystery of the Coniunctio: Alchemical Image of Individuation (Inner City, 1994), which included an "Introduction to Jung's Mysterium Coniunctionis" and "A Psychological Interpretation of the *Rosarium* Pictures," which Jung drew on in writing "The Psychology of the Transference."

The Mysterium Lectures: A Journey Through C. G. Jung's "Mysterium Coniunctionis" (Inner City, 1995), which was a massive line-by-line—or, better, image-by-image—study of Mysterium Coniunctionis.

The Aion Lectures: Exploring the Self in C. G. Jung's "Aion" (Inner City, 1996), which similarly explicated *Aion*, which many consider Jung's most complex work, line-by-line and image-by-image.

Each of these three works is intended to serve as a useful companion volume for someone who is reading Jung's original work at the same time. Edinger's emphasis is on opening up this difficult material for his listeners (now his readers) by concentrating on the alchemical images through which Jung tells his tale. Many readers may find this an unfamiliar way to approach a complex book.

Discussing *Mysterium* (though it is equally applicable to all three volumes), he says, "To learn about these uniformities of imagery we have to take images seriously, and that goes against a major individual and collective predisposition to the contrary." (19f)

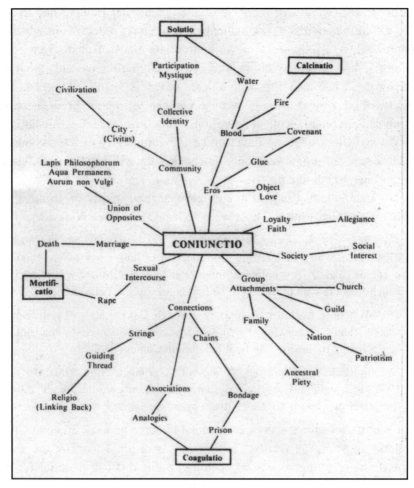

Figure 3. Cluster Chart of the Coniunctio.

However, Edinger properly insists that this is the only way to address this material and argues that "this book can't be read the way one reads an ordinary book—it has to be worked on the way one works on a dream." (18)

Miscellaneous Volumes

The Living Psyche: A Jungian Analysis in Pictures (Chiron, 1990) is "an attempt to demonstrate graphically the reality of the living psyche. It is based on a series of 104 paintings done over a period of five years during the course of a Jungian analysis which lasted twice that long." (xiii)

As such, it is in some ways a comparable effort to what Jung did with his longitudinal study of Wolfgang Pauli's dreams in *Psychology and Alchemy*. Each of the 104 paintings is included (unfortunately, only in black and white, except for the last two), together with a short description by the analysand and a short comment by Edinger. Throughout, "the personal aspects have been treated only very briefly . . . [because of Edinger's] conviction in any case that the archetypal aspect of the material is of far greater general interest."

One of Edinger's last published volumes was another compilation of lectures: *Transformation of Libido: A Seminar on Jung's Symbols of Transformation* (C. G. Jung Bookstore of Los Angeles, 1994). In this small, aptly-named volume, Edinger does indeed trace the various stages of transformation through which libido passes from "attention, to interest, to desire, to attachment, to enthusiasm, to compulsion, to worship." (21) He includes several more of his wonderful cluster diagrams similar to those in *Anatomy of the Psyche* (and, before that, in *Ego and Archetype* with "the Blood of Christ")—this time on the themes of sun, fire, city and tree.

The Bible and the Psyche

In *The Bible and the Psyche: Individuation Symbolism in the Old Testament* (Inner City, 1986), Edinger further develops the idea of the evolution of the God-image as presented in the Bible:

The Old Testament documents a sustained dialogue between God and man as it is expressed in the sacred history of Israel. It presents us with an exceedingly rich compendium of images representing encounters with the *numinosum* [the mysterious sacred] These are best understood psychologically as pictures of the encounter between the ego and the Self, which is the major feature of individuation. (12)

The first seventeen books of the Old Testament, from Genesis to Esther, are "the historical books in which Yahweh deals with Israel, collectively as a nation." The last seventeen, from Isaiah to Malachi, are "the prophetic books, each named after a great individual who had a personal encounter with Yahweh and was fated to be an individual carrier of God-consciousness." (12f) "In the middle are the poetical-wisdom books, with Job at their head. Job is the pivot of the Old Testament story. This is why Jung focused his Bible commentary on Job."

In *The Christian Archetype: A Jungian Commentary on the Life of Christ* (Inner City, 1987), this evolution of the God-image takes its next natural step:

> The life of Christ, understood psychologically, represents the vicissitudes of the Self as it undergoes incarnation in an individual ego and of the ego as it participates in the divine drama. In other words the life of Christ represents the process of individuation (15)

Edinger traces Christ's life through "the incarnation cycle" as an example of the individuation process, identifying a series of twelve stages that wrap back on themselves: the Annunciation, the Nativity, and Flight into Egypt, Christ's Baptism, his Triumphal Entry into Jerusalem, the Last Supper, his bitter suffering in the Garden of Gethsemane, his Arrest and Trial, Flagellation and Mocking, culminating in the Crucifixion, Lamentation and Entombment, and—finally—the Resurrection and Ascension. A thirteenth stage, Pentecost, forms a new "Annunciation." And the cycle begins again, this time with the Church as the "Body of Christ." If, however, the Church is destined to complete its incarnation cycle some time before the "last day," then we can expect the cycle to be circled once again, perhaps this time with the individual as the vessel of the Holy Spirit. This brings us to Jung's idea of continuing incarnation. (129)

Edinger then quotes Jung:

Thus man is received and integrated into the divine drama. He seems destined to play a decisive part in it; that is why he must receive the Holy Spirit. . . The Spirit is destined to be incarnate in man or to choose him as a transitory dwelling-place. . . That is why he must not be identified with Christ. We cannot receive the Holy Spirit unless we have accepted our own individual life as Christ accepted his. (129f)

At this numinous point, I would like to conclude this review of Edinger's books with a quotation from the book with which I began, *The New God-Image*:

Jungian psychology is a redemptive power. Not only did Jung redeem alchemy, he also redeemed ancient philosophy, mythology and all of the more primitive aspects of existence by virtue of demonstrating that they are manifestations of the psyche—not just the past psyche, but the permanent, eternal, ever-living psyche that we can be in touch with right now. For me Jung's work has been a vast redemptive process. (45)

For many readers, Edinger's work may itself serve as a redemptive process . . . .[3]

---

[3] This essay concludes with a paragraph anticipating future volumes which have since been published.—Eds.

Figure 4. Edward F. Edinger (1994).

PART II

AN AMERICAN JUNGIAN

Edward F. Edinger in Conversation
with Lawrence W. Jaffe[4]

1. Introduction

This interview is being conducted in the West Los Angeles home of the internationally known Jungian analyst, Edward F. Edinger, and his partner, Dianne Cordic, who is also a Jungian analyst. I am Lawrence Jaffe, a Jungian analyst from Berkeley, California, and the author of a book on Jung's and Edinger's work called, "Liberating the Heart: Spirituality and Jungian Psychology."[5]

Dr. Edinger has for a generation been in the forefront of those who have carried forward the work of the great Swiss psychiatrist, Carl Gustav Jung. Dr. Edinger received his medical degree from Yale University in 1946. He is a former supervising psychiatrist at Rockland State Hospital in Orangeburg, New York; he is also a founding member of the C. G. Jung Foundation of New York and the C. G. Jung Institute of New York. He served as president of the New York Institute from 1968 to 1979, when he was also a member of the faculty.

An analysis of the content of his many books and more than fifty published articles discloses four major areas of interest: clinical, cultural, alchemical, and Jung's myth for modern man, i.e., the psychological redemption of traditional religion. A single unifying theme runs through them all, namely, the ego's relationship and encounter with the Self.

---

[4] This three-part video interview was conducted in 1990 by Jungian analyst Lawrence W. Jaffe, Ph. D., now deceased. It is here transcribed and edited, with footnotes, by George R. Elder. Most of Part 3 has already appeared in print, albeit in a somewhat different style. See "Transforming the God-Image" in *Psychological Perspectives* 25 (Fall-Winter 1991), pp. 40ff.—Eds.

[5] Later replaced by *Celebrating Soul: Preparing for the New Religion* (Inner City, 1999).

Personal Life and Development

Ed, it's been a privilege to read your books, and I'm glad to have the opportunity to sit and talk to you in the flesh. I was relating to you just a bit before an incident that happened with my youngest son who knew that I was going to be interviewing an eminent psychiatrist. When I was going over some of the questions I'd be asking you, he was struck by the fact that you were born in America. And he was really surprised and started prancing around the room, saying, "An American, an American!" He said that he thought all eminent and creative psychologists or psychiatrists were born in Europe and, I guess, had Viennese accents. Do you have any response to that?

Well, I'm proud to be able to feel that I am one of the early American-born Jungian analysts who had a contribution to make. It pleases me to hear that because it's very much a part of my psychological identity—the fact that I'm an American. And that has pluses and minuses; needless to say, it has a lot of negatives to it. But that's where my roots are, and that's where I am.

Most of your childhood was spent in Indiana. Can you tell us something about your boyhood?

Well, let me give you the whole story in outline. I was born in 1922 in Cedar Rapids, Iowa. That's the year that T. S. Eliot's poem, "The Waste Land," was published; that's the year the second volume of Spengler's *Decline of the West* was published; and it's the year after Yeats' poem, "The Second Coming," was published. Those are all significant things to me. I lived the first nine years of my life in Iowa.

I have what I would call a very early pre-memory. I think it's something like the reverie of a nursing infant, my very earliest recollection. The reverie didn't even have visual images attached to it; it was a tactile reverie that contrasted beautiful, wonderful smoothness and ugly, disagreeable roughness. It was a tactile image of the rough and the smooth. I assume it derives from the fact that my mother probably wore a silk or

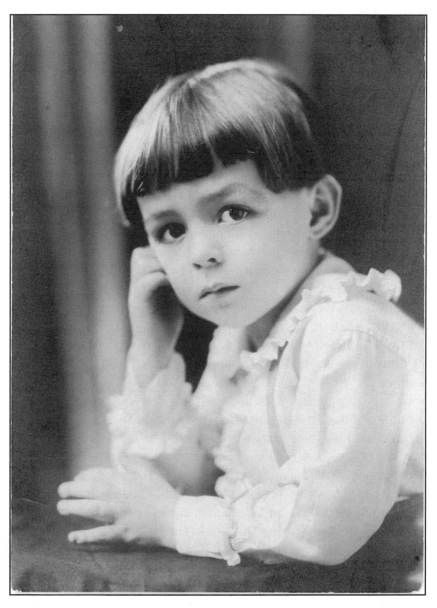

Figure 5. Edinger as a Young Boy (1926).

satin dressing gown when she nursed me; and there was probably some rough woolen blanket around somewhere—I assume that sort of thing. But what's so interesting to me about the memory is that right at the very dawn of my existence the "problem of the opposites" was constellated. I don't call that an earliest memory because there wasn't really any consciousness associated to it.

But there was another interesting event that I learned in the course of my analysis. At the beginning of my analysis, I discovered what I thought was my earliest memory; but in the course of the analysis that memory gave way to an even earlier one—which is an interesting phenomenon, I think. The first memory was when I was about six years old. I was playing outside the house of my maternal grandparents, and my mother came to the door and announced to me that my grandfather had died. And I went on playing as if nothing had happened. But, later, I recalled an earlier memory in which I was playing with my grandfather in the living room. We were bouncing a ball back and forth, and the ball hit a vase on the mantelpiece that was a particular favorite of my mother and smashed it into many fragments. My grandfather proceeded laboriously to put that vase back together with chewing gum.

I think of those two memories as having a larger reference. I think of the death of my grandfather as having in the background the event of the death of the Western God-image. And I think of the other memory as being a picture of the reconstitution of our broken mythological container. So, all those things happened when I was in Iowa.

But when I was nine years old, I moved to Bedford, Indiana. My father was a prosperous cut-stone contractor who had stone mills—one in Bedford, Indiana, and another in Cedar Rapids. But when the Depression came, it wiped him out. He closed down the Iowa mill, and we moved to Bedford and carried on the Indiana mill for a period of time—although that closed for a while, too. That was a terrible time for my father. He told me once that if it hadn't been for his religion, he could not have survived the catastrophic change in fortune that was forced on him. It was interesting to me, when I had a couple of brief opportunities to talk to Jung many years later, that this is one of the things I found myself telling him—about my father's remark, that without his religion he could not have survived the Depression. Jung's reply was, "That reminds me of my talk with Mountain Lake who told me that his tribe and his religious operations helped the sun come up." They're analogous events, you see. Anyway, we moved to southern Indiana, and that's where I feel I really put down roots. I've got a "Hoosier" soul, I think. I once had a dream in which a "Voice" announced, "Here comes the Hoosier gold-maker." And that established for me that my roots are Hoosier. We lived in a semi-rural setting, and I had an opportunity for a lot of leisurely strolling in the fields and the woods and following the streams and exploring the ponds in the region. It meant a great deal to me as a boy.

So, was it a brother who was born?

I have a brother who is seven years younger than myself. That's enough of a gap that I think it's safe to say that I have to a large extent an "only child's psychology." My mother was an exceedingly loving and doting mother; I got the very best kind of loving attention that a young boy could get. But the other side of that was—especially as I got older—that she was quite possessive. And I had to fight my way out of that tangle. She was a trespasser, a psychological trespasser. The result was that it gave me an elaborate sensitivity to psychological trespass. Once I worked through the worst part of that mother complex, it became a very useful sensitivity to have in psychotherapy. Because you can point out to patients when trespassing is going on, psychological trespassing of which they are totally oblivious.

As far as my father is concerned, he never seemed very problematical to me. He was straightforward, decent, somewhat stern, but a very honest and reliable man that I sort of took for granted. There is one interesting issue that comes up concerning the father side of the family—an ancestral problem has been passed on through my father's side of the family. I came to a full realization of it only when my father died, and I had a dream that brought up my paternal grandfather. The dream led to this realization; and I think it's worth recounting because it's instructive.

Figure 6. Edinger in High School (1939).

My father told me as a boy many times the story of an event that happened in his own childhood. The oldest child of my father's family was a little girl named Ruby. She was the first-born of the family—a couple years older than my father—and the absolute delight of my grandfather. And she was a couple years older than my father was. When she was five years old, she died of diphtheria. That was an absolute catastrophe for my grandfather, and the consequence of it was that it destroyed his faith in God.

Now, what followed was—I can't prove this as a causal sequence, but I'm convinced of it by all sorts of circumstantial evidence—that the problem my grandfather had with God got transferred to my father. And, in adolescence, he became a religious missionary. He became totally devoted to a religious sect called the International Bible Students' Association—which later came to be called the Jehovah's Witnesses—and he decided to devote his life to being a missionary.[6] He would have done so except that his father got sick and asked him to come back home and run the family business. After some reflection and advice from religious elders, my father eventually dutifully complied, gave up his missionary work, and came back to run the stone business. Then, that issue that my father did not have an opportunity to engage totally got passed on to me. And I think that's basically why Jungian psychology—when I finally found it—registered so profoundly with me. Because it answered my grandfather's question about his dealing with God. The answer, of course, is in Jung's *Answer to Job*.[7] But that's part of the psychological

---

[6] See Herbert Hewitt Stroup, "Jehovah's Witnesses," in *The Encyclopedia of Religion*, ed. Mircea Eliade (New York: Macmillan Publishing Company, 1987). The article begins, "Along with the Mormons, the Christian Scientists, and perhaps a few other groups, Jehovah's Witnesses is one of the few truly American expressions of religion." Their name is based on the conviction that the biblical deity is properly called Jehovah and the correct name for a follower of Jehovah is not Christian, but Witness.

[7] See C. G. Jung, "Answer to Job," in *Psychology and Religion*, vol. 11 of *The Collected Works of C. G. Jung* (Princeton: Princeton University Press, 1953-1979). [Hereafter, in this book, the *Collected Works* will be designated as *CW* without publication data.—Eds.]

heritage that my father passed on to me.

What Jung called, "God's tragic contradictoriness."

Exactly. What Jung elaborates so beautifully in *Answer to Job* is what the "Job experience" means for the individual who's going through it.[8] Because that's what my grandfather had—he was having a Job experience, you see. His dearest possession, his little girl, was taken away from him. And he couldn't forgive God for that act. And Jung spells it all out; that's what *Answer to Job* is all about.

And when your brother came along at age seven or eight, did that help extricate you from your mother's clutches?

Not that I know of. What did come along two or three years later was a major event in my life—an emerging fascination with chemistry. Starting out with just a little elementary chemistry set, I gradually accumulated a larger and larger home laboratory. It was a major object of fascination. It's very interesting to me as I look back over my life to realize that in order to be happy and functioning well I have to have a connection with an object of fascination. The first object was chemistry. I was just entranced by what goes on in chemical reactions, the transformations that take place under various circumstances. And, as I grew a little older, the fascination moved to biological science. I would go pond hunting in the springtime and bring back frog's eggs and fish eggs and pond water to examine for protozoa and things of that sort. So, the phenomenon of life, then, became the object of fascination. In turn, that very gradually shifted to the most complex living organism of all, namely, man. And that's what led me to medical school.

After medical school and internship, however, that object of fascination paled. I was in a period of emptiness and lostness. But, then, I dis-

---

[8] See Edinger's discussion of the "Job archetype" behind this experience in *Transformation of the God-Image: An Elucidation of Jung's "Answer to Job,"* p. 29.

covered Jung, and the object of fascination became the psyche—and that's held firm ever since, you see. But it's the way the *numinosum* has manifested itself in my life. And I think the reason that it expressed itself so intensely in my case was because of my experience of my parents' religion.

It's really quite a remarkable experience for a child, a thoughtful child, to grow up in the environment of a fundamentalist apocalyptic Christian sect. It's amazing! As I came to realize later, they are duplicating the primitive Christian communities of the first and second centuries. Those primitive communities were living with the anticipation of the imminent Second Coming of Christ; that was their conviction. And they could hardly pay any attention to making a living, because the Second Coming was going to happen so soon. The only thing they could do was to spread the message so as many people could be ready for it as possible. This is precisely what the Jehovah's Witnesses were doing.

It was evident to me, at quite a young age, that there's something wrong with this intellectually; but, emotionally, it was very powerful. And that's where chemistry came in. My psyche had to erect a contrasting entity that could stand over and against the emotional power of that collective religious conviction. What I did in effect was erect an alternative God—"science" was my God. And that's what protected me from being swallowed up.

It was absolutely appalling to me that, when it came to their religion, my parents were utterly devoid of intellectual critical self-reflection. In all other respects, they were reasonable people. But they were caught up in what amounted to a collective psychosis. The fact that it was collective and contained made it "containable," but it is an astonishing phenomenon.[9] Here, again, nothing except Jungian psychology could have enabled me to integrate so thoroughly that experience. Because it's the only thing in the world that has penetrated to the level of the religion-creating archetypes; it explained to me what was going on. And only

---

[9] Psycho-religious "containment" is an important theme in Edinger's writings. See the discussion in his *The New God-Image*, pp. 9f.; also the many references to "container" in the index of his *Archetype of the Apocalypse*.

through that understanding was I released from bitterness and rebellious-
ness against my parents.

*So, were you already a physician when you came across Jung or were
you still in medical school?*

I didn't have the slightest interest in psychiatry when I encountered it in
medical school. Jung wasn't even mentioned. And it never entered my
head that I'd be interested in psychiatry; I intended to go into internal
medicine. But when I finished the internship and had to spend a couple
of obligatory years in the army—largely in the Panama Canal Zone—it
came in on me with considerable impact that I was lost, that I didn't
know where I was going. I used to have dreams that I was driving in my
car and the windshield was fogged over; I couldn't see where I was going, and I was desperately trying to stick my head out the window to see
where I was going. I knew perfectly well what those dreams meant. They
were telling me I didn't know where I was going—and I didn't. Because
I knew that I couldn't live my life as a physician treating physical ill-
nesses; the meaning wasn't there. And so everywhere I perceived missing meaning, everything seemed meaningless. And that's, of course, because I'd lost the sense of meaning within myself. I'd lost connection
with that object of fascination. And that went on for some time until I
discovered Jung.

I discovered him in an interesting way, by reading the book *Generation of Vipers* by Philip Wiley, a kind of sardonic author of the 1940s.
He's probably not remembered much, but one of his issues was "Momism."[10] Anyway, he had made the acquaintance of Jung and was extolling

---

[10] In *Generation of Vipers*, published in 1942, Wylie exposed the shadow side of
"Americanism," including the worship of "Mom": "Mom is everywhere and
everything and damned near everybody, and from her depends all the rest of the
U. S. Disguised as good old mom, dear old mom, sweet old mom, our loving
mom, and so on, she is the bride at every funeral and the corpse at every wed-
ding." The book is currently available from Dalkey Archive Press, Champagne-
Urbana, 1996. Marie-Louise von Franz refers to this work in her essay, "The

Figure 7. Edinger in the Army (1948).

Religious Background of the Puer Aeternus Problem," in *Psychotherapy* (Boston: Shambhala, 1993), p. 314.

his virtues; and I thought, "This is somebody I'd better look into." I proceeded to do so, and when it finally took hold—when it finally registered what he was saying—I knew that was it. It took a while, but one morning—it was in October of 1950; I can't tell you the exact date, I think it was somewhere between October 12ᵗʰ and October 19ᵗʰ—I woke up and realized that I must become a Jungian analyst. Suddenly, everything fell into place. And then all I had to do was do it! That's the easy part. Once a person's got direction and knows what he's supposed to do in life, then the easy part is doing it. The hard part is finding one's assignment.

Did you know what a Jungian analyst was?

Well, I knew what Jung was talking about was it. And I was right.

Were you a psychiatrist at this point?

No, no, I hadn't even entertained psychiatry. I was in Connecticut at the time going through a residency in internal medicine. But I had come across *Psychic Energy* by Esther Harding and paid her a visit.[11] And she said, "Well, if that's what you have in mind, the first step is to go into analysis and into a psychiatric residency." So, I got a residency at Rockland State Hospital in Orangeburg, New York—way outside of New York City—and started analysis the following year.

Can you tell us something about your personal analysis with Esther Harding?

It was a first-rate analysis. She did a wonderful job of combining the reductive aspect of the analytic process with the synthetic aspect.[12] That

---

[11] M. Esther Harding, *Psychic Energy: Its Source and Its Transformation* (Princeton: Princeton University Press, 1948; revised, 1963).

[12] Jung explains in "The Synthetic or Constructive Method": "I had first to come to the fundamental realization that analysis, in so far as it is reduction and nothing more, must necessarily be followed by synthesis, and that certain kinds of

balance isn't often kept, you know; it's easy to get out of balance. She did a wonderful job of keeping that together, and I worked with her for about six or seven years. I'll read to you my very first dream. As you know, initial dreams are often especially important. I've used this in *Ego and Archetype*:

> After some difficulty, I caught a golden-colored fish. It was jumping up from the floor; I managed to catch it with a particular method. And then my task was to extract the blood from that fish and heat it until it reached a permanently fluid state. So I was in a laboratory, and I had a beaker of this fish blood that was being heated to make it permanently fluid. And the danger was that the blood might clot during this process. As I was in the laboratory boiling the blood of this fish, an older man—he was a scientist, a man that I had worked with in a research capacity—came into the laboratory. I described him in the book as a "spokesman for the scientific tradition," and he told me what I was doing would never work. The blood was sure to clot, he said. But I didn't think so, and I was going to continue heating it. I felt quite sure that it was going to succeed.[13]

Now, that was my initial dream. It had reference to a very painful personal issue that involved concupiscence—which is one of the symbolic meanings of the fish. But, as I came to realize later, it had the much larger reference that Jung discusses in *Aion*—the transformation of the whole Christian era and the extraction of the "blood," the living essence, from one form into another. Of course, that wasn't realized until a long time later.

Another major event that happened during my analysis was my discovery of what chemistry had meant to me as a boy. I'd forgotten all about that by then. You know, young men—I was in my twenties—don't think about what was significant in boyhood; they're thinking about the future. But I had a dream in which I was in my boyhood home, taking a

---

psychic material mean next to nothing if simply broken down. . . . so the synthetic procedure integrates it into a universal and intelligible statement." (*CW* 7, par. 122).

[13] See the slightly different anonymous version in Edinger, *Ego and Archetype*, p. 257.

walk down the road, and I came to a beautiful blue iris flower—one of the late blooming kind. I picked that flower. Then, as I was walking along, I blew upon it; and, as I blew on it, it opened up fully. Then, it's as though it took on a life of its own, and it broke away from my hand and started floating up in the air. And it went through some branches of some trees. I was afraid for a moment that it might get stuck in the trees, but it didn't. And it kept floating along, and I followed it. It led me back to my home, to the backyard of my home, to a little outbuilding that at one time had been a chicken coop and a woodshed and that I had turned into a chemistry laboratory. The flower floated directly to that little laboratory building; and, when it touched the roof, it burst into flame, into a blossom flame.

That dream taught me the numinosity that my love of chemistry carried for me, you see. And these two come together—the flower and the backyard laboratory—it's a *coniunctio.* There's a conception when they come together, and the result is a "flame" which at the same time is a "rose." That was one of the high points of my analysis.

Another particularly interesting event in my analysis that I think is instructive to people in general is the dream I had at the time that my analysis was ending. An event happened that made me recognize the psychological limitations of Esther Harding, and that had the effect of breaking the transference. When that occurred, I dreamed that a gigantic tree in the side yard of my childhood home had fallen over and now must be cut up into firewood. I've had occasion to mention that dream every now and then to patients when they have dreams of that sort. Because the image indicates that a rather sizeable sum of libido that has been confined to a vegetative mode of existence has fallen and is undergoing transformation from one manifestation to another. But I was very fortunate to have Esther Harding as my analyst; and I am very grateful to her.

What is your view of transference and countertransference?

It was a stroke of genius on the part of Freud to have discovered both the personal unconscious and the personal dimension of the transference. Brilliant! It's been in front of everybody's eyes for as long as human civilization has existed and was never seen before. And, then, Jung added to it by discovering the collective unconscious and the archetypal dimension of the transference. It's such a big subject that it's hard to know what to say about it. Perhaps the first question to be asked is: How does one define it?

It's not so easy to answer, but I define it as the emotional attachment or involvement that a patient has with his analyst based on the projection or induction of unconscious contents. There's so much to say about the transference that I don't know where to begin. What's so interesting to me is the profound mystery of how the internal and external factors come together in creating psychological experience. You see, an analysis with one analyst is a very different experience from an analysis with another analyst. What the analyst contributes is a unique psychological equation stemming from his own basic identity that determines very significantly how the analysis proceeds. Even though we examine diligently all the dream material of the analysand and do our best to concentrate on what emerges from within the analysand, the psychological presence of the analyst has an incalculable effect. I'm certain of that.

Let's say that you're a patient of mine, and you find yourself in a transference; you find yourself fascinated by me, and interested in me. And let's say it's a positive transference which is the most fruitful kind. You will look forward to your time with me and want as much of it as possible; and contact with me will have the effect of opening, and releasing, and enlivening you. You'll have dreams that will refer to it. Now the question comes up: What's the source of that transference, that state of mind? Are you projecting from your own unconscious, are you projecting positive feeling, enlivening contents of which you have been unconscious? Is it primarily a projection phenomenon that accounts for the transference? Or is it an induction phenomenon? I mean, could it be that just being exposed to the nature of my being—just what I am psychologically—has the effect of inducing in your psyche something of the same condition that exists in my psyche? That's not projection, that's induction. And that depends on me and the state of my psychology, the state of my consciousness.

The question can't be answered, because I think it's always a mixture of the two. But I do believe that we need to pay a great deal of attention to the induction phenomenon. That means, then, that a very major portion of the therapeutic experience derives from the consciousness of the analyst. That is what made Jung such a superlative analyst, I'm sure. He induced in those with whom he had contact a connection with depths in themselves—just by virtue of the fact that he was in contact with those depths, you see.

Those are some of the aspects of transference. Of course, Jung has written a whole book on the subject; and it's interesting into how large a framework he places the subject when he writes his *Psychology of the Transference.*[14] He uses the ten *Rosarium* pictures from an alchemical text to talk about the phenomenology of transference. And we're still left with the major task, then, of applying that rich symbolic imagery to specific occasions.

How would you distinguish transference from love?

I think it's distinguished by the degree of consciousness that accompanies it. Love, what I would call object love—as opposed to love based on unconscious factors which always has a degree of possessiveness attached to it—sees the reality of the object and relates to that reality as it is. A person caught up in a transference is not relating to the carrier of that transference in his or her full reality at all; he's relating to a piece of his own psychology that he sees in the mirror of the other person. It's a totally different thing.

It's almost as if the induction predominates in the induction-projection mixture. And it's closer to love perhaps.

If it's perceived as induction. I think it all depends on how conscious it

---

[14] Currently published as the second half of Jung's *The Practice of Psychotherapy, CW* 16, but first published in book form as *Die Psychologie der Übertragung* (1946).

is. The problem always is: How does one get out of the transference? It's not so easy to answer. And I think that's the real test of being an expert analyst—the ability to disengage the patient from a full-blown transference. One of the things that makes it difficult is that a positive transference is a seductively flattering thing, because the patient experiences you as more than you are. But it can be so subtle that that appraisal can creep in—because it's so flattering. And, then, there's a tendency to identify with the transference content. As long as that's the case, the situation remains stuck; nothing will happen. That can go on indefinitely—each side enjoying the experience with the other. But it's not really going to further consciousness on the part of the patient. I think an important way to start handing back the transference to the patient is to start revealing one's personal reality in a way that makes visible one's limitations and deficiencies that will encourage the patient to see there's really a sizeable difference between the reality of the analyst and the image that the patient has of him. The more that can be seen, the more the transference can start to be integrated.

Another very major way to give back the transference is to do active imagination. That is the real agency that integrates the transference. I will often recommend—if it's a very strong transference—that the patient do active imagination with the image of me. Now, that's not the same as me, you see; it's an image of me. The image of me belongs to the patient. And so, before long, he or she discovers that the image of me says things that I'd never think of saying. Then other images, other figures, that come up in dreams can also be used. As that process develops, it becomes an alternative to the dialogue with the analyst; the inner dialogue comes to replace the dialogue with the analyst. And the analysis isn't needed so much anymore.[15]

The patient begins to make a distinction between you and the image of you.

---

[15] Edinger elaborates on this topic in his essay "The Transference Phenomenon" in *Science of the Soul: A Jungian Perspective,* pp. 99ff.

Exactly. That's it. And, of course, another feature of transference is the distinction between the personal and the archetypal transference. I'm not sure it always gets as much attention as it deserves. The personal transference will usually have at its basis the transfer onto the analyst of behavior and experiences deriving from childhood and the relation to the parents, that sort of thing—the personal dimension. But when the archetypal layer is touched, then another whole dimension opens up; and the analyst takes on—subtly, to be sure; but, nonetheless, really—attributes of deity! In other words, the analyst can very often, in a strong transference, carry the Self to a significant extent.

The classic example of that is the one Jung used. His patient dreamed that she was in a wheat field and being rocked in his arms, and he was flowing with the wind and with the waves of the wheat.[16] He had become an embodiment of the Nature Goddess herself. And he uses that as an illustration of how the archetypal transference can take over.

2. The Psyche in Culture

What does the vocation of psychotherapy mean to you?

There's so much I could say I don't know where to begin. But it's something I want to talk about, because the psyche is my object of fascination. I feel so grateful to have been born in the 20th century, to be able to witness the discovery of the psyche and the emergence of a whole new basic vocation. Now, that doesn't happen very often. New jobs and new crafts open up. But it's not very often that there is born a fundamentally new vocation orientation. And I think psychotherapy is such an entity. As I see it, it's got roots in three noble traditions: first of all, the tradition of medicine; second, the tradition of religion—as a priestly endeavor—that

---

[16] Recounted by Jung in "The Houston Films," in *C.G. Jung Speaking*, ed. William McGuire and R. F. C. Hull (Princeton: Princeton University Press, 1977), 346. For a different version and longer discussion, see Jung, *Two Essays on Analytical Psychology*, CW 7, pars. 211ff.

mediates the manifestations of deity to man; and, third, the tradition of philosophy. The complete psychotherapist, as I see it, is one who has a living connection to all three of those traditions—to the healing tradition, to mediation of the transpersonal, and to the reflective task of rational human consciousness, which is what philosophy is.

So, to be a psychotherapist means, to me, to be an heir of all three of these traditions and at the same time to be doing something totally new. Because the psyche has never existed before *empirically*. It's existed embedded in other contexts—like a religious or mythological context— but it's never existed before as a living, empirical, organic reality. And it's a wonderful privilege to be in on the birth of that.

How can the study of culture—for instance, religion, history, or litera- ture—repay the psychotherapist?

I'd put the question a little differently. Rather than the "study" of culture, I would say the "experience" of the various culture forms. It's the same thing, of course, because you can't experience them if you don't study them. But just intellectual study of them isn't quite what does it. Think of the example of Friedrich Nietzsche who was in love with the opera *Car- men*. He saw it at least twenty times in his life, and it wasn't as easy then to see opera as it is now. In that opera, an army officer is seduced by an anima; he's seduced to abandon his army unit, to go AWOL. And, then, once she abandons him for another lover, he murders her in his despair. That's the story of *Carmen*. Of course, it's got beautiful music, and it's a seductive thing to witness: because it does to the audience the very thing it's picturing being done. But the fact that Nietzsche was so enamored of that opera tells me something about Nietzsche's psychology. It's a picture of his relation to his anima. And it describes from the inside, so to speak, the whole phenomenology of his inflated psychology and how it eventually abandoned him, how it had aspects that were ultimately suici- dal.

I bring that up as an example of how culture forms hold up the mirror to our psyche so that we can see what we are. Jung says some place—I think it's in *Symbols of Transformation*—that the theater is where we go to work out or experience *collectively* our complexes.[17] That's another way of putting it, that what it is we respond to, what it is that moves us, is an expression of our own psychic reality. And different things move different people. I remember a patient from the 1950s who saw the movie *East of Eden,* based on the novel by John Steinbeck. This novel is a modern version of the Cain and Abel myth—about two brothers, one of whom was the favorite loved one of his father and the other who was the rejected one. In the course of this movie, the patient got so agitated that he could not stand to see the whole thing—because he was identified with the rejected brother. It was so painful to see his situation mirrored on the screen, he couldn't stand it. This is an example of the function of culture. I think of it as that "mirror shield" that Athena gives to Perseus when he is on his way to encounter the Gorgon Medusa. Medusa is of such dreadful mien, her appearance is so horrible, that anyone who looks at her straight on is petrified. I see that image as the nature of Raw Being—life is too terrible to endure in its raw form. Most people don't know that, because they've never seen it in its raw form. They've been acculturated, and they are operating from a surface level. They're hedged in by protections of such magnitude that they never see the raw form. If you've ever seen it, you know it's unendurable. Then you know why there has to be culture if the human psyche is going to exist. Even in its acculturated form, it was more than that young man could endure. I first met him at Rockland State Hospital; he eventually committed suicide. He had seen the Gorgon, and the sight was more than he could endure.

It's a marvel to me. Just consider opera—I mentioned *Carmen*—consider the standard opera that people attend for so-called entertainment. The content of almost all operas is murder, suicide, incest—horrible events. The basic content is violent and terrible. But it's sugar-coated by beautiful music, and beautiful dialogue, and beautiful costumes, and beautiful settings—and probably a nice dinner beforehand. And so you can just bear to look at the reality of life when it is built

---

[17] See Jung, *Symbols of Transformation, CW* 5, par. 48: "One might describe the theatre, somewhat unaesthetically, as an institution for working out private complexes in public."

within the structure of beauty. The reason we go to see it is that it puts us in touch with the reality of the primordial psyche. What happens on the stage is the nature of the psyche, but it's made endurable by being presented in a beautiful form. And the whole function of beauty is very impressive to me there. It lures us into consciousness somehow. It's something like the story of Helen and Paris—when Paris, the shepherd boy, is lured into life by the beauty of Aphrodite. So, those are some of my thoughts about culture.

I know many years ago, back in the 1960s, I was asked by Union Theological Seminary in New York to give a course; and they gave me the title of what they wanted me to teach. They wanted me to talk about "Jung's psychology of religion and culture." I agreed to do that; but the first remark I made at the beginning of that course was to turn that title around and say, "Religion and culture are psychology." Another way of putting it is that "religion and culture" is the human psyche manifest. It's one of the major ways that it reveals itself to us. It *is* the psyche. But those who are interested in literature, and art, and philosophy, and the various culture forms, are very much like the theologians. They deal with the psyche, but they deal with it second-hand; they deal with it embedded in another form and not in its own living reality. The job of the psychologist, the Jungian psychologist anyway, is to "extract" the psyche from religion and culture as it manifests—and reveal it in its living state.[18]

I wanted to ask you more about "beauty"—but I don't know quite what to ask you. Can you say a bit more about it?

Well, I've thought about it. There are some people for whom beauty is the supreme meaning of life. I've met such people for whom the aesthetic factor is the crucial factor. And I can only conclude that for some people that's the way they experience the *numinosum*—through beauty. Keats said, "A beauty is truth, truth beauty, that's all we know and all we

---

[18] Consider the "extraction" imagery in Edinger's initial dream upon entering analysis.

need to know."[19] Well, I love Keats, but one could question that; it's a little too nondiscriminatory for me. Beauty can lead one into terrible evil. There is the old notion that "beauty and goodness" go together. In Greek philosophy, *kalokagathia* is a hyphenated single term—meaning the "good-beautiful."[20] Although often translated "the good and the beautiful," the ancients thought of it as a unit—so that everything that's beautiful has to be good, and everything that's good has to be beautiful. In ordinary terms, that's not true.

Jung doesn't talk much about beauty. He does speak about the danger of the aesthetic attitude by itself—when it leaves out of account the ethical dimension.[21] In effect, he's saying that the ancient idea of the "good-and-the-beautiful" is not a proper identity. It's as though the ancients hadn't differentiated the opposites, so that that which is aesthetically pleasing is not necessarily ethically good.

However, thank God for beauty. It makes life bearable, just like the operas reveal.

You use the term, the "ethical" element. Could you say a little more about what you mean by that?

I've paid a lot of attention to Jung's comments on this subject. He talks about it very earnestly concerning one's dealings with the unconscious. We do our best to understand our dreams and to engage the unconscious in active imagination; and he says it's very important to extract the

---

[19] John Keats, last two lines of "Ode on a Grecian Urn" (May, 1819): "'Beauty is truth, truth beauty,' that is all / Ye know on earth, and all ye need to know."

[20] Technically, this term for an ideal Greek citizen is a combination of *kalos* ("beautiful"), *kai* ("and"), and *agathos* ("good").

[21] See Jung *Psychological Types*, *CW* 6. par. 232: "The aesthetic approach immediately converts the problem into a picture which the spectator can contemplate at his ease, admiring both its beauty and its ugliness, merely re-experiencing its passions at a safe distance with no danger of becoming involved in them. The aesthetic attitude guards against any real participation, prevents one from being personally implicated, which is what a religious understanding of the problem would mean."

meaning from unconscious contents. Of course, the aesthetic dimension, the *image*, must come up; and so that dimension is important in the process of just realizing a content. And very often it comes up in striking and beautiful terms. But, then, Jung goes on to say that's not enough. One must also respond to the emerging content by asking the question: "What does this content demand of me ethically? What must I do with it?" If I don't engage that question of what I do with it, if I'm just satisfied with enjoying the image aesthetically or just satisfied with an intellectual "enjoyment" of its meaning, the whole relation to the unconscious can turn negative—dangerously negative. That can happen if the ethical responsibility that the unconscious content evokes is not integrated.

So, the ethical idea has to do with integrating contents into one's life.

Yes, so that it becomes a living reality.

Hanging over your mantelpiece are pictures of Jung, Lincoln and Emerson. I know that you've written a paper on Emerson, and you've written a book called "Melville's Moby-Dick". Can you tell us something of what these great Americans have meant to you?

Well, yes I can. You've named three Americans, so I'll take them up in turn. Abraham Lincoln grew up in southern Indiana. He was born in Kentucky; and about the age of seven, he moved to southern Indiana and grew up, I think, all the way to age twenty before the family moved on to Illinois. So his determinative years were spent in Indiana; that gives me a connection right away. When I was a boy, there was a copy of Sandburg's *Prairie Years* on the family bookshelf; and it's now on my bookshelf.[22] I remember reading it when I was quite young. I've always been

---

[22] The reference is to Carl Sandburg's influential two-volume work, *Abraham Lincoln: The Prairie Years*, published in 1926. The remaining four volumes of the biography, *Abraham Lincoln: The War Years*, were published in 1939. Sandburg distilled these six volumes into a single volume of 800 pages, published in 1954, now available as a Harvest Book, Harcourt, Inc.

interested in Lincoln, and in my later years I was able to put it psychologically. He combined uniquely the virtues of both extravert and introvert in an unparalleled way. He's an obvious extravert as a politician, a highly successful politician, who could relate to people just marvelously out of his homely wit. But he's also a profound introvert; that's evident in his writings.

This ties in with my interest in American history. I don't know whether anyone's given very much attention to it or not, but American history has followed the same archetypal pattern as that of the ancient history of Israel. The Puritans were consciously aware of the fact that they were realizing the myth of the Israelites going to the Promised Land. That was explicit in the way they talked about themselves. This land was the Promised Land, but neither the Israelites nor the Puritans got it effortlessly. Once the Israelites arrived, they still had to drive out the Canaanites; once the Puritans got here, they still had to drive out the Indians—the original "Canaanite" inhabitants. Then, there is a period of a unified kingdom: just as the Kingdom of Israel was unified, so the Republic was unified for seventy or eighty years. Then, Israel split apart after the death of Solomon. And America would have split apart, too, if it hadn't been for Lincoln; at that point, the archetypal pattern was broken. Ancient Israel did not have anything equivalent to the Civil War, and there was no equivalent to Lincoln. Israel and Judah just went their separate ways—both to their destruction, sooner or later, you see. Now, the history of America veered off at this point because Lincoln arrived on the scene, and the nation did not split—at a terrible cost.

I've often reflected on the question: What gave Lincoln the strength, the endurance, through these terrible years of defeat and retreat? What kept him going? All he had to do was to agree to the splitting of the country, that's all. But the notion of "union" was the supreme image to him; and I see the Coniunctio archetype as operating there. That's the only thing that could have enabled him to endure. It's a miracle to me that we didn't split. How our history is going to unfold, I don't know; but I think it's psychologically true—as popular culture has it—that we're the "last best hope in the world." I think that's true, that the psychological factors America is carrying are of the same order as the ones that ancient Israel carried, you see. Lincoln's all tied up with this thinking.

Now, let's turn to Melville. I didn't read *Moby-Dick* until I was thirty years old, and I think that was very fortunate. If it had been spoiled as a schoolboy exercise, I probably would never have gone back to it. But the fact that I read it only in my maturity—when I already had some exposure to Jung—enabled me to see what was going on. It's the American *Faust*, that's what it is. Melville saw what others were beginning to see in the 19th century—but he saw it precociously, and he saw it more clearly. He saw the paradoxical nature of God. But that could not be discussed in any kind of open terms then. He wrote another book about six or seven years after *Moby-Dick* entitled *The Confidence Man*. It's about a confidence man that shows up in various guises in the course of a boat trip on the Mississippi River. And if you read between the lines, the "confidence man" is God. Melville is talking about religion's call for "faith" as the operations of a Confidence Man—that shows you the level of his reflections. And that's all in the background of *Moby-Dick*. It's a terrible and wonderful story of a descent into the unconscious—in many respects much more gripping and more vital than Goethe's *Faust*, although it's not as wide-ranging and profound. But it really goes into the depths, and it almost killed Melville to do it. He just barely escaped a psychosis.

Then there's Emerson. I think Lincoln and Emerson are the finest products of America. They're what make me proud to be an American, that our nation could bring to birth two such human beings as Emerson and Lincoln, who were quite opposite in the way they expressed themselves. Emerson was a supreme introvert! And what a remarkable thing that probably the most extraverted country the world has ever known could bring forth the superlative introvert that Emerson was. Lincoln, as I've already said, was a highly extraverted man. Emerson was appreciated in the nineteenth century and at the beginning of the twentieth, but I don't think people pay much attention to him anymore. I don't think his complete works are even in print. I've got a copy of the collected works, and they may be in print in some limited edition, but nobody pays attention to them anymore in the secondary schools. And he's the harbinger of Jungian psychology in America. Joe Henderson told me in a personal conversation that Jung said to him, "If you understand Emerson, you'll understand my psychology."[23] Jung refers to Emerson a number of times in the *Collected Works*. Nietzsche himself was a devotee of Emerson; unfortunately, he took him one step farther. But the insights that reside in Emerson's writings are just remarkable in the light of twentieth century psychology. So, he's a great love of mine.

I've had the opportunity to read all of your books, including Goethe's Faust: Notes for a Jungian Commentary. *I found this the most difficult and somehow different from the others. Was there something different about that book?*

Well, there may be. I got interested in studying *Faust* more closely after giving a course here on Jung's *Aion*.[24] Because what he demonstrates in that volume very clearly is that the Christian eon that is now coming to an end has built into it an *enantiodromia*. That means a "turning into the opposite," a reversal of prevailing principles. It's based upon the astrological sign of Pisces with its two "fish" pointing in different directions. Jung establishes that the first fish corresponds to Christ, and the second fish corresponds to Antichrist. And the emergence of the principle of Antichrist has been particularly prominent in the last quarter of the Christian eon, i.e., in the last 500 years. That was when the great explosion took place—the Renaissance, the Reformation, the scientific revolution, and the great world explorations. All that started around 1500. Jung establishes that these events are associated in the collective unconscious with the emergence of Antichrist—in the gradual evolution of the collective unconscious. And the legend of "Faust" began at precisely the same time. There was supposedly an historical Faust. He's said to have lived

---

[23] Joseph Henderson, M.D., now deceased, was an eminent Jungian analyst in San Francisco, California.

[24] Jung, *Aion: Researches into the Phenomenology of the Self, CW* 9ii; see also Edinger, *The Aion Lectures*.

from 1480 to 1540, and all the legends that gathered around him started at that time. Thus, he's a kind of corollary or an addition to the coming of Antichrist. He's an image of modern man—what you might call "post-Judeo-Christian man"—who has turned his back on that religious or mythological containment and has taken up with the contrary principle. That's the principle of egohood. It's the Luciferian principle of rebellion against bondage to nature—or bondage to any dogmatic or mythological structure. So it's an image of the ego and the two sides of it: one side being the presumptuous, inflated, hubristic ego that risks annihilation through inflation; and the other side being the heroic, Promethean ego that dares to take on new responsibilities and open new areas of awareness for the purpose of the enlargement of consciousness. That is what *Faust* is about.

Actually, the figure of Faust returned to embrace nature which the strict spiritual Christian standpoint had repressed to a sizeable extent. You see, nature had become equated with Satan who took on attributes of Dionysus and Pan—the goat god of nature—with goat hoof and such things. What got Faust started was he had reached an impasse. Goethe's play begins with Faust sitting in his study in a state of despair; he's ready to commit suicide. And in that state of desperation, he takes a walk with his assistant Wagner; and they meet the black poodle. This dog starts circling around them. And Faust immediately realized something big was happening here, this was no ordinary dog. In fact, the dog followed him home; and eventually he turned into Mephistopheles. Then, they reach an agreement, they reach a pact. And Faust sets off on his travels with Mephistopheles as his servant-companion, so to speak.

One of the reasons I felt obliged to study *Faust* in some detail was that it meant so much to Jung. Jung was profoundly identified with Goethe's *Faust*, and that told me for sure that there's something vitally important in this story for all of us. It's a little hard for Americans to get into it because it's a little remote in its imagery; it's much easier for Europeans to get into it. But our version is Melville's *Moby-Dick*; it's the same story with a little different slant. But *Faust* is very, very much worth one's study.

One last question on Faust. *Your book ends with a Coniunctio image, with the image of Helen. Can you say something about that?*

Well, Helen is the principal figure in Part II of Goethe's *Faust.* In Part I, the Coniunctio takes place between Faust and Gretchen. And it's a tragedy in human terms; because she's left pregnant, he deserts her, and she kills her baby and dies in prison. It's a terrible human tragedy. But *Faust* II involves Faust's quest for the mythological Helen of Troy. So the whole drama shifts from the personal dimension to the archetypal dimension. Thus, my book ends with a discussion of Helen of Troy as an archetypal image, because that is the central image sought for in the drama of *Faust.*

Do you think that has anything to say to modern people who are struggling to withdraw their projections from each other and to relate to the soul within each of them?

That's all very relevant, yes, the whole matter of the discovery of the anima—which Jung has accomplished for us. You know, it's really quite a sizeable individual task psychologically to discover the anima for one's self—as opposed to experiencing it in one or more women who happen to be the carriers of its projection. It's a major accomplishment for a human being to be able to discover the reality of the anima as a living psychic organism—and then to form a relationship with her as something separate from the relationship to the woman who evokes the projection. That's one of the things that *Faust* is about, that's true.

To many people, a myth is not a very important thing. So, can you speak to that?

Yes, yes. I obviously am using "myth" in a special sense. You know, somebody said, "Myth is somebody else's religion." So I could just as well use the word "religion." It's the living structure or container that

conveys the sense of a connection to the transpersonal dimension of existence. I use the word "myth" in that larger generic sense—but I realize
that is open to misunderstanding if I don't explain it.

Why is loss of our myth such a tragedy?

The human psyche is so built, so structured, that it requires a connection
to the transpersonal dimension of existence in order to survive. I think
our study of primitive societies and history teaches us that. It's only
modern man, in the last few hundred years, who thinks he can get along
without a living connection to deity. I think Jung has demonstrated pretty
conclusively that the relation to a religion provides the ego with a connection to the Self, the transpersonal center of the psyche, which is vital
for psychic existence.

*Mary Bancroft, an early follower of Jung, claimed that many Americans
have found their way to culture through Jung.*[25]

Well, I agree with that. I think it's true of myself. It reminds me of the
larger fact—a marvelous fact to me—that Jung's discovery of the objective psyche, of the collective unconscious, has had the effect of redeem-
ing a whole series of earlier human activities that otherwise would be
cast aside as irrelevant and meaningless to modern man. A good example
is that I would never have been interested in ancient Greek philosophy by
itself. Because what is it? It's just a series of primitive gropings after
some understanding of the nature of the universe—that's how it appears
to scientific understanding. So, why bother with paying attention to those
things? What Jung demonstrated is that these so-called "primitive gropings" are actually expressions of the archetypal dimension of the psyche.
And they're still alive in us today! That means that, in effect, he's redeemed—for me, anyway—the whole field of ancient Greek philosophy.

---

[25] For an account of the American Mary Bancroft's association with the Jungians
of Switzerland, see Deirdre Bair, *Jung: A Biography* (Boston: Little, Brown, and
Company, 2003), pp. 487ff.

The same thing applies to the whole history of religion, religious heresies, alchemy. And, as Mary Bancroft says, many people who aren't aesthetically inclined can relate to culture forms—once they have some understanding of what they mean psychologically. And I'm one of those.

In your essay, "The Tragic Hero: An Image of Individuation," you discuss the Oedipus plays of Sophocles.[26] You make the interesting distinction between the mythological hero and the tragic hero; and you identify Oedipus with the tragic hero. Can you tell us something about how you see Oedipus?

I wrote that paper on the Oedipus plays in particular because Freud started with that. You see, Freud discovered the first archetype. He didn't call it an archetype; he called it a personal complex, the "Oedipus complex." But, as Jung demonstrated, behind every major complex there is a core which is an archetype. So, Freud actually discovered the first archetype, which is the "Oedipus archetype." It is sort of characteristic of Freud that he applied only the first Oedipus play to the psyche, namely, *Oedipus Rex*—with Oedipus blind, exiled, and in despair. But the second Oedipus play, *Oedipus at Colonus*, is the play of transformation in which—through his sufferings—Oedipus has actually turned into a sacred object. As the oracle stated, "Wherever Oedipus' tomb shall lie, that land will be blessed"—because he had become a sacred object.

It's a wonderful image of what I call the "archetypalizing" of the ego that had gone through the individuation experience, you see. And these plays are particularly relevant to depth psychology. Freud picked them up and elaborated the first half in personal terms while Jung—who didn't speak in detail about Sophocles or Oedipus—elaborated the second half, the archetypal dimension of the human journey.

In another paper, "Romeo and Juliet: A Coniunctio Drama," you dis-

---

[26] Originally published in the first issue of *Parabola*, no.1 (Winter 1976), this essay can be found as "*Oedipus Rex*: Mythology and the Tragic Hero" in Edinger, *The Psyche on Stage: Individuation in Shakespeare and Sophocles*.

cussed the Shakespearean tragedy from the point of view of the "union of opposites," as Jung says, "in love and in enmity."[27]

This is an example of how one can see the basic archetypal pattern shining through a given work of art when one is familiar with these archetypal patterns. In this case, the pattern is the Coniunctio that Jung has written about so extensively. Once one is familiar with the phenomenology, one can see that the Coniunctio involves not only the attraction of opposites in "love" but also the hostility of opposites in "enmity"—those are the two sides of the Coniunctio phenomenology. So love and war go right together. And that's why Aphrodite and Ares are lovers in Greek mythology, you see, because they belong to the same basic psychological phenomenon. Since that is revealed so clearly in *Romeo and Juliet*—if you have eyes to see—I used that example to elaborate it. I wrote that paper for Joe Henderson's 75th birthday *festschrift.* He was a little surprised that I could find alchemy even in Shakespeare; but there it is.

You often illustrate your books with the works of Rembrandt. What is your assessment of this artist?

Rembrandt is an awesome figure, just awesome. I have a book right behind me on my shelf, a rather thick book, that contains just his biblical etchings and woodcuts. But they are the ones, I think, you refer to chiefly. What they demonstrate is that Rembrandt—in his artistic individual experience—really integrated those biblical figures he was making visible to us. That's the sense I get from looking at those pictures. He's not just photographing them from without, so to speak; he's revealing them from the intimate experience of them, from within. They reveal that he has a remarkable magnitude as a psychological human being; it's very impressive to me.

---

[27] Originally published in *Shaman from Elko: Papers in Honor of Joseph L. Henderson on His Seventy-fifth Birthday*, ed. Gareth S. Hill (San Francisco: C. G. Jung Institute of San Francisco, 1978), later included in Edinger, *The Psyche on Stage.*

3. Jung's Religious Message

One reason, apparently, that some of Jung's books are difficult to follow is that his thinking was so far ahead of our own. Would you say that much of your work has the goal of rendering more understandable Jung's religious message, understood broadly?

I think of myself as a mediator between Jung and a wider audience. Jung is this gigantic presence that is profoundly intimidating to all of us little ones. And we're all little ones in comparison to him. I've been studying Jung as my major life endeavor for forty years, and the more I study him the more impressed I am by his magnitude—and the more I can understand why so many people don't want to get anywhere near him. Because it's just too painful to experience one's smallness in comparison to such a massive entity.

Often, I think it's a sound instinct of self-preservation that keeps people away from Jung. You know, we have many different schools of psychotherapy. And I think that's for a good reason: we have as many different schools of psychotherapy as there are basic attitudes and typological categories in relation to the psyche. In other words, the psyche creates for itself the schools of psychotherapy that serve it. Human beings may think they create the schools, but I don't think so. I think the unconscious does it, you see. And everyone should find the school that fits him best. When that's done, however, there are not very many Jungians; because Jung's particular approach doesn't seem to be relevant to the majority of people . . . *yet*. I think that's only a short-term phenomenon. But I'm trying to make it a little easier to relate to Jung by mediating.

What does Jungian psychology have to do with religion?[28]

Everything, everything. You see, Jung has demonstrated that the religious function resides in the psyche and is an integral part of human psy-

---

[28] From this point, Part III of "An American Jungian" has already appeared in print. See first footnote of this interview.

chology. And that just means that the ego—in order to be healthy—needs to have a living connection to a transpersonal center. There are two etymologies for the word, "religion."[29] One etymology emphasizes the meaning of "linking back"—which I think goes back to Augustine. The idea is that the religious function links the ego back to its origin, its background, to the larger entity from which it came. The other etymology of "religion"—the one that Jung really preferred—points to *religio* as "careful consideration," i.e., the careful consideration of the background of one's life. This is the opposite of the root of the word, "neglect," and the opposite of neglecting the background of one's life. Although Jung preferred one meaning, he acknowledged the importance of the other, since the human psyche has a religious function in both senses—a need to link back and a need to give careful consideration to the source of one's being.

The religious process, then, is one in which the ego has a living organic connection to a larger whole. That, of course, is the function that the traditional religions have always served. They've done so by way of their collective structure, their dogmatic formulations—the whole concept of God and man's relation to God—provided the believer. Traditional religion has given the individual a religious container in which he has the sense of being connected to the larger whole.

Now, modern man—especially the "creative minority" of modern man—has lost that connection provided by the traditional religions; because they're too concrete.[30] They haven't kept pace with modern man's mental development, so they're not in tune with modern categories of understanding. The great service that Jung has performed by his discovery of the collective unconscious, and the archetypes, and the Self is that he's penetrated to the psychological basis that underlies all the world religions. Thereby he's verified and redeemed for modern consciousness the reality of religious operations as they express themselves in *all* religions. That's been achieved. And I don't think we can appreciate the

---

[29] For a more technical discussion, see Edinger, *The New God-Image*, p. 35.

[30] Below, Edinger attributes the phrase "creative minority" to the English historian Arnold Toynbee.

magnitude of that achievement—because it means that the psychological basis has been laid for the realization of a unified world. We've got the basis now for a unification of all the factional divisions among the world religions; and once that is achieved, I think political unification is bound to follow. It's been accomplished! One man has done it.

I wish I could communicate this fact that I see so clearly concerning Jung's discovery of the basis of all the world religions. He's achieved by this discovery the psychological basis for the unification of the world. It's really a pitiful sight to see the world split up into these separate warring fragments of religious identifications, of nationalistic identifications, of ethnic identifications—all at war with one another. They're all operating out of the energies of connection with the same transpersonal image of Wholeness. They are all operating out of their connection to deity, to the Self, as it is constellated and perceived within their local religious or nationalistic context. It's the same psychic Self. And what Jung has done has penetrated to that Source—that's the "paradoxical God" he talks about. He's seen it. And once he's seen it, it can no longer split up into these various ethnic and religious factions and fight against itself. One human being has seen the "back of God," so to speak, so that means he's going to be eventually unified. The world will be unified politically, sooner or later, as an inevitable consequence of that event of human consciousness.

Jung has taught us that the leading idea of a new religion will come from the symbolism of the religion that preceded it. Applied to modern times, this means that the leading idea of the era that we are now entering will be based on the Judeo-Christian myth. Do you have a comment on this?

Yes, I do. It leads us right into a major pronouncement that Jung makes in his late work, especially in *Answer to Job* where he speaks about the new mode of existence, what he calls, "continuing incarnation." Now, that requires some explanation, because I think few people will get right away just what he means by continuing incarnation. You see, the central image of the Judeo-Christian myth is that Yahweh—the God of the Old

Testament—was obliged to incarnate, according to Jung, because he had an encounter with Job. And so he's born in the form of a human being in Jesus Christ as his Son. That's the basic image of the entire Judeo-Christian myth. And that's the issue that Christianity has picked up and elaborated and that Judaism has declined to pick up. Christianity is really just a Jewish heresy that has mushroomed so much that it has sort of obscured its "mother." But the Jewish scriptures and the Christian scriptures share the same idea of a divine Son. The difference between them is that the Jews think he's coming in the future, and the Christians think he's already come. But the basic idea is the same. Jung's point is that that image of the "incarnation of deity in a human being"—which was symbolically manifested in Christ—is now to be realized empirically in a few individuals who are able to go through the process of individuation. Because Jung considers the individuation process to be equivalent to the symbolic imagery of the incarnation of God in a human being.

What that means psychologically is that the ego—in the process of establishing a conscious living relationship with the Self—becomes the "ground" for the incarnation of deity. As Jung puts it some place, the ego is the "stable" in which the Christ child is born.[31] This symbolism has now become available for empirical psychological understanding. It no longer has to be worshipped as a metaphysical or theological hypostasis which is how it appears in projection as a religious image. In such a form, it is not yet realized as a psychic reality, as an aspect of psychological experience. But that's what Jung has achieved.

He's achieved in his own life the "incarnation of deity." And he puts it modestly, that there's now the opportunity for many to do likewise. He describes that at the conclusion of *Answer to Job*. He puts it so well that I'd like to read it. He's talking about the relation between the ego and the

---

[31] See Jung, "A Psychological Approach to the Trinity," in *Psychology and Religion, CW* 11. par. 267: "The more unconscious we are of the religious problem in the future, the greater the danger of our putting the divine germ within us to some ridiculous or demoniacal use, puffing ourselves up with it instead of remaining conscious that we are no more than the stable in which the Lord is born."

Self, and he says that a "reciprocal action" is established when the ego and the Self are consciously related:

> [The] reciprocal action between two relatively autonomous factors which compels us, when describing and explaining the processes, to present sometimes the one and sometimes the other factor as the acting subject, even when God becomes man. The Christian solution has hitherto avoided this difficulty by recognizing Christ as the one and only God-man. But the indwelling of the Holy Ghost, the third Divine Person, in man, brings about a Christification of many. . . . (par. 758)

That's what I wanted to get to, "the indwelling of the Holy Ghost, the third Divine Person, in man, brings about a Christification of many." Now, if I translate that symbolic imagery into banal psychological terms, then I would say the achievement of consciousness of the ego-Self axis—the connecting factor between the ego and the Self, i.e., the "Holy Ghost"—brings about a realization that the life of the ego is manifesting a transpersonal purpose and meaning. That's what's meant by the symbolic imagery of the "incarnation of God in man through the agency of the Holy Ghost."

That's hard to grasp. But as with so much of Jung's writings, I think the way to go at it is to read the relevant passages—such as the last paragraph of *Answer to Job*—over, and over, and over again. Because they really have the quality of scripture. Jung is speaking from a consciousness that transcends that of all of us; therefore, we must read what he has to communicate over, and over, and over again. And, then, it begins to dawn on us just what he means.

Jung said that certain aspects of his work sounded like religion but was not. Would you say the same about your work?

There is so much in Jung's work that it's very difficult to characterize it. And, of course, Jung says different things at different times and under different circumstances. You have to keep that in mind. I consider Jung's work—as I think he did—to be primarily a scientific accomplishment. What he did was discover—through his own personal experience both individually and with patients—the objective psyche, the psyche as an objective entity in contrast to just a subjective entity. And that led him into a region of such immense dimensions that he spent the rest of his life trying to describe and present some of the major aspects of the nature of the objective psyche. So, Jung is primarily, fundamentally, a scientific genius who has made a totally new discovery. A totally new dimension of being has been laid bare. Following that discovery, he was obliged to create a whole new methodology for approaching it: since it's a new object, it cannot be approached by the old methodology used by physical science. Physical science requires a methodology different from the science of depth psychology, because the nature of the subject matter is different. The psyche requires a methodology that engages the whole person. Physical science, by its nature, excludes a significant portion of the whole person as irrelevant. But dealing with the psyche requires an engagement of the whole person—that's a totally new approach. And people have yet to learn it. Jung teaches us how to do it, but we still have to learn it. Anyway, he was obliged to create that whole new methodology in order to deal with the new subject that he discovered—the subject of the objective psyche—and this is what he's done in all his mature work. Fundamentally, that's how I think of him.

When he discovered the objective psyche and started exploring it, Jung could see that it is the source of religion, philosophy, art, mythology, and world views of all kinds. And although we say quite accurately—"No, Jungian psychology is not a religion, it's not a philosophy, it's not a *Weltanschauung.*"—nonetheless, it deals with the source of all of those. Also, in the course of realizing the practical aspect of encounter with the psyche, Jungian psychology has discovered that psychotherapy—if it is going to be complete in the individual case—involves the individual's discovery of a religious standpoint and of a *Weltanschauung.* When Jungian psychology is applied, therefore, it does lead to a religious consciousness and to the emerging awareness of a new world view. And this is true even though Jungian psychology itself is not a religion or a world view. It's as though it's more fundamental than that. Because Jung talks about religious imagery and religious phenomenology, many people superficially think he's a "religionist" or even a "mystic."[32] That's not true. He's an empirical scientist of the psyche. That's what he is.

Ed, you have spoken of Jung as an "epochal man," and you have explained by that a man whose life inaugurates a new age in cultural history. Can you tell us more of this idea? And have there been other epochal men?

You see, I have a perception of Jung that I'm afraid practically nobody shares. I'm almost alone in that, speaking of being "alone." I mentioned earlier that he's a whole new species. And we know from history that when an individual who is carrying a major new consciousness arrives on the scene, that often inaugurates a new epoch. The two examples that I'm thinking of in particular are Christ and Buddha. I believe that Jung belongs to that order of individual, you see. When a major new level of consciousness emerges, it has to have some huge collective effect that may take several hundred years to bring into visibility. But, eventually, that will be seen for what it is. That's how I see Jung.

I want to refer to a remark that Jung makes on this subject; it comes from page 311 of volume two of his *Letters.* I believe that it puts in a nutshell the basic idea behind "continuing incarnation." He says:

> Buddha's insight and the Incarnation in Christ break the chain through the intervention of the enlightened human consciousness, which thereby acquires a metaphysical and cosmic significance.

Now, of course, you're not going to get that in one reading. But he's referring there to the Buddhist notion of the "chain of suffering" that involves desirousness, leading to frustration, and finally to death—repeating itself endlessly. And he says that two things break it: he says "Buddha's insight" breaks it and the "Incarnation in Christ" breaks it. He doesn't say, "broke it," he doesn't use the past tense; he uses the present

---

[32] See McGuire and Hull, eds., *C. G. Jung Speaking,* for the following comment in "The Houston Films": "Everyone who says I am a mystic is just an idiot. He doesn't understand the first word of psychology," p. 333.

tense. This means, then, that "Buddha's insight" and the "Incarnation in Christ" are current happenings which have the effect of breaking the chain of suffering "through the intervention of the enlightened human consciousness, which thereby acquires a metaphysical and cosmic significance."

Now, that's what happened in the Book of Job as Jung spells it out in *Answer to Job*. Job got a glimpse into the nature of the primordial psyche. As Jung puts it, he got a glimpse of the "back side" of God, the "abysmal world of shards." He saw it. That "seeing it" is "Buddha's insight." And it had the effect of bringing about the "Incarnation of Christ." In fact, Job was a kind of prefiguration of the "Incarnation in Christ," because he was the victim: his suffering was the sacrifice that had to be paid in order to achieve the insight that he got. So "Buddha's insight" and the "Incarnation in Christ" are illustrated in the Book of Job—they achieve the "intervention of the enlightened human consciousness, which thereby acquires a metaphysical and cosmic significance." It takes on divine attributes, and that corresponds to the incarnation of God. That enlightened human consciousness acquires a "metaphysical and cosmic significance" means that it is a carrier of the God-image. It's all there in that one sentence, and I was delighted when I came across it.

So, as human beings attempt to carry consciousness, they participate in the "transformation of God"?

Ah, there is another major image concerning the same issue. Jung says somewhere that it may very well be that his insights will have the effect of bringing about a major change, a major evolution, in the God-image.[33]

---

[33] It is not clear what reference Edinger has in mind. Jung does say in *Answer to Job*, "Whoever knows God has an effect on him" (par. 617). And Edinger often quotes Jung thus: "Just as Job lifted his voice so that everybody could hear him, I have come to the conclusion that I had better risk my skin and do my worst or best to shake the unconsciousness of my contemporaries rather than allow my laxity to let things drift towards the impending world catastrophe. Man must know that he is man's worst enemy just as much as God had to learn from Job

So, he's telling us quite explicitly that the consciousness of an individual human being does have the capacity of "transforming" the God-image. The question, of course, is: How does that happen? How are we to understand that; how are we to apply it to psychological experience that we can grasp? I'm not sure I can communicate how that's done, but I'm going to try. I spoke earlier about the objective psyche as being a pervading medium like the atmosphere in which we live. We participate in it, it's within us and is expressed through us; and it's also without. It's the medium we exist in that is usually invisible. The human ego is a part of that objective psyche. But it's a part that owes its existence to the fact that it's been able to separate itself and exist like a separate island; but it's still a part. So it's got an organic living connection between the medium out of which it was born and its own separateness.

Now, in the science of depth psychology, in the course of studying the objective psyche, the only means we have of studying it is the individual human ego—that's the only "I" there is. That means, however, that whenever the ego looks at the medium it influences the medium in the process of looking at it. Because the individual human ego has an organic attachment to the medium that it's studying—they're connected, they're not totally separate entities.

Well, that complicates things. It means that to some extent or other, the observing ego—as it studies the objective psyche—is "subjectifying" what it's studying. The ego can't help that; it's built into the situation. But, if we're aware of that fact, then we'll make allowances for it; and that will, at least, mitigate its effects. Now, that's the situation. The God-image is the central archetype, as Jung describes it, in that pervading medium of the objective psyche or the collective unconscious. And when the ego sees the God-image, when it consciously sees it for what it is, that very perception has the effect of altering it, you see—because of the nature of the connection between the ego and the Self. They're part of the same total organism, a total state of being; and, therefore, what hap-

---

about His own antithetical nature." (Gerhard Adler and Aniela Jaffé, *eds., C. G. Jung Letters*, vol. 2: 1951-1961 (Princeton: Princeton University Press, 1975), p. 239.

pens to one has an effect on the other. That's the mechanism, so to speak, whereby God undergoes transformation by being "seen" by a human ego.

Now, that's just an abstraction. But when you've had some living experiences that illustrate it, they're very impressive. Because what happens—in the course of a really deep analysis—is that the unconscious changes. It isn't just the ego that changes; the unconscious changes. And the rule of thumb that Jung has taught us is that the unconscious takes the same attitude toward the ego as the ego takes toward it. That's one aspect of how the unconscious changes when the ego pays attention to it. But the unconscious also changes when the ego has seen with its own "eyes" the raw view of the primordial psyche. Believe me, it's a terrible thing to see. There is an image of that in the Blake series on "Job" where Yahweh is showing Job his "back side"—the terrible monsters, Behemoth and Leviathan [See Figure 7, opposite].[34] It's an image of getting a glimpse of what the primordial psyche looks like, what God's "back side" is, you see. And when one has that view—not just hearsay knowledge—when one *sees* it in shuddering knee-knocking reality, that changes the nature of the primordial psyche. It does so first of all in oneself; and we have reason to believe that the effect goes beyond just one's own personal psyche.

Do you believe, as I do, that Jung will be remembered by future generations not primarily as a theoretician of depth psychotherapy but for the religious aspects of his work?

I'm not a prophet, but I have a perception, in broad outlines, of what I expect to happen. It's obvious to any thoughtful person that Western society is hurtling toward some terrible catastrophe. That's obvious. That means we are going to be exposed to massive suffering, something along the order of what went on 2,000 years ago with the disintegration of the Roman Empire—when the established social structures broke down and chaos intervened. Something like that's going to happen. And, in such a

---

[34] See Edinger, *Encounter with the Self: A Jungian Commentary on William Blake's "Illustrations of the Book of Job."*

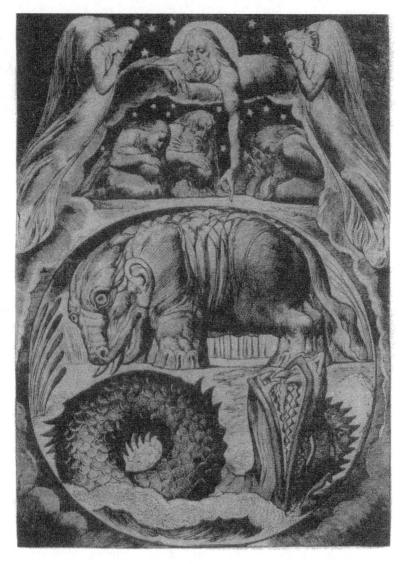

Figure 7. William Blake's Image of the "Back Side" of God—
Behemoth and Leviathan.

case, there will be reversions to more primitive modes of behavior, there will be a regressive movement backward. There will be a regression to tribalisms of all kinds, I'm sure, to primitive structures, more localized structures. There will be a regression to concrete and fundamentalist religions of various kinds. And I hope that the collective suffering on such a vast scale will force reflective individuals—what Toynbee calls the "creative minority"—to look around desperately for some kind of understanding of what's happening to them. If they're able to resist the regressive tendency to revert to more primitive modes of functioning, if they can hold on to their consciousness enough, then they might discover Jung. They might pick up *Answer to Job* and read Jung really attentively and realize that what's being experienced collectively on such a vast scale is a "Job experience" of humanity. That's what's in store for us, because we've lost our previous religious moorings. And the only way to a new religious connection, I think, is through the "Dark Valley."

Jung's *Answer to Job* spells it all out. It tells us what the "Job experience" means. And when humanity on a sizeable collective scale has had the Job experience, if they can locate *Answer to Job* at that point and study it diligently, it will give them their bearings. They will know the meaning of what they are experiencing—and that will make the suffering bearable. Because they'll realize that there's a purpose in it, and that the purpose is the "transformation of God," the emergence of a new God-image and the possibility—as I mentioned earlier—of a genuine unification of both the individual and the world. I think that in the long run, that's what's in store for the Age of Aquarius—after a terrible time of troubles.

In your book, The Christian Archetype: A Jungian Commentary on the Life of Christ, *you write, "The goal of the incarnation cycle , like the goal of individuation, is the Coniunctio. The time has come for the psychic opposites—heaven and earth, male and female, spirit and nature, good and evil—which have long been torn asunder in the Western psyche, to be reconciled." (p. 137) Can you elaborate on this idea?*

The basic question is: What is this thing called the "Coniunctio"? You know, Jung's last book-length work is on that subject. The title is *Mysterium Coniunctionis—The Mystery of the Coniunctio*—a very sizeable tome.[35] And it was the theme that really preoccupied him in his last years. During his illness in 1944, he had some profound experiences of the Coniunctio which he reports in his *Memories, Dreams, Reflections*.[36] The question is: How are we to understand the symbolic image? You see, it comes from alchemy. I mentioned earlier that the goal of the alchemical process was the Philosophers' Stone. And it was created, so the alchemists thought, by the Coniunctio of "purified opposites." So, their basic image was the Coniunctio of "Sol and Luna"—Sun and Moon create the Philosopher's Stone. Thus, the Coniunctio is that process which achieves the Philosophers' Stone, which achieves Selfhood, which achieves the living connection to the God-image. And it was pictured as a "marriage" or as an act of "sexual intercourse."

Now, we know that just on the biological level the goal of existence is the creation of offspring—achieved through intercourse. That's the reason Nature has built into us the experience of supreme bliss at the peak of sexual intercourse. Nature, of course, knows what she's doing. So, the physical "Coniunctio" is the goal of our existence as a biological organism. What Jung has demonstrated is that the psychological "Coniunctio" is the goal of existence as a psychological organism.

Now, the only difficulty is being able to grasp what that means. It's easy enough to grasp what sexual intercourse means, we can encompass that in a definition. But the psychological Coniunctio is an image of the achievement of totality which transcends the ego—transcends, therefore, the rational ability to define it. Therefore, we can't define it. We can talk about it, and we can sort of circumambulate it and bring up images that express it. But we can't grasp it or contain it rationally, because it's bigger than we are.

There's reason to believe that the Coniunctio is only experienced in its

---

[35] Jung, *Mysterium Coniunctionis, CW* 14.

[36] See C. G. Jung, *Memories, Dreams, Reflections*, ed. Aniela Jaffé (New York: Vintage Books, 1961), chap. 10, "Visions."

complete form in death, in physical death. And I think that's good to know, because there's a real need to reappraise in the modern world the nature and significance of death. Death is the goal of life. And in a different sense than Freud meant it, there really is a "death instinct." We've got the instinctual equipment built into us to take care of all the basic occurrences in human existence; these are the archetypal patterns that are built into us. Our physical life ends in death, and we've got the instinctual wisdom to relate to that phenomenon properly if we're in touch with that wisdom. Part of that wisdom, I think, is the realization that one level of psychological existence is achieved and fulfilled in the process of physical death—the Coniunctio is realized probably to the fullest extent at that time. Jung's visions of the Coniunctio occurred during a near-death experience; he almost died during that 1944 illness. But they contained images of great joy and fulfillment.

The Coniunctio, then, is the biological experience of sexuality on the psychological plane. And that's why sexual images have to be used to refer to it. Perhaps our finest document concerning it is the Song of Songs in the Bible.[37] Of course, there's more to be said about it. It's an image of totality. It's an image of the reconciliation of opposites. On the simplest level, it's the reconciliation of the opposites, "male and female." But those images can be used to express all the pairs of opposites. The Coniunctio, then, is an image of harmony beyond the conflict of all the opposites that make up the struggle and agony of existence.

---

[37] See Edinger, *The Bible and the Psyche: Individuation Symbolism in the Old Testament,* chap. 14, "Coniunctio: The Song of Songs."

Figure 9. Edinger teaching in Los Angeles (1994).

PART III

JUNG DISTILLED

An Outline of Analytical Psychology[38]
Edward F. Edinger

Analytical psychology is the school of depth psychology based on the discoveries and concepts of Carl Gustav Jung. Jung gave the broadest and most comprehensive view of the human psyche yet available. His writings include a fully-developed theory of the structure and dynamics of the psyche in both its conscious and unconscious aspects, a detailed theory of personality types and, most important, a full description of the universal, primordial images deriving from the deepest layer of the unconscious psyche. These primordial images are called *archetypes of the collective unconscious*. The latter discovery has enabled Jung to describe striking parallels between the unconscious images produced by individuals in dream and vision, and the universal motifs found in the religions and mythologies of all ages.

The concept of the collective unconscious gives Analytical psychology an added dimension in comparison with other schools of psychotherapy. It takes the theory and practice of psychotherapy out of the exclusive realm of psychopathology and relates it to the whole history of the evolution of the human psyche in all its cultural manifestations. The practice of Analytical psychology thus becomes not only a therapy for neurosis but also a technique for psychological development applicable to normal and superior individuals.

An abstract, theoretical presentation is alien to Jung who always strove to engage the response of the whole man, not just the intellect. This presentation should thus be recognized as no more than a two-dimensional sketch of a three-dimensional reality.

---

[38] This essay was originally published in *Quadrant* 1 (1968), pp. 1ff.—Eds.

Libido

The psychic energy that directs and motivates the personality is called *libido*. Interest, attention, and drive are all expressions of libido. The libido invested in a given item is indicated by how highly it is valued. Libido can be transformed or displaced but not destroyed. If the libido attached to one object disappears, it reappears elsewhere. Libido is the dynamism of the life process manifested in the psychic sphere.

The theory of libido is closely connected with the *law of opposites*. The processes of the psyche depend on a tension and interplay between opposite poles. If one side of a pair of opposites becomes excessively predominant in the personality, it is likely to turn into its contrary. This is called *enantiodromia*. A one-sided conscious attitude constellates its opposite in the unconscious. See Jung's essay "On Psychic Energy."[39]

Psychological Types

Analytical psychology distinguishes several psychological types. These refer to innate differences in temperament that cause individuals to perceive and react to life in different fashions. There are two *attitude types*, the *extravert* and the *introvert*.

The *extravert* is characterized by an innate tendency for his libido to flow outwards, connecting him with the external world. He naturally and spontaneously gives greatest interest and value to the *object*—people, things, external accomplishments, etc. The extravert will be most comfortable and successful when functioning in the external world and human relationships. He will be restless and ill at ease when alone without diversion. Having little relation to the inner world of subjectivity, he will shun it and tend to depreciate subjective concerns as morbid and selfish.

The *introvert* is characterized by a tendency for his libido to flow inwards connecting him with his subjective, inner world of thought, fantasies, and feelings. He gives greatest interest and value to the *subject*—the inner reactions and images. The introvert will function most satisfactorily on his own and when he is free from pressure to adapt to external cir-

---

[39] In Jung, *The Structure and Dynamics of the Psyche*, CW 8, pars. 1ff.

cumstances. He prefers his own company and is reserved or uncomfortable in large groups.

Both introvert and extravert have the defects of their strengths, and each tends to undervalue the other. To the extravert, the introvert is self-centered and withholding of himself. To the introvert, the extravert seems shallow, opportunistic, and hypocritical.

Every individual possesses both tendencies, but one is usually more developed than the other. As a pair of opposites, they follow the law of opposites. Thus, an excessive, one-sided emphasis on one attitude is likely to lead to the emergence of its opposite. The opposite, however, because it is undeveloped and undifferentiated, will appear in a negative, crude, and unadapted form. Thus, the extreme extravert will become a victim of negative inferior introversion in the form of depressions. The extreme introvert is likely to have episodes of compulsive extraversion which are crude, ineffectual, and unadapted to outer reality.

In addition to attitude types, we also distinguish four function types. The four basic psychological functions are *thinking, feeling, sensation,* and *intuition.*

Thinking is the rational capacity to structure and synthesize discrete data by means of conceptual generalizations. *Feeling* is the function that determines value. It is the function that values and promotes human relationships. *Sensation* is that function which perceives and adapts to external reality via the senses. *Intuition* is defined as perception via the unconscious, that is, the perception of representations or conclusions whose origin is obscure. These four functions arrange themselves into two pairs of opposites: thinking—feeling, and sensation—intuition.

Although every individual has all four functions potentially at his disposal, in actuality one function is usually more fully developed than the others. This is called the *superior function.* The one least developed is the one that is most primitive and unconscious—the *inferior function.*

Often a second function will have achieved considerable development which approaches that of the superior function. This is an *auxiliary function.* Since any one of the four functions may be superior, we have the possibility of four function types: the *thinking type, feeling type, sensa-*

tion type, and *intuitive type*.

The *thinking type* is found chiefly among men. A man's mental life is concerned largely with the creation of intellectual formulae and the fitting of all life experience into these forms. To the degree that he is identified with the thinking function and unconscious of the other functions, his thinking will tend to be autocratic and his formulae Procrustean beds which do violence to the fullness of life. Since feeling will be the inferior function, its values will suffer the most neglect. Human relationships will be quickly sacrificed if they interfere with the ruling formula.

The *feeling type* is found chiefly among women. The development and sustenance of personal relationships is the major aim. A sensitivity to human needs and a willingness to meet them is its outstanding characteristic. It finds its greatest satisfaction in rapport with others. In its extreme, this function type can be objectionable in its excessive emphasis on personal matters. Since thinking is the inferior function, its capacity for abstract, impersonal judgments will be neglected or denied. Thinking will be accepted only so long as it plays a subservient role to the interests of feeling relationships.

The *sensation type* is characterized by his excellent adaptation to simple, matter-of-fact reality. He is content to relate to life on its most elementary terms without subtlety, reflection, or imagination. The sensation type appears stable and earthy but rather dull. Vision and imagination which could mitigate this earthbound state are products of intuition, which is the inferior function of this type. The sensation type, in fact, will depreciate all intuitive expressions as unrealistic fantasies and thus deprive himself of badly needed leaven for his own heaviness.

The *intuitive type* is motivated chiefly by a steady stream of new visions and possibilities that derive from his active intuition. The new, the strange, and the different are a constant lure. He often perceives obscure connections between things that seem separate and unrelated. His mind works in quick jumps that others can't follow. When asked to proceed more slowly, he is apt to become impatient, considering his listeners dull-witted. This type's weakness lies in its inferior sensation function. His relation to reality is poor. The hard work required to bring a possibility into actuality or to make an intuitive flash generally accepted seems too onerous. He thus often remains misunderstood—and his insights, if they are to bear fruit, must be patiently developed by others.

The function types are seldom as definite as would appear by these descriptions. Usually the development of an auxiliary function will soften and modify the sharp characteristics here described. In addition, we have a further complication. According to the attitude type, each of the function types may have either an introverted or an extraverted orientation.

Ideally, all four functions should be available to the individual in order for him to have a complete response to life experience. It is one of the goals of Jungian psychotherapy to bring into consciousness, and to aid the development of, the inferior undeveloped functions in order to approach psychic wholeness.

Many conflicts in human relationships and disputes can be understood through the theory of psychological types. For instance, Jung has explained the difference between the psychological theories of Freud and Adler on this basis. Freud's theory is concerned chiefly with the individual's need for and love of the object. Thus, it is an extraverted theory. Adler's theory is based on the individual's need to maintain his own self-esteem, prestige and power. Adler emphasizes the inner, subjective need; hence, his is an introverted theory.

Differences in type can underlie difficulties in interpersonal relationships. Marital conflicts are often related to differences in psychological type. Knowledge of one's own type and of the fact that other equally valid types exist can often help to relativize one's own personal reactions and can lead to more conscious and fruitful human relationships.[40]

Structure of the Psyche

The psyche can be divided into *conscious* and *unconscious* aspects. The *ego* is the center of consciousness and the starting point for all empirical psychology. It is the seat of individual identity, and all contents which

---

[40] Jung, *Psychological Types, CW 6.*

are conscious must be connected with it. The *unconscious* includes all psychic elements that are outside conscious awareness and therefore not connected with the ego.

Contents of the unconscious are first encountered as *complexes*. A *complex* is an emotionally charged unconscious psychic entity made up of a number of associated ideas and images clustered around a central core. On investigation this core is found to be an *archetypal image* (see below). One recognizes that a complex has been struck by the emergence of an affect which upsets psychic balance and disturbs the customary function of the ego.

The ego stands between the inner world and the outer world, and its task is to adapt to both. By its extraverted orientation, it relates itself to external reality. By introversion, it perceives and adapts to inner, subjective reality. The requirement for external adaptation leads to the construction of a psychic structure that mediates between the ego and the external world of society. This mediating structure is called the *persona*, the Latin word for the ancient actor's mask. It is the partially calculated public face an individual assumes towards others. The persona is composed of various elements: some based on the individual's personal propensities, and others derived from the society's expectations and the early training of parents and teachers.

The persona is a mediating compromise between individuality and the expectations of others. It is the role one plays in society. It is also a protective covering that shields from public view what is personal, intimate, and vulnerable. The characteristic symbol for the persona is the clothes we wear. Dreams involving missing or inappropriate clothes refer to a persona problem. Ideally a persona should be appropriate, well-fitting, and flexible. It is especially important that the individual realize that he is not identical with his persona.

The persona sometimes lends one a prestige and authority belonging to the collective group which is not properly used for personal ends. To identify with the persona can cause inflation and alienation from reality. Other persona disorders include a lack of persona which leaves the individual sensitive and exposed to every social touch and a too rigid, defensive persona which is a barrier to realistic adaptation. For further discussion of the persona, see Jung's *Two Essays on Analytical Psychology*.[41]

Just as the persona stands between the ego and the outer world, so another psychic entity stands between the ego and the inner world of the unconscious. This entity is called the *shadow*. The shadow is a composite of personal characteristics and potentialities of which the individual is unaware. Usually the shadow, as indicated by the word, contains inferior characteristics and weaknesses that the ego's self-esteem will not permit it to recognize.

The persona may be personified in dreams by such figures as criminals, drunkards, and derelicts. Technically, it must be of the same sex as the dreamer. As with all unconscious contents, the shadow is first experienced in *projection*. This means that an unconscious quality of one's own is first recognized and reacted to when it is discovered in an outer object. So long as the shadow is projected, the individual can hate and condemn freely the weakness and evil he sees in others, while maintaining his own sense of righteousness. Discovery of the shadow as a personal content may, if it is sudden, cause temporary confusion and depression. This will be most likely if the ego's previous attitude had been especially inflated.

The shadow is the first layer of the unconscious to be encountered in psychological analysis. It is not always a negative content. In many cases, unconscious positive potentialities of the personality reside in the shadow. In such cases, we speak of a *positive shadow*. Furthermore, the evil and dangerous aspect of the shadow is often due more to its circumstances than to its essence. Just as animals that have become vicious by starvation and brutal treatment can be changed into loyal companions by loving care, so the shadow loses much of its negative aspect when given conscious acceptance and attention.

The problem of the shadow and its projection applies to collective psychology as well. The persecution of the Jews by the Nazis is a terrifying example of the extent to which a collective shadow projection can go. The same psychological mechanism operates in discrimination

---

[41] Jung, *Two Essays on Analytical Psychology*, CW 7, pars. 243ff., 305ff.

against black people and other minority groups. For more on the shadow, see von Franz.[42]

The first layer of the unconscious, the shadow, is also called by Jung the *personal unconscious* as distinguished from the *collective unconscious*. The personal unconscious or shadow contains personal contents belonging to the individual himself which can, and properly should, be made conscious and integrated into the conscious personality or ego. The collective unconscious, on the other hand, is composed of transpersonal, universal contents which cannot be assimilated by the ego. Between these two layers of the unconscious—the personal and the collective—is another entity with, so to speak, one foot on each side. This is the *anima* in a man and the *animus* in a woman.

The *anima* is an autonomous psychic content in the male personality which can be described as an inner woman. She is the psychic representation of the contrasexual elements in man and is depicted in symbolic imagery by figures of women ranging from harlot and seductress to divine wisdom and spiritual guide. She is the personification of the *feminine principle* in man, the principle of *Eros*, pertaining to love and relatedness. The projection of the anima is responsible for the phenomenon of a man's "falling in love." Identification of the ego with the anima causes the man to become effeminate, sensitive, and resentful—behaving as an inferior woman.

Anima moods or states of *anima possession* can be recognized by their characteristic features of resentment and emotional withdrawal. Such a condition renders a man psychically paralyzed and impotent, reduced to the state of a sulky child. It is most likely to occur in relation to a woman with whom he is emotionally involved, especially his wife. With full psychological development, the anima leads the man to the full meaning of human relationship and provides him an entrance to the deeper layers of the psyche, the collective unconscious.

The *animus* is the corresponding representative of the masculine contrasexual elements in the psychology of women. It can be expressed in

---

[42] Marie-Louise von Franz, "The Process of Individuation," in *Man and His Symbols*, ed. C.G. Jung (New York: Dell Publishing Company, 1964), pp. 171ff.

symbolic imagery by a multitude of male figures, from frightening, aggressive men threatening rape to divine light-bringers. It is the personification of the *masculine principle* in women, the principle of *Logos*, which is the capacity for rationality and consciousness. A woman's "falling in love" is likewise due to the projection of the animus. Subjective identification of the ego with the animus causes the woman to lose contact with her feminine nature and behave as an inferior man. She becomes rigid, aggressively bitter, and opinionated.

The animus-possessed woman is more interested in power than in relatedness. As with the man's anima, the animus is most often activated in relation to an emotionally significant man, especially the husband. Indeed, the anima and animus have a marked affinity for each other. The slightest evidence of one is likely to evoke the other in the partner. With maturity and maximum development, the animus can become a valuable psychic entity, enabling the woman to function with objective rationality and—similar to the anima in a man—opens to her the collective unconscious. Further discussion of anima and animus is in Jung and von Franz.[43]

The *collective unconscious*, more recently termed the *objective psyche*, is the deepest layer of the unconscious which is ordinarily inaccessible to conscious awareness. Its nature is universal, suprapersonal, and non-individual. Its manifestations are experienced as something alien to the ego, numinous or divine. The contents of the collective unconscious are called *archetypes* and their particular symbolic manifestations, *archetypal images*.

The concept of the archetype has a close relation to the concept of *instinct*. An instinct is a pattern of behavior which is inborn and characteristic for a certain species. Instincts are discovered by observing the behavior patterns of individual organisms. The instincts are the unknown motivating dynamisms that determine an animal's behavior on the biological level.

An archetype is to the psyche what an instinct is to the body. The exis-

---

[43] See Jung, *Two Essays*, *CW* 7, pars. 296ff., and von Franz, "Individuation," in *Man and His Symbols*, pp. 186ff.

tence of archetypes is inferred by the same process as that by which we infer the existence of instincts. Just as instincts common to a species are postulated by observing the uniformities in biological behavior, so archetypes are inferred by observing the uniformities in psychic phenomena. Just as instincts are unknown motivating dynamisms of biological behavior, archetypes are unknown motivating dynamisms of the psyche. Archetypes are the psychic instincts of the human species. Although biological instincts and psychic archetypes have a very close connection, exactly what this connection is we do not know any more than we understand just how the mind and body are connected.

Archetypes are perceived and experienced subjectively through certain universal, typical, recurring mythological motifs and images. These *archetypal images*, symbolically elaborated in various ways, are the basic contents of religions, mythologies, legends, and fairy tales of all ages. Such images also emerge from the collective unconscious of individuals through dreams and visions in cases of deep psychological analysis, profound subjective experience, or major mental disorder. The experience of encountering an archetypal image has a strong emotional impact which conveys a sense of divine or suprapersonal power transcending the individual ego. Such an experience often transforms the individual and radically alters his outlook on life.

Archetypal images are so various and numerous that they defy comprehensive listing. For our purposes, we shall describe four broad categories of archetypal imagery.

1) *The Archetype of the Great Mother*, the personification of the feminine principle, represents the fertile womb out of which all life comes and the darkness of the grave to which it returns. Its fundamental attributes are the capacity to nourish and to devour. It corresponds to Mother Nature in the primordial swamp—life being constantly spawned and constantly devoured. If the Great Mother nourishes us, she is good; if she threatens to devour us, she is bad. In psychological terms, the Great Mother corresponds to the unconscious which can nourish and support the ego or can swallow it up in psychosis or suicide. The positive, creative aspects of the Great Mother are represented by breast and womb.

The negative, destructive aspects appear as the devouring mouth of the *vagina dentata*. In more abstract symbolism, anything hollow, concave, or containing pertains to the Great Mother. Thus, bodies of water, the earth itself, caves, dwellings, vessels of all kinds are feminine. So also is the box, the coffin, and the belly of the monster which swallows up its victims. See Neumann.[44]

2) *The Archetype of the Spiritual Father*. As the Great Mother pertains to nature, matter and earth, the Great Father archetype pertains to the realm of light and spirit. It is the personification of the masculine principle, of consciousness symbolized by the upper solar region of heaven. From this region comes the wind, *pneuma, nous, ruach*—which has always been the symbol of spirit as opposed to matter. Sun and rain likewise represent the masculine principle as fertilizing forces which impregnate the receptive earth. Images of piercing and penetration such as phallus, knife, spear, arrow, and ray all pertain to the Spiritual Father. Feathers, birds, airplanes, and all that refers to flying or height are part of this complex of symbols which emphasizes the upper heavenly realms. In addition, all imagery involving light or illumination pertain to the masculine principle as opposed to the dark earthiness of the Great Mother. Shining blond hair, illumination of the countenance, crowns, halos, and dazzling brilliance of all kinds are aspects of masculine solar symbolism.

The image of the *Wise Old Man* as judge, priest, doctor, or elder is a human personification of this same archetype. The positive aspect of the Spiritual Father principle conveys law, order, discipline, rationality, understanding, and inspiration. Its negative aspect is that it may lead to alienation from concrete reality causing inflation, a state of spiritual hybris, or presumption that generates grandiose thoughts of transcendence and results in the fate of Icarus or Phaethon.

3) *The Archetype of Transformation* pertains to a psychic process of growth, change, and transition. It can express itself in many different

---

[44] Erich Neumann, *The Great Mother: An Analysis of the Archetype* (New York: Pantheon, 1955).

images with the same underlying core of meaning. Perilous journeys to unknown destinations, exploration of dark places, purposeful descent to the underworld or under the sea or into the belly of a monster to find a hidden treasure are expressions of this archetype. The theme of death and rebirth as well as the symbolism of initiation rites in all of their various forms; the crossing of rivers or waters or chasms, and the climbing of mountains; the theme of redemption, salvation, or recovery of what has been lost or degraded wherever it appears in mythological or unconscious symbolism—all of these are expressions of the archetype of transformation.

The theme of the birth of the Hero or Wonder-Child also belongs to this archetype. This image expresses the emergence of a new, dynamic content in the personality presaging decisive change and enlargement of consciousness.[45]

A rich and complex example of this archetype is provided by the symbolism of medieval alchemy. In alchemy the psychic transformation process was projected into matter. The goal of the alchemists was to transmute base matter into gold or some other supremely valuable object. The imagery of alchemy derives from the collective unconscious and belongs properly to the psychological process of transformation.[46]

4) *The Central Archetype,* the *Self,* expresses psychic wholeness or totality. The *Self* is defined by Jung as both the center and circumference of the psyche. It incorporates within its paradoxical unity all the opposites embodied in the masculine and feminine archetypes. Since it is a borderline concept referring to an entity which transcends and encompasses the individual ego, we can only allude to it and not encompass it by a definition. As the central archetype is emerging, it often appears as a process of centering or as a process involving the union of opposites.

Alchemical symbolism gives us numerous examples of the central archetype as a union of opposites. For example, the Philosophers' Stone, one of the goals of the alchemical process, was depicted as resulting

---

[45] See Jung, *Symbols of Transformation, CW* 5.

[46] See Jung, *Psychology and Alchemy, CW* 12.

from the marriage of the red king and the white queen, or from the union of sun and moon, or fire and water. The product of such a union is a paradoxical image often described as hermaphroditic. Other images which are used to express the union of opposites are the reconciliation of opposing partisan factions and the reconciliation of good and evil, God and Satan.

The emerging central archetype gives rise to images of the *mandala*. The term mandala is used to describe the representations of the Self, the archetype of totality. The typical mandala in its simplest form is a quad-rated circle combining the elements of a circle with a center plus a square, a cross, or some other expression of fourfoldness.

Mandalas are found everywhere in all times and places. They seem to represent a basic unifying and integrating principle which lies at the very root of the psyche. Mandalas can be found in the cultural products of all races. A fully developed mandala usually emerges in an individual's dreams only after a long process of psychological development. It is then experienced as a release from an otherwise irreconcilable conflict and may convey a numinous awareness of life as something ultimately har-monious and meaningful in spite of its apparent contradictions.[47]

Psychological Development

Psychological development is the progressive emergence and differentia-tion of the ego or consciousness from the original state of unconscious-ness. It is a process which, ideally, continues throughout the lifetime of the individual. In contradistinction to physical development, there is no time at which one can say that full psychic development has been achieved. Although we may distinguish various stages of development for descriptive purposes, actually one stage merges into another in a sin-gle fluid continuum.

In the early phase, the ego has very little autonomy. It is largely in a

---

[47] See Jung, "Concerning Mandala Symbolism," in *The Archetypes and the Col-lective Unconscious*, *CW* 9i, pars. 627ff.; also von Franz, "Individuation," in *Man and His Symbols,* pp. 230f.

state of identification with the objective psyche within and the external world without. It lives in the world of archetypes and makes no clear distinction between inner and outer objects. This primitive state of ego development is called, after Lévy-Bruhl, *participation mystique*, and is shared by both the primitive and the child. It is a state of magical participation and interpenetration between the ego and its surroundings. What is ego and what is non-ego are not distinguished. Inner world and outer world are experienced as a single totality. This primitive state of participation mystique is also evident in the phenomena of mob psychology in which individual consciousness and responsibility are temporarily eclipsed by identification with a collective dynamism.

Jung made no effort to present a systematic theory of psychological development. However, some of his followers, especially Neumann, have attempted to fill in this gap. Following Neumann, the stages of psychological development can be described as follows.[48]

The first or original state is called the *uroboric stage*, derived from *uroborus*, the circular image of the tail-eating serpent. It refers to the original totality and self-containment which is prior to the birth of consciousness. The ego exists only as a latent potentiality in a state of primary identity with the Self or objective psyche. This state is presumed to pertain during the prenatal period and early infancy.

The transition between this state and the second stage of development corresponds to the creation of the world for the individual psyche. Thus, world creation myths refer to this first decisive event in psychic development—the birth of the ego out of the unconscious. The basic theme of all creation myths is separation. Out of undifferentiated wholeness, one element is discriminated from another. It may be expressed as the creation of light—the separation of light from darkness—or as the separation of the world parents, the distinction between masculine and feminine, or the emergence of order out of chaos. In each case, the meaning is the same, namely, the birth of consciousness, the capacity to discriminate between opposites.

---

[48] See Erich Neumann, *The Origins and History of Consciousness* (New York: Pantheon, 1956).

The second stage of psychological development is called the *matriarchal phase*. Although beginning consciousness has appeared, it is as yet only dim and fitful. The nascent ego is still largely passive and dependent on its uroboric matrix which now takes on the aspect of the Great Mother. The predominant concern will be to seek her nourishment and support and to avoid her destructive, devouring aspect. The Father archetype or masculine principle has not yet emerged into separate existence. Mother is still all. The ego has achieved only a precarious separation and is still dependent on the unconscious, which is personified as the Great Mother.

The matriarchal phase is represented mythologically by the imagery of the Ancient Near Eastern Mother religions, for example, the Cybele-Attis myth. Attis, the son-lover of Cybele, was unfaithful to her. In a frenzy of regret, reflecting his dependent bondage, he was castrated and killed. The matriarchal phase corresponds to the Oedipal phase as described by Freud. However, analytical psychologists interpret incest symbolically rather than literally as was done by Freud. The matriarchal phase is the phase of original incest, symbolically speaking, prior to the emergence of the incest taboo. In the life of the individual, this phase corresponds roughly with the early years of childhood.

The third stage is called the *patriarchal phase*. The transition is characterized by particular themes, images, and actions. In an attempt to break free from the matriarchal phase, the feminine with all its attributes is rejected and depreciated. The theme of initiation rituals pertains to this period of transition. The Father archetype or masculine principle emerges in full force and claims the allegiance of the individual. Tests, challenges, rules, and discipline are set up in opposition to the sympathy and comfortable containment of the Great Mother. The incest taboo is erected prohibiting regression to the mother-bound state.

Once the transition to the patriarchal stage has been accomplished, the archetype of the Great Father, the masculine spirit principle, determines the values and goals of life. Consciousness, individual responsibility, self-discipline, and rationality will be the prevailing values. Everything pertaining to the feminine principle will be repressed, depreciated, or subordinated to masculine ends. Women will be tolerated as necessary but inferior versions of the human species. In childhood development, the patriarchal phase will be particularly evident in the years preceding puberty.

The fourth phase I designate the *integrative phase*. The preceding patriarchal phase has left the individual one-sided and incomplete. The feminine principle, woman—and, therefore, the anima and the unconscious—have been repressed and neglected. Another change or transition is thus needed to redeem these neglected psychic elements.

This transition phase also has its characteristic imagery. The most typical myth is the hero fighting the dragon. In this archetypal story, a beautiful maiden is in captivity to a dragon or monster. The maiden is the anima, the precious but neglected feminine principle that has been rejected and depreciated in the previous patriarchal phase of development. The monster represents the residual uroboric state, the Great Mother in its destructive, devouring aspect. The anima or feminine value is still attached to this dangerous element and can be freed only by heroic action. The hero represents the necessary ego attitude that is willing to relinquish the safety of the conventional patriarchal standards and expose himself once again to the unconscious, the dangers of regression and bondage to the woman, in order to redeem a lost but necessary element, the anima. If this is successful, the anima or feminine principle is raised to its proper value, modifying and completing the previous one-sided patriarchal attitude.

This is a decisive step in psychological integration that amounts to a reconciliation of opposites: masculine and feminine, law and love, conscious and unconscious, spirit and nature. In individual development of the youth, this phase corresponds to the emerging capacity to relate to girls during puberty which is subsequently followed by love for a particular woman and eventually marriage.

It should be understood that although these phases of psychic development have been related to various periods in the development of the child and young man, their meaning is not confined to these external events. The end of psychological development is not reached when a man marries. Such external happenings are only the external manifestations of an archetypal process of development which still awaits its inner realization. Furthermore, the series of psychological stages here described can be traversed not once but many times in the course of psychic development. These stages are, so to speak, successive way stations that we return to again and again in the course of a spiral journey that takes one over the same course repeatedly—but each time on a different level of conscious awareness.

The foregoing account of development refers particularly to masculine psychology. Although the same stages of development apply to a woman, they will be experienced in a somewhat different way. Relevant myths are those of Demeter and Persephone and Amor and Psyche. See Neumann.[49]

Jung's major contribution to developmental psychology is his concept of *individuation*. The term refers to a developmental process which begins in the adult individual, usually after the age of thirty-five, and if successful leads to the discovery of the Self and its replacing of the ego as the personality center.

Individuation is the discovery of and the extended dialogue with the objective psyche of which the Self is the comprehensive expression. It begins with one or more decisive experiences challenging egocentricity and producing an awareness that the ego is subject to a more comprehensive psychic entity. Although the full fruits of the individuation process only appear in the second half of life, the evolving relation between the ego and the objective psyche is a continuous one from birth to death.

The Process of Psychotherapy

Psychotherapy is a systematic examination and cultivation of the inner life. It is applicable not only to neurosis and mental disorders but also to those with a normal psychology who wish to promote their own psychological development. A unique and comprehensive technique has been

---

[49] See Erich Neumann, *Amor and Psyche: The Psychic Development of the Feminine* (Princeton: Princeton University Press, 1956).

developed. The basic instrument of this procedure is the personality of the psychotherapist. Major care and attention is thus given to the selection and training of potential psychotherapists.

The primary requirement for a psychotherapist is that he have a thorough personal analysis which leads to a high level of psychological development. It is a basic axiom that a therapist can lead his patient's psychic development no further than he himself has gone. Fundamentally, it is the patient's opportunity to have a living relationship and dialogue with a more developed conscious personality that produces the healing effect.

After the initial consultation when the decision is made to begin work with a particular psychotherapist, the procedure is started by taking a detailed *anamnesis*. This is a historical summary and discussion of all significant life experiences in chronological order that the patient can recall. Next comes an examination of the current life situation with particular emphasis on areas that are felt to be problematical. Only when the past and the present have been explored adequately, so far as they are available to consciousness, does the therapist turn his attention to the unconscious.

The major approach to the unconscious is through *dream interpretation*. A *dream* is considered to be an expression of the objective psyche describing in symbolic language the nature of the current psychic situation. The understanding of dreams thus becomes a powerful aid in the growth of consciousness.

A dream is a *symbol*. This term has a particular connotation in Analytical psychology. A symbol is not a sign and does not stand for a known meaning that could be expressed equally well in another way. A symbol is an image or form giving the best expression available to a content whose meaning is still largely unknown. On the basis of this definition, it is clear that a symbol (or dream) cannot be interpreted as though it were a sign standing for a well-known meaning. It must be approached by the method of *analogy*, which amplifies the unknown meaning to the point of visibility.

In Analytical psychology, the interpretation of dreams is undertaken by *amplification*. The method has two aspects, *personal amplification* and *general amplification*.

Personal amplification is done by asking the patient for associations to each of the specific items and figures in the dream. *Associations* are the spontaneous feelings, thoughts, and memories that come to mind concerning the given item in the dream. The total of the associations to all the elements in the dream provide the personal context of the dream and often lead to a significant meaning.

General amplification is done by the psychotherapist on the basis of his own knowledge. It provides the collective, archetypal associations to the dream elements. Here is where the therapist's knowledge of the collective or objective psyche is put to use. When a dream contains an archetypal image or theme, the therapist demonstrates this by presenting parallel imagery from mythology, legend, and folklore. General amplification establishes the collective context of the dream, enabling it to be seen as referring not only to a personal psychic problem but also to a general, collective problem common to all human experience. General amplification introduces the patient to the collective or objective psyche and at the same time helps the process of disidentifying the ego from the objective psyche. As long as the patient experiences his problems and his dreams as referring only to his personal psychology, his ego remains largely identified with the objective psyche; and he carries a burden of collective guilt and responsibility not properly personal which can paralyze his capacity to function.

In addition to dreams, imaginative and expressive activity of all kinds is encouraged. Drawing, painting, sculpture, story writing, etc., may be suggested as means of expressing emerging unconscious material. Such creative products are then examined in much the same way as dreams. Even without analytic interpretation, the effort to give verbal or visual expression to unconscious images can often be very useful. The objectification of a psychic image, by painting for instance, can help to disidentify the ego from the unconscious and may release a sum of psychic energy.

At a later stage of psychotherapy another important technique is introduced in suitable cases. This is called *active imagination*. This procedure must be learned and requires considerable experience to use. There must be discrimination in its use since in some cases there is danger that it might activate unconscious contents that cannot be controlled. Properly used, however, it is a very valuable technique.

Active imagination is a process of conscious, deliberate participation in fantasy. It often takes the form of a dialogue between the ego and a fantasy figure—perhaps the shadow or anima. It can be extremely helpful in bringing an unconscious content into consciousness especially when the ego feels it has reached an impasse. To the degree that a patient can use active imagination successfully on his own, he will have less need for the help of the therapist. Indeed, the development of this technique often leads to the termination of formal psychotherapy since the patient then has the capacity to relate to and deal with the unconscious on his own.

A very common and important phenomenon in psychotherapy is the *transference*. This refers to the emotional involvement, either positive or negative, based on unconscious factors that the patient feels for the psychotherapist. The transference is due to the projection of unconscious contents onto the therapist. Such projections may have varying kinds of content and intensity. Commonly, an early form of the projection is an expectation of being treated in the same way as the patient had been treated by the parent of the same sex as the analyst. However, in a deep transference after the analysis of these superficial aspects, it is generally found that the transference is based on the projection of the Self onto the analyst. The analyst then becomes endowed with all the awesome power and authority of the deity.

So long as this projection prevails, the relationship to the therapist will be the container for the highest life value. This is because the Self is the center and source of psychic life, and contact with it must be preserved at all cost. As long as the therapist is carrying the projection of the Self, the relationship with him will be equivalent to connection with the Self, which is vital to the patient's psyche. To the degree that this projection can be consciously recognized, dependence on the therapist will be replaced progressively by an inner relatedness to the Self. Through the intermediary step of experiencing and living through the transference, the patient will gradually reach awareness of the inner power and authority of the objective psyche as it is manifested within himself.[50]

Synchronicity

Synchronicity is the term Jung coined for a postulated acausal connecting principle to explain the occurrence of meaningful coincidences. The phenomenon of synchronicity stands on the borderline of human knowledge, and what is said about it must remain tentative. Nevertheless, there is a growing body of evidence indicating that under certain circumstances events in the outer world coincide meaningfully with inner psychic states. Evidence of extrasensory perception and parapsychological experiments indicate this.

Synchronistic events are often encountered during an analysis of the unconscious, particularly when the objective psyche has been activated. Sometimes, for instance, the pertinent associations to a dream refer to life experiences that occur *after* the dream rather than before it. Evidence is accumulating that the objective psyche functions beyond the categories of time and space. Dreams thus can allude to future events as well as to past events.

Whether or not an event can be considered an example of synchronicity depends on the individual's subjective response—whether he feels it to be a *meaningful* coincidence. Obviously such subjective judgments cannot be verified by objective statistical methods. Such subjective experiences are the empirical data of psychology. On this subjective basis it is known that synchronistic events do occur, sometimes with a numinous impact on the individual.

The full significance of synchronicity is still to be discovered. We already have hints from what is so far known that at some point the objec-

---

[50] See Jung, "The Psychology of the Transference," *The Practice of Psychotherapy, CW* 16. [See also Edinger, "The Transference Phenomenon," in Edinger, *Science of the Soul,* pp. 99ff.—Eds.]

tive psyche may emerge with outer physical reality to form a unitary reality transcending the antithesis of subject and object.[51]

The Collective Unconscious as Manifested in Psychosis[52]
Edward F. Edinger

I

Jung, in contrast to Freud and Adler, had extensive psychiatric experience dealing with hospitalized psychotic patients. The theories he later elaborated owe much to this intensive, first-hand contact with the bizarre mental contents of psychotics. Jung's ideas are, therefore, of special value for the understanding of psychosis. His theories, however, go beyond their specific application to psychiatry and throw considerable light on the general cultural manifestations of the psyche, especially religion and mythology.

Jung's fundamental contribution to psychology is his theory of archetypes and the collective unconscious. In studying the mental contents of psychotics he found recurring themes and images that showed remarkable similarity to the symbolism appearing in the religions and mythologies of the world. Such figures as the "divine hero," "the spiritual savior," or "the evil demon of darkness," such themes as "the battle with a devouring monster," "death and rebirth"—all these motifs appear with remarkable repetition in psyches. And it is these same motifs which form the basic content of religions and mythologies. Recurring psychic patterns of this type Jung has labeled "archetypes of the collective unconscious." They are considered to be psychic representations of the in-

---

[51] See Jung, "Synchronicity: An Acausal Connecting Principle," in *The Structure and Dynamics of the Psyche*, *CW* 8, pars. 816ff. [See also J. Gary Sparks, *At the Heart of Matter: Synchronicity and Jung's Spiritual Testament* (Inner City Books, 2007).—Eds.]

[52] This essay was first published in *American Journal of Psychotherapy* 9, no. 4 (October 1955), pp. 624ff. The clinical material herein was collected while the author was on the staff of Rockland State Hospital, Orangeburg, N.Y.—Eds.

stincts and are called collective because they are held in common by all mankind. They are also collective in the sense that they transcend the individual ego. They are suprapersonal, conveying energies of the race as a whole.

The relation between archetype and instinct provides a bridge between Freudian and Jungian thinking. The archetype is a kind of pictorial pattern of the instinct. As Jung says, "There are in fact no amorphous instincts, as every instinct bears in itself the pattern of its situation. It always fulfills an image, and the image has fixed qualities. . . . Such an image is an *a priori* type" [i.e., an archetype].[53]

If these psychic structures are considered infantile and pathological *per se*, then, since they appear in all races and cultures, humanity as a whole is pathological—and the term loses all meaning. It is true that in most cases these archetypal forces have been experienced in projected form personified as cosmic personages or events taking place in heaven or hell with no awareness of their psychic origin. By modern psychological standards this naive attitude could indeed be called primitive or immature. However, it is Jung's view that the archetypes themselves are healthy, normal constituents of the personality. They are psychic organs whose well-balanced functioning is as important as the performance of the heart or kidneys. What determines health or disease is the relation between these suprapersonal psychic forces and the conscious ego. If the ego loses its own boundaries and becomes identified with an archetype, or it defensively represses instinctual archetypal contents and loses all contact with them, the dynamic equilibrium of health is lost and one can speak of mental illness.

In most cases of mental illness, one finds a weak or defective ego that, to a varying degree, has identified with an archetypal image and is thus correspondingly alienated from reality. The extremes of such an identification are seen in acute psychosis. The opposite danger is the complete loss of contact with the archetypes, which are the primary sources of psychic energy. This is seen in its extreme form in simple schizophrenia.

---

[53] See Jung, "On the Nature of the Psyche," *The Structure and Dynamics of the Psyche, CW* 8, par. 398.

From this viewpoint, a living religion or mythology is considered essential for the healthy functioning of the psyche. The twin dangers, an inflated identification with the archetype and repression, with serious loss of vital energy, are avoided by providing a vessel or container for the archetypes—in most cases the dogmatic and ritualistic structure of the Church. Such a structure keeps the archetypal images in full view, so that their reality is never forgotten. At the same time, the individual is kept at a respectful psychological distance from them, thereby lessening the danger of identification.

Of course, to function properly, the mythological container must be acceptable to the conscious personality, including the critical intellect. In this respect traditional religion is currently failing for many people in its function as container for the archetypes. Jung considers his own psychological theories as an attempt to provide a new mythology or vessel for the archetypes which will be acceptable to the modern scientific mind.[54]

II

In discussing the collective unconscious as it is manifested in psychosis, no unusual clinical material is needed. The common, bizarre and grandiose delusions of the psychotics are well known. The very fact that these delusional patterns duplicate themselves so consistently demonstrates their "collective" nature. For the purpose of this paper, examples of several common themes of delusional thought will be presented briefly and examined in the light of Jungian theory.

An acute psychosis is considered to be an eruption of the collective unconscious with the fragmentation and dissociation of a weak, undeveloped conscious personality. The archetypal patterns and images that ordinarily govern life from the depths of the unconscious are suddenly exposed to view in bizarre and incongruous relations. The patient is literally living out a dream. Very often the ego undergoes an inflated identification with a highly charged, numinous archetypal figure, such as the

---

[54] See Jung, "The Psychology of the Child Archetype," in *The Archetypes and the Collective Unconscious*, *CW* 9i, par. 271.

hero or the savior. It is this pattern we see in the frequent case of delusional identification with Christ, who for Christians (and sometimes unconsciously for Jews) carries the projection of the archetype of the spiritual hero. A brief clinical example follows:

> A twenty-four-year-old white, married male who was recently ordained a
> Protestant minister suffered a sudden onset of an acute psychosis. He felt
> his congregation had elevated him to the position of Jesus Christ, and he
> began to experience auditory hallucinations in which God told him that he
> was the Messiah, carrying out the second coming of Christ. He attempted
> to fight against this message, but it was insisted upon. He was told to go
> among the churches of the world to make his mission known and preach
> the gospel.

This case illustrates a very common theme in psychosis. The patient,
an immature and unsure young man, was faced with a responsible task
far beyond his emotional capacity. In this situation, some saving force
was badly needed. The archetype of a spiritual savior, in the form of
Christ, was activated and emerged into consciousness. This could be
considered a purposeful attempt of the unconscious to remedy a serious
deficiency. However, if so, it failed. The feeble ego was overwhelmed by
this experience, lost its boundaries in an inflated identification with the
archetype—and became psychotic.

It is a basic premise of Jungian theory that psychic energy derives
from a tension between opposites.[55] Wherever one extreme attitude is
found, its direct opposite will be close at hand. This is well illustrated in
psychotics who, with their loss of conscious discrimination, become the
helpless victims of the clash between the archetypal opposites. For example, identification with the benevolent figure of Christ brings with it
the paranoid manifestations of attack by the Adversary, the Devil, or the
Evil Demon. Conversely, where paranoid phenomena predominate, a
grandiose state of inflated self-righteousness can usually be found as a
concomitant. The above patient showed no overt paranoid tendencies but
they are usually present in such cases.

---

[55] See Jung, "On Psychic Energy," in *The Structure and Dynamics of the Psyche*,
CW 8.

Another theme which occupies a central position in all religions is that of eternal life. This idea also appears not infrequently in psychosis. The following is an example:

A thirty-year-old white, divorced male college graduate, experienced a gradual onset of psychosis. He progressively neglected his responsibilities, was divorced for non-support, and wandered about aimlessly, preoccupied with abstruse problems. He became convinced that he was a "genius" and had been given special knowledge and insight into the nature of life. He was especially preoccupied with space and time. The patient claimed he had learned that "the secret of eternal life was within our grasp." Life expectancy shall increase progressively until we will eventually live forever. He considered that this knowledge should be evident to anyone who understands "the relationship of God to man." This patient denied any hallucinatory experiences, stating his knowledge came to him from his own thought.

Immortality is an image symbolizing the highest possible affirmation of life. In primitive forms of thinking it is taken concretely, where it represents the hope for a literal, eternal paradise. If taken symbolically, it can represent an intensity of living which is oblivious to or beyond time. It is well known that our sense of the passage of time varies with our interest and the emotional intensity with which we participate in life. In this patient, his pre-psychotic state was one of progressive withdrawal from responsibility with listlessness and boredom. Time hung heavy on his hands. In such a state, eternal or timeless life—namely, the chance of living fully and intensely beyond awareness of time—was needed urgently. The patient, however, failed to understand this symbolic message and, instead, became grandiosely identified with the unconscious wisdom.

A variant of the immortality theme is the alchemical attempt to produce an elixir of life. In his later years, Jung has devoted much effort to the study of alchemical symbolism. He considers the attempts of the alchemists to transform base metal into gold and to produce an elixir of life as projected symbolic images from the collective unconscious, which actually represents the possible transformation of the personality and the discovery of the sources of psychic energy in ourselves.[56] A remarkable parallel to the alchemical elixir of life appears in the delusional thought of the following patient who had never heard of alchemy:

> A sixty-four-year-old white housewife had symptoms of a delusional psychosis for three years prior to her hospitalization. She had formed an erotic attachment to a dentist, without his knowledge, and had become convinced that the dentist had discovered a miraculous medicine that would prolong life. She expected to receive this medicine as a gift from him and was planning to live a long, happy life in great wealth and with many friends. While describing these beliefs, the patient revealed her inflated state by obvious elation and a boastful, complacent manner completely inappropriate to her situation.

Dreams, delusions, and myths are spontaneous manifestations of the unconscious psyche, which is presumably telling us something about itself by means of these expressions. Supernatural and miraculous occurrences, such as a medicine that confers immortality, virgin birth, resurrection from death, etc., obviously do not refer to the real external world. However, this does not make them false if they are correctly understood. Jung believes that such supernatural elements in dream, myth, or fairy tale indicate that the material is referring specifically to the inner psychic world where the physical laws of nature do not prevail. Unconscious symbolism is figurative, metaphorical language. If such material is confused with external reality, it becomes delusion—but if taken symbolically as referring to the inner psychic world it is potential wisdom.

The above patient developed an erotic attraction to a dentist. Her sexuality and her emotional life previously had been largely repressed, and she was approaching old age without having lived fully. Her feelings for the dentist awakened new possibilities for a richer life experience. The wellsprings of life had been touched. It was *as if* she had been offered the elixir of life by the dentist. The unconscious has given a correct and meaningful interpretation of her situation in the only language it knows. If the conscious personality could have understood this message symbolically or metaphorically, she would have been forced to deal with

---

[56] See Jung, *Psychology and Alchemy, CW* 12.

the difficult reality problems presented. She was unable to do this, however, and instead became delusionally inflated with the conviction that she was to receive a literally life-giving medicine.

From the brief material presented, it is apparent that Jung considers the totality of the psyche to be purposeful and self-regulative. The contents of the unconscious lead to psychotic alienation from reality when applied to the external world; but if interpreted symbolically, they become a source of knowledge and self-understanding. It appears as if the unconscious (which is as old and wise as the body) attempted to compensate for the blindness and the inadequacies of consciousness, which is a phylogenetic newcomer. This is done by expressing the true state of affairs in the vivid imagery of dream or vision. Each symbolic content, although presented in concrete, plastic form, has a psychic or spiritual meaning. A highly developed consciousness is needed to make this distinction, and this is the very thing the psychotic lacks.

Ordinarily, the collective unconscious is visible only in occasional dreams or in the general, impersonal form of myth. However, in psychosis the conscious ego that covers the deeper layers is temporarily dissolved, leaving the eternal, recurring archetypes of the collective unconscious openly exposed to view.

Summary

Jung's theory of the collective unconscious is described briefly and its application to psychotic phenomena is illustrated. The archetypes of the collective unconscious are considered to be universal instinctual patterns of behavior that reveal themselves as recurring themes and images in religion, mythology, dream, and delusion. The emergence of archetypal images is seen to be purposeful and meaningful if referred to the inner psychic world. If confused with the outer world of reality, the archetypes become the contents of psychotic delusion.

Archetypal Patterns in Schizophrenia[57]
Edward F. Edinger

The purpose of this paper is to present briefly Jung's theory of archetypes and to illustrate it by application to specific schizophrenic delusions. Although psychiatrists in this country have shown, so far, very little interest in Jung, it is felt that this theory of personality structure offers a valuable approach to the understanding of schizophrenia.

One of Jung's major contributions has been the concept of the collective unconscious. His split with Freud began with disagreement over this idea. Freud later presented a similar concept in his "archaic heritage," but this was never elaborated nor used in his psychotherapeutic system. The collective unconscious is thought to be the basic core of the human personality, which in its general pattern of function is common to all human beings—and is, therefore, called "collective."

This personality core underlies and is prior to individual life experience and all conscious elaboration. It is the inherited part of the psyche, corresponding to the anatomical structure of the brain, which is also inherited and held in common by all human beings. The collective unconscious manifests itself in certain fundamental patterns of thought and behavior that are characteristic of the human species. These psychic patterns can be thought of as the underlying structure of the mind which is potentially present prior to any life experience but which becomes actualized only when clothed with individual life happenings and contact with a specific human culture.

The unconscious psyche is considered to be a purposeful organ of the body just as the heart and kidney are organs carrying out their functional purpose even though we are unconscious of them. The lungs of the newborn infant know how to breathe, the heart knows how to beat, the whole coordinated organic system knows how to function because the infant's

---

[57] This essay was first published in the *American Journal of Psychiatry* 112, no. 5 (November 1955), pp. 354ff. A modified version had been presented at the Downstate Interhospital Conference of the N. Y. State Department of Mental Hygiene, New York City, April 8, 1954.—Eds.

body is the product of inherited functional patterns. Considering the psyche as an organ of the body, it is reasonable to assume that it also has inherited patterns of function which it shares in common with all human minds. These inherited patterns of function are called archetypes and are considered to be psychic manifestations of the instincts. They manifest themselves in overt behavior or depict themselves in the symbolic imagery of dreams and myth. Jung has this to say about archetypes:

> The form of these archetypes is perhaps comparable to the axial system of a crystal, which predetermines as it were the crystalline formation in the saturated solution, without itself possessing a material existence. This existence first manifests itself in the way the ions and then the molecules arrange themselves. . . . The axial system determines, accordingly, merely the stereometric structure, not, however, the concrete forms of the individual crystal . . . and just so the archetype possesses . . . an invariable core of meaning that determines its manner of appearing always only in principle, never concretely.[58]

The concept of the archetype is not new. Jung borrowed the term from St. Augustine, and in many respects it corresponds to the Platonic idea.[59] However, its empirical demonstration and application to a theory of personality is original. For the study of archetypes, a comparative method is necessary. The unconscious imagery of dreams and delusions is compared with religious and mythological symbolism. This procedure is justified theoretically on the hypothesis that a myth is the dream of a people, and a religion is an elaboration of a myth of unusual power. Thus dream, delusion, myth, and religion are all considered to come from the same unconscious source. If archetypes exist, we should detect them by comparing these various products of the unconscious. It is Jung's contention that such comparative study reveals the existence of similar archetypal

---

[58] Jung. "Die psychologischen Aspekte des Mütter-Archetypes," *Eranos Year Book* (1938), 410. Quoted by Jolande Jacobi, *The Psychology of Jung* (New Haven: Yale University Press, 1943), p. 43. [Edinger apparently translated from the original German. For the *Collected Works* translation, see *Archetypes and the Collective Unconscious*, *CW* 9i, par. 155.—Eds.]

[59] See Jung, *The Archetypes and the Collective Unconscious, CW* 9i, par. 5.

themes in the mythological symbolism of all races and cultures, and also that the same motifs appear in the dreams and delusions of modern men.

The Prophet and Religious Savior

Several common patterns of schizophrenic delusion will now be considered in the light of the theory of archetypes. The theme of the prophet and religious savior is a central one in all the major world religions. In Judaism, this figure is represented by Moses, in Buddhism by Buddha. In Islam, the prophet of God is Mohammed, and in Christianity the savior is Jesus. Since our civilization is nominally Christian, it is not surprising that the delusions of our schizophrenics involve chiefly an identification with Christ. In other cultures, the delusion would show a similar pattern but would refer to a different religious figure. For a person who is not committed to any one version of religious belief, it is easy to see that the central figures in all of these religions have a remarkable similarity to one another. Since religion is a psychological phenomenon, it is valid to attempt to understand it psychologically. The interpretation here suggested is that these various religious figures, with their accompanying mythologies, represent varying manifestations of the same basic archetype that exists in the collective unconscious of all humans.

Religions, when effective, are collective containers of the archetypes and seem to be psychically wholesome if not essential. They engender humility and tend to reduce the dangerous possibility of identification with an archetypal figure. We see the results of such an identification in many cases of schizophrenia where the patient is tremendously inflated by identifying himself with the archetype of the religious savior. A brief example of this is the following:

> A 23-year-old white male with no previous religious interest has a sudden catatonic episode with excitement. He believes himself to be the second coming of Christ and thinks he has a great mission to perform. It is his duty to go throughout the world and establish faith. He states that he is in contact with the power of God. This power will suddenly come over him causing shaking tremors. Then, out of the patient's mouth the voice of the Lord will speak. He spends day and night yelling out of the window,

preaching his revealed mission. Following electroshock treatment, the patient returns to reality. When questioned, he says he can't imagine how he could have been so foolish as to consider himself Christ. Something strange came over him that he can't explain. After his recovery, the patient described his feelings during the psychotic episode. He admitted grandiose ideas of importance, but more impressive to him was the tremendous burden of responsibility that was involved in being Christ. After all, such a role leads to crucifixion.

This person's pre-psychotic personality was a very childish and irresponsible one. It is perhaps meaningful that his psychosis brought with it an overpowering sense of responsibility—something the patient seriously lacked consciously. The theory of wish fulfillment with regression to infantile omnipotence fails to explain this great burden of responsibility. It can perhaps be better understood as due to identification of the ego with a suprapersonal archetypal role.

Cases similar to this are plentiful in every mental hospital. The constant recurrence of this type of delusion suggests that some fundamental psychic pattern or archetype is involved. The only other place that such a pattern finds expression is in a collective religion where it appears normal and conducive to health. This suggests that such archetypes represent basic forces of life that are collective or social in nature and transcend the individual ego. When they are worshipped as a group activity in some religious form, they are health giving. When the ego identifies with such a figure, the conscious personality is inflated and shattered to fragments. This process of inflation has been described in detail in a recent publication by Perry.[60]

Death and Rebirth

The second archetypal theme to be considered is that of death and rebirth. This is another universal theme that is usually associated with religious symbolism. A prominent example is the Indian doctrine of trans-

---

[60] See John Weir Perry, *The Self in Psychotic Process* (Berkeley: University of California Press, 1953).

migration of souls in which a man's death is thought to be followed immediately by his birth again as an infant. The puberty initiation rites of primitives reveal the same theme acted out overtly. By a ritual ordeal, the adolescent dies as a child and is born again as a responsible adult member of the community. Often this rebirth is represented by dropping the boy through the legs of a woman—thus imitating the process of actual birth. From our knowledge of the Greek mystery cults, their central theme seemed to be a ritual death and rebirth for their members.[61] Christianity is rich in such symbolism. Christ's life portrays the theme of death and resurrection The original significance of baptism was rebirth or renewal.[62] The visions of the apocalypse prophesy a cosmic catastrophe with the birth of a new heaven and a new earth.

This archetypal motif appears commonly in schizophrenic delusions. The death and rebirth dreams of patients during insulin coma are well known. The delusion of an impending world catastrophe with or without rebirth of a new world is a common variation of the same pattern. The following cases illustrate this theme:

A 43-year-old man described an hallucinatory stupor at the beginning of his psychosis during which he thought he had died. Then he heard voices telling him that he was to be reincarnated and reborn on earth as the son of God. Since then, the voices have told him that he is reborn and living his second life.

Another patient, a 33-year-old black male paranoid schizophrenic, who believes himself to be a prophet of God, states that the world is coming to the end of a 20,000-year era. The present world order will collapse, and a new progressive organization shall take its place. This is a version of the cosmic catastrophe theme and is, of course, a projection of what is happening in the patient himself. However, one can think of the emergence of this idea in the patient's mind as a purposeful phenomenon. If the patient could recognize that this idea refers to his own desperate need for rebirth

---

[61] See H.R. Willoughby, *Pagan Regeneration* (Chicago: University of Chicago Press, 1929).

[62] See Alan W. Watts, *Myth and Ritual in Christianity* (London: Thames and Hudson, 1953).

or change in attitude, it might even have a therapeutic effect.

The archetype of rebirth seems to represent a fundamental mechanism of psychic growth. Each step in the growth of personality requires the death of the old attitude before the new one can emerge. The primitives made valuable, although unconscious, use of this pattern in their initiation rites. With an experience of death and rebirth intervening between the child and the man, there was little possibility for the adult to regress to childish attitudes and behavior. Perhaps the contemporary incidence of neurosis would be less if we had effective initiation rites for adolescents. Such a line of thought suggests that the archetypes contain a valuable source of instinctual wisdom and that the unconscious may be able to offer creative solutions to problems. Nevertheless, in psychoses, we are more impressed by their destructive power, which can shatter a feeble ego.

Cosmic Dualism

A third archetypal pattern not uncommonly found in delusional thought is the cosmic dualism of light and dark, good and evil. The classic religious example of this theme is the dualism of the Zoroastrian Parsis. According to their belief, the universe is divided into two great rival camps—that of Ahura Mazda (the God of goodness, light and health) and that of Ahriman (a Devil representing darkness, evil and disease). The same idea appears, of course, in Christian theology with God and Satan, heaven and hell. The Chinese concept of Yin and Yang is similar and yet significantly different. Yin is the principle of darkness, passivity, and feminine creativeness. Yang is the principle of light and masculine activity. There is no connotation here of good and evil, but rather both principles are considered necessary complements to each other—two polar opposites between which the constant interplay of life occurs. This is a highly developed conception which leads to a view of life as an integrated harmonious function—far different from our Western version of eternal cosmic conflict.

Nevertheless, the fundamental dualistic pattern is the same. In our modern mythology, this archetypal dualism appears in the terms conscious and unconscious. And the unconscious still carries many of the aspects of evil. This theme appears occasionally in schizophrenic delusions. For example:

> A 41-year-old single woman with paranoid schizophrenia states that in a previous incarnation she had experimented extensively with light rays. She learned that there were two kinds of light: rays of sunshine that were health giving and good, and black rays which were evil and destructive of life. She thought she was subjected to these evil rays at times and developed special ritual movements to ward them off. Another patient, the 33-year-old black male previously mentioned, described similar thoughts. He would discourse at length on what he called, "the two world principles," namely, the principle of Life represented by doing good which leads to immortality and the principle of Death which leads to doing wrong and causes one to die. The patient claimed that these two cosmic principles were at war with each other within himself and that the outcome was uncertain.

This pattern of two opposing principles seems to represent a basic characteristic of psychic function. If a psychic energy system may be compared with a system of electrical energy, it appears that a tension between two opposite poles is necessary for vital function. If the potential between the opposites is lost, psychic paralysis or entropy will result.[63]

There are, of course, many other archetypal themes and figures which have not been mentioned. One such would be Freud's Oedipus complex, which by its universality immediately qualifies as an archetypal pattern. Related to this theme of love for the mother is the Attis-Cybele myth in which the young man Attis castrates himself as a sacrifice to the Great Mother Cybele.[64] How many patients are seen who are living out unconsciously this archetypal role and have castrated themselves psychically rather than give up their dependent bond to the mother?

---

[63] See Jung, "On Psychic Energy," in *The Structure and Dynamics of the Psyche, CW* 8.

[64] See James G. Frazer, *The Golden Bough* (New York: The Macmillan Company, 1945).

A distinguishing feature of Jung's psychological viewpoint is that he takes religions seriously. This is not to say that he is a partisan of any one religious system. Jung gives as evidence of his objectivity that he once helped a Parsi by psychotherapy to find his way back to the Zoroastrian fire temple.[65] Religions have always dealt with the ultimate problems of human life. As collective expressions of the archetypes, they provide orientation concerning the collective problems of man—the questions of meaning, purpose, and goal. The schizophrenic patients described in this paper were immersed in these same problems. They gave the impression of being destroyed by ideas bigger than themselves. Each had a personal religion with some concept of the ultimate nature and purpose of human life, but each found himself to be the central religious figure. The immensity of such a burden broke their bonds with reality. A study of psychotic delusions reveals that religious contents often predominate. This suggests that one approach to the study of schizophrenia would be a search for a deeper understanding of religious phenomena of all kinds. It is this approach that was used by Jung and led him to the theory of archetypes.

Summary

The purpose of this paper is to present briefly Jung's theory of archetypes and to illustrate it with specific case material. An archetype is described as an inherent pattern of psychic function common to all human beings and thought to be inherited with the brain structure. Archetypes present themselves in unconscious symbolism as certain characteristic recurring themes and figures of a mythological nature. Since religions and mythologies come from the same unconscious source as dreams and delusions, we find the same basic archetypal themes appearing in all such unconscious productions. Thus, schizophrenic delusions are found to show many parallels with religious and mythological symbolism.

The conscious ego of the schizophrenic has been overwhelmed by these archetypal contents, and the patient often identifies himself with

---

[65] See Jung, *Psychology and Alchemy*, CW 12, par. 17.

such suprapersonal figures as the mythological hero or the religious savior. Such figures represent basic forces of life which are collective or social in nature and transcend the individual ego. Any attempt to appropriate them for personal aggrandizement leads to alienation from reality.

Figure 10. Edinger Pondering (1995).

PART IV

SOUL MATES

Paracelsus and the Age of Aquarius[66]
Edward F. Edinger

Introduction by Maurice Krasnow

Welcome to the third lecture in our series, "Lead into Gold," commemo-
rating the 500th Anniversary of the birth of Paracelsus—a predecessor of
the psychological thought of C. G. Jung and in whom Dr. Jung found an
analogy to his own understanding of our modern day experience as well
as today's psychological disorders.

Tonight I have the pleasure to introduce Dr. Edward F. Edinger. I
cannot express myself more eloquently about Dr. Edinger than these
words Paracelsus himself is rumored to have said. Listen: "It is the phy-
sician who reveals to us the diverse miraculous works of God." In our
modern psychological language we could say that's the objective psyche.
"And having revealed them, he must use them" in the "true" way. "What
is in the sea [he brings to] the light of day. He should make it manifest. .
. so that many people may be able to see the works of God and recognize
how they can be used to cure disease." The true physician must "know
the constellation of the Whale, the monster of the sea." He must know
"what the Apocalyptic Beast is and what is Babylon." For everywhere
"the blindness [of] the death of the soul" prevails. And then Paracelsus
completes his thought with this: Our science "is full of mysteries and
must be studied like the words of Christ. These two callings – the prom-

---

[66] This essay was first published in *Psychological Perspectives* 33 (Spring
1996), pp. 10ff. It was delivered originally as a lecture in New York City, 1994,
under the auspices of the C. G. Jung Foundation of New York. Maurice Krasnow, Ph.D., is a Jungian analyst in New York City.—Eds.

ulgation of the word of God and the healing of the sick—must not be separated from each other. . . . the two are connected, and the one must open access to the other."[67]

Dr. Edinger has revealed to a generation of individuals the depths of meaning found in the psychic images of the unconscious and in our individual experience of psychological life. More than any other author, the work of Dr. Edinger—through his evocative and clear explication—has revealed to us, has brought within our grasp, the profundity of the thought of C. G. Jung and its meaning in our everyday lives. Indeed, in my opinion, Dr. Edinger is the largest container of the reality of the living psyche in the world today.

For those of you who are new to the C. G. Jung Foundation, Dr. Edinger, a Jungian analyst who lives in Los Angeles and is currently on the faculty of the C. G. Jung Institute of Los Angeles, has his professional roots here in the east coast. He received his medical degree at Yale University School of Medicine, was a supervising psychiatrist at Rockland State Hospital in Orangeburg, New York. He is a founding member of the C. G. Jung Foundation here in New York, as well as a founding member of the C. G. Jung Institute of New York. For many years he served as its chairman. He practiced here in New York, and he was an integral part of the New York Jungian community. . . .

In all of Dr. Edinger's works, you will find that he grapples with the encounter with the Whale, the Apocalyptic Beast, Babylon—the paradoxical opposites we face in ourselves and in our lives. He brings to light the various representations of the God-image, the central archetype of the psyche, the Self. And he opens access to the healing of our inner experience from that encounter.

Ladies and gentlemen, please welcome Dr. Edward Edinger, a true physician in the spirit of Paracelsus who never separates transpersonal reality from the healing of the psyche. His topic tonight: "Individuation Symbolism in Paracelsus."

---

[67] See Jolande Jacobi, ed., *Paracelsus: Selected Writings*, trans. Norbert Guterman, Bollingen Series (New York: Pantheon Books, 1958), pp. 67f.—Eds.

I must begin with a confession. I have not made a serious study of Paracelsus. To be candid about it, it's been hard for me to like Paracelsus. He makes so little effort to accommodate the needs of his readers. He uses obscure neologisms of his own construction, doesn't always explain them, and lets readers figure them out as best they can. Furthermore, his temperament is violent and contentious—and those qualities are distasteful to me. But the fact is that Paracelsus had need of such qualities. He was dealing with psychic factors of such a magnitude that he was fortunate to retain his sanity. Certainly he is one of the great-souled ones of history, and that makes him worthy of our attention. However, my primary reason for focusing on Paracelsus is that he was important to Jung. In his autobiography, Jung writes:

> The writings of Paracelsus contain a wealth of original ideas, including clear formulations of the questions posed by alchemists, though these are set forth in late and baroque dress. Through Paracelsus I was finally led to discuss the nature of alchemy in relation to religion and psychology—or, to put it another way, of alchemy as a form of religious philosophy. This I did in *Psychology and Alchemy* (1944). Thus I had at last reached the ground which underlay my own experiences of the years 1913-1917 [the time of Jung's confrontation with the unconscious]; for the process through which I had passed at that time corresponded to the process of alchemical transformation discussed in that book.[68]

Because of my limited knowledge of Paracelsus, I am not competent to engage in a comprehensive survey of his work. I can only offer personal reflections on his place in the evolution of the Western collective psyche and on his significance for depth psychology. Indeed, I really have just three basic ideas to convey.

1) The first one concerns Paracelsus' main symbolic image—his concept of the lower heaven—which is of overwhelming importance in his writings. He also calls it "star," "light to be found in nature," and "iliaster." His pupil, Gerhard Dorn, even went so far as to write an alchemical recipe whereby this lower heaven could be extracted from matter.

---

[68] Jung, *Memories, Dreams, Reflections,* p. 209.

2) The second idea is that Paracelsus is representative of sixteenth-century man. His concept of the lower heaven was very relevant to the larger issues astir in the collective psyche of his time. The sixteenth century was a momentous period in the history of the Western world. It was then that heaven, which heretofore had been the dwelling-place of the God-image, fell out of the sky into matter, and into the human psyche.

3) The third idea is the psychological meaning of the lower heaven. Depth psychology recognizes and elaborates the full consequences of this change in the God-image. We can now see how Dorn's extraction procedure—using matter, chemicals and chemical apparatus—was a symbolic precursor to depth analysis, whose basic aim is to extract the God-image from the unconscious and bring it into full conscious relation to the ego.

The Lower Heaven: "Stars in Us"

Jung tells us that the word "iliaster," which Paracelsus used synonymously with "lower heaven," is one of his neologisms and is probably a combination of two Greek words: *hyle*, meaning "matter," and *aster*, meaning "star." So iliaster would mean the "star-in-matter." Another related name given to the same concept is *lumen naturae*, the "light of nature." This refers to the wisdom and vision that comes from below rather than above, from matter and nature rather than the upper regions of the spirit or divine revelation as dispensed by the Church.

Paracelsus was gripped by the archetype of heaven, which in earlier ages was projected onto the sky, so that "heaven" and "sky" were synonymous. As soon as we start talking about a *lower* heaven, then we know that the archetype has fallen out of the sky—sky and heaven are no longer the same, and the psychic content that had been projected onto the sky is now starting to be withdrawn. Jung says: "In his conception of the inner heaven he glimpsed an eternal primordial image, which was implanted in him and in all men, and recurs at all times and places."[69] Jung

---

[69] See Jung, "Paracelsus the Physician," in *The Spirit in Man, Art, and Literature, CW* 15, par. 31.

quotes Paracelsus as saying: "The heavens are a spirit and a vapor in which we live just like a bird in time. Not only the stars or the moon, etc., constitute the heavens, but also there are stars in us, and these which are in us and which we do not see constitute the heavens also. . . ."[70]

For Paracelsus, this inner heaven is the major source of knowledge. Jung gives Paracelsus high praise for this insight:

> The firmament is not merely the cosmic heaven, but a body which is a part or a content of the human body. . . . The firmamental body is the corporeal equivalent of the astrological heaven. [What he calls a *corpus sydereum*, "star body"] is the source of illumination by the *lumen naturae*, the "natural light," which plays the greatest possible role not only in the writing of Paracelsus but also in the whole of his thought. This intuitive conception is, in my opinion, an achievement of the utmost historical importance, for which no one should grudge Paracelsus undying fame.[71]

As with every major archetypal image, the image of heaven clusters around itself a whole symbol system of associated images and ideas. This is the nature of an archetypal image. It functions like a magnetic field. I am rather fond of charting that kind of phenomenon because it helps me to visualize, all at once, the entire network of associated images. So I have constructed a chart that presents some of these associated images that cluster around the archetypal image of heaven (Figure 11, opposite).

The first association that comes to mind in response to the notion of heaven is the image of the sky. As long as the physical sky and the psychic content of heaven are merged in the psyche, the sky will carry the projection—or will function as the projection screen, so to speak—of this entire symbol system. What we're actually looking for, then, is not the phenomenon of the physical sky but of the collective unconscious, which has been projected onto the sky. The chief attributes contained in this projection are transcendence of this burdensome earth, i.e., destiny, paradise, the afterlife, eternity, infinity, dwelling-place of the deity. The prayer, the Pater Noster, begins, "Our Father who art in heaven." And in

---

[70] Ibid., par. 31n.
[71] Ibid., par. 29.

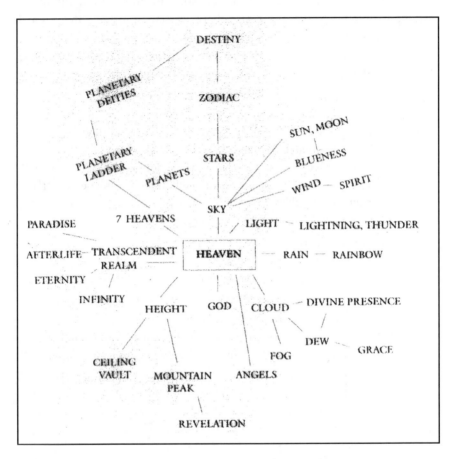

Figure 11. Cluster Chart of the Archetype of Heaven.

the teachings of Christ, the kingdom of God and the kingdom of heaven were synonymous. They meant exactly the same thing because *the sky and the psychic contents were not distinguished.* The wind was the spirit; thunder and lightning—the dynamic manifestations of the divine presence—were the source of all grace and revelation. All these sacred associations belong to the symbol system of this archetype of heaven. And this is the grand entity that has finally fallen down to earth—thanks, in large part, to Paracelsus—and has become available for extraction out of matter by those alchemists who followed Paracelsus. This is an amazing image: Heaven is now within the grasp of humanity. And the alchemists, if they do their work right, can get hold of it, heaven itself. It is a very big deal.

Historically, the image of heaven goes back to the earliest cosmologies, which began with the idea that the original chaos gave way to a separation of heaven and earth; those were the two antithetical elements. Psychologically, we understand earth to refer to the ego because earth is where humanity lives, and it is out of earth that flesh is born. So, psychologically speaking, the beginning is a birth of ego consciousness and separateness out of what had previously been nothing but unconscious deity. Early on, humans attributed transpersonal powers to the sky. According to the scholar A. B. Cook, in primitive Greek religion, Zeus was conceived of as the animate or living bright sky. It was only later that Zeus took on his anthropomorphic aspects and gradually evolved from being the *sky as a whole* to being, specifically, the *sky god.* Cook makes a very interesting observation in this regard:

> The shift from sky to sky god was a momentous fact, a fact which modified the whole course of Greek religion, and its ultimate consequence was nothing less than the rise of faith in a personal god, the ruler and father of all.[72]

This historical sequence has a very interesting parallel in the psychological development of the individual in relation to the collective uncon-

---

[72] A. B. Cook, *Zeus: A Study in Ancient Religion*, vol. 1 (1914; repr., New York: Biblo and Tannen, 1964), p. 9.

scious. In the course of analysis, one's first encounters with one's own psychic contents correspond to recognizing the transpersonal dimension as being something like the diffuse sky. We call it the collective unconscious, with its contents of the archetypes, but there is a diffuseness about it. It is only later, with further development, that this diffuse numinosity is focused down to an awareness of an individual unified essence of the collective unconscious—the Self. This sequence happens quite regularly in analysis. I find it very interesting that Cook makes the same observation in regard to the course of historical development.

Quite early on, humankind began to think of itself as the offspring of both heaven and earth. Orphic gold tablets, dug up from graves dating back to the second or third century B.C., contained instructions for the deceased as to how to negotiate their way past the gatekeepers into paradise. Those Orphic gold tablets instructed the deceased to say: "I am a child of Earth and the Starry Heaven, / but my race is of Heaven alone." Such imagery corresponds to the widely held belief, general at the time and extending historically for centuries, that death brings about a final separation between the soul and the body. The soul was thought to have its parentage in heaven, and the body was something that had to be endured for a while. With death, the body was cast off and, freed of that inconvenience, one could return to one's original spiritual, heavenly nature. The end result, then, would be a final separation of body and soul.

This is a far cry from the Paracelsian notion of the heaven within matter itself. What Paracelsian imagery implied—and what Jungian psychology has made explicit—is that the supposed separation between heaven and earth that leaves the body behind is unsatisfactory, leaving us in a chronic dissociated state that the modern mind will no longer accept. The modern mind requires wholeness, and that means that the body has to be redeemed—egohood, the earth, and matter itself, have to be redeemed. The earlier religious symbol systems did not attempt this integration. Alchemy started to work on it, and depth psychology has carried it to completion, a whole new world view.

As Jung tells us, the alchemical notion of Mercurius is essentially synonymous with Paracelsus' idea of the "lower heaven." Mercurius is to be found in the darkness of matter. It is a spirit, a light, that does not derive from heaven but is generated out of the earth and comes about through human efforts. This notion contrasts greatly with the message of Christ who, as an emissary from the upper heavens, descends to earth to acquaint humankind with the higher realm and hopefully lead everyone back to heaven.

As Jung points out, alchemy provided a compensatory counterpoint to the Christian cosmology in the figure of Mercurius, which manifests from below as the son of the world of matter. This view of spirit coming from below completes the spirit of Christ coming from above. Jung says:

> With the incarnation of Christ . . . the higher, the spiritual, the masculine inclines to the lower, the earthly, the feminine; and accordingly, the mother, who was anterior to the world of the father, accommodates herself to the male principle. And she does that by producing a son rather than producing a daughter. And so with the aid of the human spirit, alchemy, she produces a son who is not the antithesis of Christ, but rather his chthonic counterpart. Not a divine man, but a fabulous being conforming to the nature of the primordial mother. And just as the redemption of man, the microcosm, is the task of the upper son, which is Christ, so the lower son has the function of the savior of the macrocosm.[73]

Jung is saying that to be the savior of the macrocosm is to be the redeemer of the *world*, of matter itself. Christ would pluck humankind out of the world and help us find our way back to his heavenly origin, leaving the world to its hell. Instead, the alchemical savior of the greater world is going to redeem the world of *matter*. Psychologically, this refers to the redemption of egohood, which does not get very good press in the Christian and Gnostic symbol systems. To contemplate the redemption of the carnal ego is no small undertaking.

Paracelsus: A Sixteenth-Century Man

From the standpoint of archetypal history, it is highly significant that the legendary figure of Dr. Faustus lived contemporaneously with Paracelsus. Faustus' dates are generally given as 1480-1540; Paracelsus' dates,

---

[73] Jung, *Psychology and Alchemy, CW* 12, par. 26.

1493-1541—almost exactly the same. In fact, it has been widely sur-mised that Paracelsus himself was the actual Dr. Faustus. Paracelsus' connection with the Faust legend establishes him as perhaps the preemi-nent historical figure who anticipates the predicament of the modern psy-che. I think this helps to explain why Jung found both Faust and Paracel-sus so very relevant to his own life and work. Like Faust, Paracelsus courted inflation. When depth psychologists encounter this attribute, we shudder with the knowledge of the danger. For example, consider Paracelsus' famous remark:

> I under the Lord, the Lord under me. I under him outside my office, he under me outside his office.[74]

This is pretty dangerous stuff, but it is characteristic of the sixteenth-century mentality. As Jung elaborates in his book, *Aion*, the sixteenth century was a crucial transition point in the unfolding of the Christian eon. It was a kind of watershed in the evolution of the Western psyche, in what might be called the collective individuation process of Western humanity. It was at this point that the process of replacing the figure of Christ (who had been the dominant of the first millennium) with the fig-ure of the Antichrist (the dominant of the second millennium) began in earnest. And by 1500, the Renaissance, the Reformation, the great geo-graphical explorations, and the scientific revolution were all underway.

What had happened psychologically to bring about all these tremen-dous, energizing changes was that the God-image had fallen out of the sky and into the human psyche. In other words, the God-image was no longer mediated or contained by the metaphysical system of the Church. The transpersonal energies contained in the God-image thus became more available to the human ego which—now mobilized by these ener-gies—engaged in new explorations of all kinds. A vast expansion of ego consciousness manifested in all fields of endeavor. At the same time, a secular rationalistic inflation and hubris also appeared that have finally culminated in the desperate plight of our modern world, which is totter-ing on the brink of apocalyptic catastrophe. And it is out of this desperate

---

[74] Jung, *Alchemical Studies*, *CW* 13, par. 151.

plight that depth psychology has been born.

Of course, for the sixteenth-century person, these developments all lay in the future. The immediate effect of the fall of the God-image out of the sky was a tremendous upsurge in human confidence. This state of affairs was well described by Pico Della Mirandola in *Oration on the Dignity of Man*, which was written in 1486. Russell Kirk comments on this Renaissance document:

> Pico's *Dignity of Man* is the manifesto of humanism: man regenerate. This visibly is the primary meaning of the Renaissance, the rebirth of man in the likeness of God. The man of the Middle Ages was humble, conscious of his almost always fallen and sinful nature, feeling himself a miserable foul creature watched by an angry God. Through pride fell the angels, but Pico and his brother humanists declared man was only a little lower than the angels, being capable of descending to unclean depths, indeed, but also having within his power to become godlike. How marvelous and splendid a creature is man. This theme of Pico's oration was elaborated with all the pomp . . . that begins to characterize the rising humanist teachings. In this idea there lay a colossal hubris unknown to the Middle Ages, but also tremendous spiritual impulse such as only modern times can show.[75]

What Kirk calls "a tremendous spiritual impulse" has culminated in what Jung describes as the psychology of modern man and modern woman:

> The man we call modern, the man who is aware of the immediate present, is by no means the average man. . . . The man who has attained consciousness of the present is solitary. The "modern" man has at all times been so, for every step towards fuller consciousness removes him further from his original, purely animal *participation mystique* with the herd, from submersion in a common unconsciousness. Every step forward means tearing oneself loose from the maternal womb of unconsciousness in which the mass of men dwells. Even in a civilized community the people who form, psychologically speaking, the lowest stratum live in a state of unconsciousness little different from that of primitives. Those on the succeeding

---

[75] G. P. D. Mirandola, *Oration on the Dignity of Man,* ed. Russell Kirk (Chicago: Gateway Henry Regnery Co., 1970), pp. xiiif.

strata live on a level of consciousness that corresponds to the beginnings of human culture, while those of the highest stratum have a consciousness that reflects the light of the last few centuries. Only the man who is modern in our meaning of the term really lives in the present; he alone has a present-day consciousness, and he alone finds that the ways of life on those earlier levels have begun to pall upon him. The values and strivings of those past worlds no longer interest him save from an historical standpoint. Thus, he had become "unhistorical" in the deepest sense and has estranged himself from the mass of men who live entirely within the bounds of tradition. Indeed, he is completely modern only when he has come to the very edge of the world, leaving behind him all that has been discarded and outgrown, and acknowledging that he stands before the Nothing out of which all may grow. . . .

An honest admission of modernity means voluntarily declaring oneself bankrupt, taking the vows of poverty and chastity in a new sense, and—what is still more painful—renouncing the halo of sanctity which history bestows. To be "unhistorical" is the Promethean sin, and in this sense the modern man is sinful. A higher level of consciousness is like a burden of guilt. But, as I have said, only the man who has outgrown the stages of consciousness belonging to the past, and has amply fulfilled the duties appointed for him by his world, can achieve full consciousness of the present. To do this he must be sound and proficient in the best sense—a man who has achieved as much as other people, and even a little more. It is these qualities which enable him to gain the next highest level of consciousness.[76]

So to be a modern person, according to Jung, means to be unhistorical. I understand that to mean that such a person is no longer contained in a tradition, which is the gist of history. In other words, the individual identity is no longer propped up by unconscious containment in a religious, cultural or ethnic identification. The modern person is alone and without a myth. When this state of affairs happens to a large number of people, it really causes a problem for society as a whole. And when that is the state of affairs, as it is today, the only viable solution—if one is not to revert or attempt to recover the lost heaven in some archaic, atavistic, regres-

---

[76] Jung, *Civilization in Transition, CW* 10, pars. 149ff.

sive fundamentalism—is to extract the inner heaven from the psyche it-self. This entails a confrontation with the unconscious, an activation of the process of individuation, through which one experiences a reconnection with that lost image of heaven, the God-image.

What Jung calls modernity began in the sixteenth century, and Paracelsus was one of its major progenitors. The consequence was the opening up of an inner conflict that Jung describes in *Aion* as a conflict between Christ and Antichrist. For Paracelsus, that conflict remained unconscious, though Jung speculates that the existence of that conflict in Paracelsus was the source of his astonishing energy during his forty-eight years of life. Jung says:

> To me it seems certain that Paracelsus was just as unconscious of the full implications of these teachings as Khunrath was, who also believed he was speaking "without blasphemy." But in spite of this unconsciousness, they were of the essence of philosophical alchemy, and anyone who practiced it thought, lived and acted in the atmosphere of these teachings, which perhaps had an all the more insidious effect the more naively and uncritically one succumbed to them. The "natural light of man" or the "star in man" sounds harmless enough, so that none of the authors had any notion of the possibilities of conflict that lurked within it. And yet that light or *filius philosophorum* [son of the philosopher] was openly named the greatest and most victorious of all lights, and set alongside Christ as the Savior and Preserver of the world! Whereas in Christ God himself became man, the *filius philosophorum* was extracted from matter by human art and, by means of the opus, made into a new light-bringer. In the former case the miracle of man's salvation is accomplished by God; in the latter, the salvation or transfiguration of the universe is brought about by the mind of man—"Deo concedente," [God willing] as the authors never fail to add. In the one case man confesses "I under god," in the other he asserts "God under me." Man takes the place of the Creator. Medieval alchemy prepared the way for the greatest intervention in the divine world order that man has ever attempted: alchemy was the dawn of the scientific age, when the daemon of the scientific spirit compelled the forces of nature to serve man to an extent that had never been known before. It was from the spirit of alchemy that Goethe wrought the figure of the "superman" Faust, and this superman led Nietzsche's Zarathustra to declare that God was dead,

and to proclaim the will to give birth to the superman, to "create a god for yourself out of your seven devils." . . .

The inner driving-force behind the aspirations of alchemy was a presumption whose daemonic grandeur on the one hand and psychic danger on the other should not be underestimated. Much of the overbearing pride and arrogant self-esteem, which contrasts so strangely with the truly Christian humility of Paracelsus, comes from this source.[77]

Jung explicitly states that Paracelsus had two mothers—the Church and nature:

Even though he endeavored to conceal the conflict between the two maternal spheres of influence, he was honest enough to admit its existence. . . .Thus he says: "I also confess that I write like a pagan and yet am a Christian."[78]

And in spite of the existence of the acknowledgment of that conflict, it still remained unconscious because he could blissfully go on his way and not reconcile the contrasting requirements of the two.

His work bore such fruitful consequences because it valued concentrating on the authenticity of one's *experience*. Faith was the operative principle of the bygone eon, and experience is going to be the principle of the coming eon. Paracelsus was a major exponent of the authenticity of experience, but he did not face fully the conflict that he had opened. Jung says:

Though this liberating act had the most fruitful consequences, it also led to that conflict between knowledge and faith which poisoned the spiritual atmosphere of the nineteenth century in particular. Paracelsus naturally had no inkling of the possibility of these late repercussions. As a medieval Christian, he still lived in a unitary world and did not feel the two sources of knowledge, the divine and the natural, as the conflict it later turned out to be.[79]

---

[77] Jung, "Paracelsus As a Spiritual Phenomenon," in *Alchemical Studies, CW* 13, pars. 163f.

[78] Ibid., par. 148.

[79] Ibid., par. 149.

So this great movement in the collective psyche, which really got going in the sixteenth century and gained momentum in the succeeding centuries, had the effect of depositing the *numinosum*, which had fallen out of the sky, into matter and into nature. The result was that these areas became fascinating to people, and that fascination is what generated science. From my own earlier scientific period, I know that science really does have a religious foundation to it—a foundation that derives from the fact that the *numinosum* was now exerting its fascination from below— from the bowels of matter.

By the nineteenth century, this simmering conflict between the light of the upper heaven and the light of the lower heaven became an open battle. The upper heaven, the sky, was no longer viewed as the abode of the deity. For example, in his poem, "The Lid," Baudelaire wrote about seeing the sky as a harsh lid on a pressure cooker containing the whole human race, rich and poor, educated and ignorant, the ascetics and the libertines, all classes, all suffering the same fate, treading on this bloody ground. That is quite a change; the sky of heaven becomes a lid on a pressure cooker for the nineteenth-century poet.

The Psychological Meaning of the Lower Heaven

As I mentioned earlier, Jung found alchemy, in general, and Paracelsus, in particular, very helpful in assimilating his experiences of the collective unconscious. He came to understand alchemy as a projection of the unconscious psyche into matter:

> The real nature of matter was unknown to the alchemist: he knew it only in hints. In seeking to explore it he projected the unconscious into the darkness of matter in order to illuminate it. . . . while working on his chemical experiments, the operator had certain psychic experiences which appeared to him as the particular behavior of the chemical process. Since it was a question of projection, he was naturally unconscious of the fact that the experience had nothing to do with matter itself. . . . He experienced his projection as a property of matter; but what he was in reality experiencing was his own unconscious.[80]

---

[80] Jung, *Psychology and Alchemy, CW* 12, pars. 145f.

This statement applies very much to the remarkable recipe of Gerhard Dorn. Jung devotes a great deal of attention to it in his final chapter of *Mysterium Coniunctionis*. Dorn was a disciple of Paracelsus and used much of his imagery, especially that of the lower heaven or what Dorn called *caelum*. Dorn's elaborate recipe involved the extraction of this *caelum*, this lower heaven, out of matter as part of the process of achieving inner unity. Jung provides a succinct overview of this process:

> The production of the *caelum* is a symbolic rite performed in the laboratory. Its purpose was to create, in the form of a substance, that "truth," the celestial balsam or life principle, which is identical with the God-image. Psychologically, it was a representation of the individuation process by means of chemical substances and procedures, of what we today call active imagination.[81]

Thus, the lower heaven is a God-image located in the unconscious; it is the task of the ego to extract this image through the process of active imagination. When such an extraction is accomplished, the person has a conscious encounter with the Self, a numinous experience, and at that point becomes *experientially*—not abstractly and theoretically—aware of the existence of the second transpersonal center of the psyche. This is the consequence of the extraction of the lower heaven. This is a decisive event when it happens, and it transforms whosoever's ego experiences it. The very nature of that ego changes forever: It is no longer an ego-centered ego but becomes a Self-centered ego by virtue of this extraction procedure.

Images of the lower heaven do show up in dreams. For example, I had such a dream many years ago—1960, to be exact. It was a brief and simple dream:

> I am examining a one-celled organism. It is just a blob of protoplasm, like an amoeba. As I look at it, I notice that its nucleus is missing. In its place is a hole that provides a glimpse into another world. As I peek through that hole, I see a patch of blue sky, heaven.

That is the whole dream. Upon awaking, the first thing I thought of

---

[81] Jung, *Mysterium Coniunctionis*, *CW* 14, par. 705.

was the rabbit hole in *Alice in Wonderland*. To me the one-celled amoeba, what I called "just a blob of protoplasm," represents organic existence at its most elementary, its most basic. Such a creature is concerned only with devouring food and reproducing itself by simple division. I see an image of elemental desirousness—greedy, lusting protoplasm—the stuff of which all living organisms are made.

This dream came at a time when I was feeling in a hole. I was frustrated and resentful because I wanted some things I couldn't have. Another way of saying it is that my protoplasmic urges were being deprived. The dream seems to be saying that there is an empty hole at the center of a purely biological existence, but if one looks more closely through the hole, it becomes a window to another realm. As I pondered the dream after awaking, I thought of Jung's "Liverpool" dream and the mandala that he painted as a result. He said of that mandala, of that dream: "The whole thing seemed like a window opening into eternity."[82] I understand my dream to picture symbolically the transpersonal or eternal basis of our psychological existence. That transpersonal dimension is revealed to be at the very heart of our elemental desirousness, the very things that are labeled the so-called deadly sins: anger, pride, envy, greed, lust, sloth, and gluttony. The "seven deadly sins" are characteristic of protoplasm and the basic constituents of our fleshly being.

In Galatians 5:19-21 (New King James version) the apostle Paul appraised the works of the flesh:

> Now the works of the flesh are evident, which are these: adultery, fornication, uncleanness, licentiousness, idolatry, sorcery, hatred, contention, jealousy, outbursts of wrath, selfish ambition, dissensions, heresies, envy, murder, drunkenness, rivalry and the like.

—all protoplasmic stuff, yet my dream seems to be saying that a window into eternity lies at the very heart of this pool of iniquity. So how are we to understand that? I think we get a clue from a remark Jung makes in *Mysterium Coniunctionis*. This remark comes when he is interpreting an alchemical text concerning sulfur, which symbolizes (among other

---

[82] Jung, *The Archetypes and the Collective Unconscious, CW* 9i, par. 655.

things) desirousness. He asks the question, "What is behind all this desirousness?" Then he answers: "A thirsting for the eternal. . . ."[83] I think that is exactly what my dream is saying.

I understand the dream to mean that we encounter the transpersonal, the eternal dimension of existence, the inner heaven of Paracelsus, by penetrating consciously to the core, to the very springs of our protoplasmic libido, the pleasure and power drives of the infantile psyche—because these are driven by the energies of the primitive unconscious cell. They are transpersonal energies in their essence that take on this destructive form only because they are manifesting through an unconscious ego, an ego that doesn't know its own transcendent nature. The ego that acts out these drives unconsciously is identified with the unconscious Self and thus is in a state of what we could call "psychological sin." But those same energies, when penetrated by consciousness, are perceived as having a transpersonal—heavenly—origin. And then they become life imperatives from the inner God-image. When they are lived out consciously, they have a totally different effect and totally different consequences.

In *Symbols of Transformation*, Jung describes this encounter with the unconscious god:

> He [the unconscious god] appears at first in hostile form, as an assailant with whom the hero must wrestle. This is in keeping with the violence of all unconscious dynamism. In this manner, the god manifest himself and in this form he must be overcome. The struggle has its parallel in Jacob's wrestling with the angel at the ford Jabbok. The onslaught of instinct then becomes an experience of divinity. . . .[84]

That is the punch line. "The onslaught of instinct then becomes an experience of divinity"—provided that we do not succumb to it. That means we do not act it out blindly or follow it blindly. We must defend our humanity against the animal nature of divine power. Or, to put this another way, the onslaught of protoplasmic urges becomes an experience

---

[83] Jung, *Mysterium Coniunctionis, CW* 14, par. 192.

[84] Jung, *Symbols of Transformation, CW* 5, par. 524.

of the inner heaven, provided these urges are made conscious and thereby humanized. This is the reconciling, unifying, and healing alternative to dissociated repression.[85]

Since primitive times, heaven has represented the dwelling place of the *numinosum*. It has been the spiritual realm, the abode of the gods, the plane of eternity and the infinite, as contrasted with our brief and painful life span. But that projection is now gone. This first withdrawal of the projection does not annul its psychic content, it merely—yet profoundly—changes its location. Francis Thompson, the nineteenth-century poet, put it in these words:

> Not where the wheeling systems darken,
>
> And our benumbed conceiving soars!—
>
> The drift of pinions would we hearken,
>
> Beats at our own clay-shuttered doors.[86]

The movements of the spirit now come from below, out of our own clay. For a truly modern person, as Jung uses the word "modern," connection with the eternal transpersonal God-image is found not by looking out and up but by looking *down* and *in*, to what Paracelsus called the "lower heaven." Nothing is more important than the search for that lower heaven.

---

[85] This phrase "dissociated repression" spoken in the lecture was erroneously published originally as "depression."—Eds.

[86] From Francis Thompson, "The Kingdom of God: In No Strange Land" in *The Norton Anthology of English Literature*, ed. M. H. Abrams, et al., vol. 2 (New York: W. W. Norton & Company, 1968), p. 1214.

Ralph Waldo Emerson: Naturalist of the Soul[87]
Edward F. Edinger

Emerson and his writings are well known to all Americans and have been the subject of many commentaries. Even so, I venture to hope that as a psychotherapist I may have something to add to the understanding of this great man by using the new insights of Analytical psychology. Moreover, the time has come to apply the discoveries of depth psychology as widely as possible to literary and artistic creation.

Jung has led the way in taking empirical psychology out of the consulting room of the therapist and applying it to all the products of the human mind. We who are carrying on the work that Jung began must continue to examine the products of human culture in the light of his psychology. Jung's psychology is profound and provocative just because it transcends the narrow specialism of a particular scientific discipline. It is a science in its form and in its origin—appropriately so since it is a child of the modern scientific age. But in its content and its applications it transcends all the separate categories by which human thoughts and actions are divided and classified.

Just as Bacon took all knowledge to be his province, so Jung took all manifestations of the psyche as his field of inquiry. According to this view, all that man has ever done or thought is pertinent to psychology. Religion, mythology, history, philosophy, art, literature, and political affairs—all being manifestations of the psyche—are included in psychology. Perhaps, at some future date, even mathematics and the exact sciences can be considered as aspects of psychology since the subject matter of these sciences is experienced and understood only through the perception-forms and knowledge-categories of the psyche. As Cassirer has put it, "Our objective is *a phenomenology of human culture.*"[88]

---

[87] This essay was originally published in *Spring 1965,* pp. 77ff. The author read it first at a meeting of the Analytical Psychology Club of New York, May 15, 1964.—Eds.

[88] Ernst Cassirer, *An Essay on Man* (New Haven: Yale University Press, 1944), p. 52.

This is a grand conception and needs to be tempered by modesty. However, an adequate approach to the psyche must be grand and comprehensive because its subject is grand. No lesser approach will do it justice. The psychology whose aim is to make man conscious of his wholeness must itself encompass the whole. It cannot fulfill its purpose if it is no more than a specialized fragment of human knowledge. Only a psychology of cosmic proportions can lead the individual to the realization that he is a microcosm, a miniature universe.

Jung has laid down the broad outlines for such a comprehensive psychology. In the process, he has helped to bring to birth an entirely new world view which has as its central principle and supreme value the human psyche with its unique phenomenon of consciousness. The whole historical endeavor of man, individually as well as collectively, is seen as a striving toward consciousness; and all the arts and sciences have the same goal. But the only carrier of consciousness is the individual. It is he who actualizes the cosmic urge to self-realization. Hence, a study of culture (art, literature, philosophy, and so on) will be most valid if it is grounded on the empirical facts of individual psychology.

If the new world view is to take place as a new cultural dominant, a long process of reorientation and assimilation is required. Just as emergent Christianity required the devoted efforts of generations to assimilate the previous Greek learning, so modern psychology will gradually assimilate into its own forms and modes of understanding the products of human culture that have preceded it. This task I take to be the responsibility of the analysts and psychologically informed laity of the present and the future.

One of the best ways to promote an understanding of the new psychological view is to compare its discoveries with the intuitions of the wise men and poets of the past and thus to throw new light on old and familiar material. Such a procedure serves two purposes. It holds up to general view the new *Weltanschauung* by demonstrating its application to a particular subject matter, and at the same time it contributes to the long-range process of assimilating the old culture to the new orientation. These are my purposes in presenting this brief paper on Emerson.

Since my first discovery of Analytical psychology, I have been impressed by the numerous parallels between the intuitive insights of Emerson and the empirically established psychology of Jung. I had known and loved Emerson long before I had heard of the existence of Jung. I had heartily approved such ringing phrases as: "Trust thyself; every heart vibrates to that iron string;" "Envy is ignorance. . . imitation is suicide;" "Whoso would be a man must be a nonconformist. . . nothing is at last sacred but the integrity of your own mind." These dicta seemed self-evident truths, and they were later verified psychologically when I came to know the writings of Jung. Thus, for many years, I have wanted to write something that would link the work of Emerson and Jung. Emerson was a kind of intuitive proto-psychologist who adumbrated the depth psychology of Jung that was to come almost a century later. Emerson considered himself a psychologist. He called himself a "naturalist of the soul," and this picturesque term describes him aptly.[89] Also, Jung was well acquainted with Emerson and referred to him several times in his writings.[90]

Ralph Waldo Emerson was born in Boston in 1803, the son of a Congregational minister and the third of eight children. When he was eight years old, his father died and his mother was left with the difficult task of rearing a large family alone. As a boy, he was quiet and well behaved, avoiding contact with the rougher children of the neighborhood. Already, his introverted disposition was evident. Although he showed no particular brilliance in his studies, he was an earnest and diligent student. He attended successively the Boston Latin School, Harvard College, and later Harvard Divinity School. After holding a pastorate for three years, he resigned it because he could not endorse the forms of traditional Christianity. He wrote in his journal at the time:

> The profession [of the ministry] is antiquated. In an altered age, we worship in the dead forms of our forefathers. Were not a Socratic paganism

---

[89] F. O. Matthiessen, *American Renaissance* (New York: Oxford University Press, 1941), p. 16.

[90] See Jung, *Symbols of Transformation, CW* 5, par. 102n; *CW* 11, par. 92; *CW* 12, par. 445n.

better than an effete, superannuated Christianity?[91]

At the age of twenty-six, Emerson married Ellen Tucker, but two years later she died. He married a second time at the age of thirty-two, but his encounters with premature death were not over. The previous year, his brother Edward Emerson had died; and in the year following his second marriage another brother, Charles, was dead. The severest blow of all came in 1842 with the death of his five-year-old first-born son, Waldo. The year of his second marriage Emerson bought the well-known large white house in Concord, Massachusetts, where he was to live for the rest of his life. From here, he made various lecture tours around the country; here he cultivated the friendships of Henry Thoreau, Bronson Alcott, and Ellery Channing; here he kept his voluminous journals and polished the gemlike sentences of his essays; and here he finally died in 1882 at the age of seventy-nine.

As one surveys the life and writings of Emerson from a psychological viewpoint, perhaps the first and most powerful impression that emerges is the fact that he was a classic introvert. Like Immanuel Kant who never traveled more than forty miles beyond his native Königsberg, and Carl Jung who described his life as being "singularly poor in outward happenings,"[92] Emerson's outer life had the typical introverted character of being quiet and apparently uneventful. Numerous passages in his journals reveal that Emerson had the introvert's typical fear of the object. At the age of twenty-one, he wrote in his journal:

> There exists a signal defect of character [in me] which neutralizes in great part the just influence my talents ought to have. . . . . Its bitter fruits are a sore uneasiness in the company of most men and women, a frigid fear of offending and jealousy of disrespect, an inability to lead and an unwillingness to follow the current conversation, which contrive to make me second with all those among whom chiefly I wish to be first.[93]

---

[91] Bliss Perry, ed., *The Heart of Emerson's Journals* (Boston: Houghton Mifflin Co., 1926), 57.

[92] Jung, *Memories, Dreams, Reflections,* p. 5.

[93] Perry, *Journals,* p. 19.

In the same vein, he writes at age twenty-nine:

> In all practick, in driving a bargain, or hiding emotion, or carrying myself
> in company as a man for an hour, I have no skill. What under the sun canst
> thou do then, pale face? Truly not much, but I can hope.[94]

Again, at the age of thirty-four, he makes fun of his own doctrine of self-subsistence:

> The self-subsistant shakes like a reed before a sneering paragraph in the
> newspaper, or even at a difference of opinion, concerning something to be
> done, expressed in a private letter from just such another shaking bullrush
> as himself. He sits expecting a dinner-guest with a suspense which para-
> lyzes his inventive or his acquiring faculties. . . . Let him not wrong the
> truth and his own experience by too stiffly standing on the cold and proud
> doctrine of self-sufficiency.[95]

These passages express clearly the introvert's fear of the object and they help to explain Emerson's preoccupation with certain themes. For instance, his essay on "Self-Reliance" is just the sort of admonition the introvert needs if he is to be true to his own disposition and not fall victim to his dread enemy, the object. The introvert's urge to anonymity, his tendency to wrap around himself a cloak of invisibility so that he can move about unnoticed and unremarked, free from the dangerous bondage to the object, is beautifully expressed in the following passage:

> Man is as it were clapped into jail by his consciousness. As soon as he has
> once acted or spoke with *éclat* he is a committed person, watched by the
> sympathy or the hatred of hundreds, whose affections must now enter his
> account. . . . Ah, that he could pass again into his neutrality! Who can thus
> avoid all pledges and, having observed, observe again from the same unaf-
> fected, unbiased, unbribably, unaffrighted innocence—must always be for-
> midable.[96]

---

[94] Ibid., p. 64.

[95] Ibid., p. 119.

[96] Ralph Waldo Emerson, "Self-Reliance," in *The Complete Essays and Other Writings of Ralph Waldo Emerson*, ed. Brooks Atkinson (New York: Modern Library, 1940), p. 147. Unless noted, Emerson references are to this work.

A corollary to the danger of being dependent on the opinions of others is dependence on one's own past state of being. In Emerson's words:

> The other terror that scares us from self-trust is our consistency; a reverence for our past act or word because the eyes of others have no other data for computing our orbit than our past acts, and we are loath to disappoint them.

> But why should you keep your head over your shoulder? Why drag about this corpse of your memory, lest you contradict somewhat you have stated in this or that public place?. . . A foolish consistency is the hobgoblin of little minds. . . .Speak what you think now in hard words and tomorrow speak what tomorrow thinks in hard words again, though it contradict everything you said today.—"Ah, so you shall be sure to be misunderstood."—Is it so bad then to be misunderstood? Pythagoras was misunderstood, and Socrates, and Jesus, and Luther, and Copernicus, and Galileo, and Newton, and every pure and wise spirit that ever took flesh. To be great is to be misunderstood.[97]

This eloquent passage makes an important point, but it is obviously one-sided. Emerson seems to protest too much. We understand why when we read the self-revelations in his journals. Such an intense declamation against consistency and conventionality must be accompanied by an equally intense tendency in the opposite direction. Indeed, in his private life, Emerson was a most consistent and conventional man. He was lacking in the spontaneous, the irrational, and the unpredictable and often spoke of himself as deficient in animal spirits. Thus, Emerson's emphasis on self-reliance derives to some extent from subjective factors and will not be equally applicable to all. An English reviewer took Emerson to task on just this point. His criticism was that Emerson failed to consider "what a bedlam of egoists would be turned loose in the world 'if this indiscriminate self-reliance was generally adopted as the sole regulating principle of life.' "[98]

This criticism has some validity but it misses Emerson's most impor-

---

[97] Ibid., pp. 151f.

[98] R. L. Rusk, *The Life of Ralph Waldo Emerson* (New York: Charles Scribner's Sons, 1949), p. 285.

tant point. Collective standards and conventionality need no spokesmen. Everything speaks in their favor. It is the private subjectivity of the inner man that is universally neglected and despised, having no external validation of its worth. Indeed, Emerson's essay on self-reliance is one of the very few human documents that consciously honor and uphold the primary validity of subjectivity itself. I know of no better single sentence that epitomizes fidelity to the inner life than this: "to believe that what is true for you in your private heart is true for all me—that is genius."[99] This is the credo of the introvert and one need not be a genius to adopt it.

Emerson himself recognized the two classes of men that Jung has differentiated by the terms extravert and introvert. He gives a succinct description of the two classes in the following sentence, although his bias in favor of the introvert is evident by his use of the word poet for introvert and sensual man for extravert: "The sensual man conforms thoughts to things; the poet conforms things to his thoughts."[100] Emerson was an introvert and wrote out of a profound understanding of that life orientation. His writings will thus be most appreciated by introverts. It is perhaps a meaningful irony of history that one of the most extraverted societies ever to exist has given birth to one of the most articulate exponents of the introverted way.

Let us turn now to the question of Emerson's function type. Intuition is obviously his major function. This is evident in everything he wrote. His essays are a series of almost disconnected intuitive insights with very little systematic thinking to hold them together. In one essay we find this remark:

> The least hint sets us on the pursuit of a character which no man realizes. We have such exorbitant eyes that on seeing the smallest arc we complete the curve. . . .[101]

This is no description of man in general. It applies only to the intuitive man. Only he rushes to complete the curve on seeing the smallest arc.

---

[99] Emerson, "Self-Reliance," p. 145.

[100] Emerson, "Nature," p. 29.

[101] Emerson, "Nominalist and Realist," p. 435.

Emerson is describing himself. In his journal, he says:

> I have. . . . a strong imagination, and consequently a keen relish for the beauties of poetry. . . . My reasoning faculty is proportionally weak. . . .[102]

Again:

> Seldom, I suppose, was a more inapt learner of arithmetic, astronomy, geography, political economy, than I am. . . . My memory of history. . . is as bad; my comprehension of a question in technical metaphysics very slow. . . .[103]

These passages tell us that his imagination (intuition) is good but his relation to facts and figures (sensation) is poor. Emerson's inferior sensation function was very evident to his contemporaries. Melville was told that Emerson was "full of transcendentalisms, myths, and oracular gibberish."[104] A friend of Melville wrote him that Emerson "tho' a denizen of the land of gingerbread, is above munching a plain cake in company of jolly fellows, and swigging off his ale like you and me." To this, Melville replied, "that's his misfortune, not his fault. His belly, sir, is in his chest, and his brains descend down into his neck and offer an obstacle to a draught of ale or a mouthful of cake." Emerson recognized his deficiency on the earthy sensation side and wrote reminders to himself to pay attention to this aspect. Who but an introverted intuitive type must remind himself in his journal that:

> A man must have aunts and cousins, must buy carrots and turnips, must have barn and woodshed, must go to market and to the blacksmith's shop, must saunter and sleep and be inferior and silly.[105]

Emerson's second or auxiliary function is less clearly evident. The lack of organization and systematic presentation in his writings indicates that thinking was not well developed. But there is much in his journals

---

[102] Perry, *Journals*, p. 18.

[103] Ibid., pp. 63f.

[104] Eleanor Melville Metcalf, *Herman Melville* (Cambridge: Harvard University Press, 1953), pp. 58f.

[105] Perry, *Journals*, p. 131.

that corresponds to Jung's description of introverted feeling. Emerson's external coldness does not speak against a well-developed introverted feeling function. Jung says about this type:

> The relation to the object is, as far as possible, kept in a secure and tranquil middle state of feeling, where passion and its intemperateness are resolutely proscribed. Expression of feeling therefore remains niggardly. . . [such a type has] a rather cold and reserved demeanor.[106]

Introverted feeling expresses itself via the subjective inner life. Thus it relates more to universals than to particular persons. This is exemplified in the journal entry where Emerson states, "I like man, but not men."[107] An intense concern with the problem of morals, which are value judgments generalized, can also be considered as evidence of introverted feeling. Emerson's passionate quest for the realization of a moral ideal is demonstrated by the following passage from his journals:

> Milton describes himself . . . . as enamoured of moral perfection. He did not love it more than I. . . . It has separated me from men. It has watered my pillow, it has driven sleep from my bed. It has tortured me for my guilt. It has inspired me with hope. It cannot be defeated by my defeats. It cannot be questioned, though all the martyrs apostatize. . . . Keeping my eye on this, I understand all heroism, the history of loyalty and of martyrdom and of bigotry, the heat of the Methodist, the nonconformity of the Dissenter, the patience of the Quaker.[108]

One can scarcely deny that this is an intensely feeling statement in spite of its universal rather than personal reference. My tentative conclusion, therefore, is that Emerson's auxiliary function is feeling, operating through the introverted mode. Although Emerson's life and writings are colored by his auxiliary feeling function, predominantly they were an expression of his pronounced introversion and his superbly developed

---

[106] Jung, *Psychological Types* (London: Routledge & Kegan Paul, 1923), p. 493. [See also Jung, *Psychological Types, CW* 6, pars. 640f. for a slightly different translation.—Eds.]

[107] Perry, *Journals*, p. 217.

[108] Ibid., p. 80.

intuition.

Once when Emerson was preparing the *Essays* for the press, he had a dream. He dreamed that he was floating at will in the ether. Not far off he saw the world diminished to the size of an apple. An angel's voice commanded him to eat it, and he did.[109] It would take a man of Emerson's stature to be able to get away with a dream like this! It is patently a dream of a transcendentalist, one who views life and human affairs from a remote distance. From the viewpoint of one floating in the ether, the perspective and overall view is magnificent. It is the ideal position for making universal generalizations. Its deficiency, of course, is the lack of earthy, personal contact with concrete reality. By all ordinary criteria, this dream portrays inflation. But Emerson was no ordinary man, and we must be careful in applying this term to him. Nothing in his private or public writings suggests inflation—one-sidedness, yes, but not inflation.

Then, the dreamer is requested to eat the apple of the world and does so. This is a striking image. What density must be packed into the world condensed to the size of an apple! I am reminded of the dream of another introverted intuitive type who dreamed that he was eating a lead cast of Christ on the cross. In the dream, he wondered if the heavy lead was digestible. Such dreams are typical for the extreme intuitive type. Intuition is weightless air, sensation is heavy earth. The intuitive is confronted by the unconscious with the need to assimilate heavy earthiness. He needs it for ballast if he is to remain in the real world. We are also reminded of Socrates' recurrent dream in which he is told to make music. Just as Socrates' one-sided thinking function needed compensation with feeling (music), so Emerson's intuition needed balancing by its opposite (eating the earth). The unconscious is attempting to correct the one-sided remoteness of Emerson's Olympian ego attitude. Emerson's dream is also reminiscent of the paradise myth of Genesis where a request to eat the apple was likewise made.

The parallel suggests that Emerson's personal problem was the need to be born into the real world. He tended to live in the eternal realm of

---

[109] Rusk, *The Life*, p. 283.

universals prior to the birth of finite particulars, and needed to be prodded into eating the apple that would plunge him into the painful conflicts
and vicissitudes of fleshly existence. The dream portrays precisely both
the strength and the weakness of the introverted intuitive type and what
he must do not to fall victim to the one-sidedness of his temperament.
However, the dream can also be taken in another way. It describes, in an
image of heroic proportions, the nature of Emerson's accomplishment.
(Remember, it came while he was preparing his *Essays* for the press.)
Who but a giant can take the whole world into himself and assimilate it?
This is what Emerson accomplished through the power of his introverted
vision.

Given Emerson's psychological type and given his greatness as a human being and his gifts of expression, it is understandable why he wrote
what he did. Being an introverted intuitive, he was ideally suited typo-
logically to be what he styled himself, a naturalist of the soul. This type
is best fitted to perceive the eternal forms or *universalia* of the objective
psyche. And this is precisely what Emerson spent his lifetime doing.
Practically all his writings center around a description of the archetypal
patterns of life. Among all the archetypal themes and images that Jung
has demonstrated empirically, there is scarcely one that Emerson has not
at least touched upon. This in itself should make Emerson of interest to
Analytical psychologists. Beyond this fact are Emerson's capacities as a
creative artist. Not only does he describe the archetypal laws and images
of life, but he does so with a beauty and conciseness of expression that
has enriched our psycho-cultural heritage. His essays are studded with
brilliant phrases, precious jewels, which reveal new facets of meaning
each time we encounter them. His finest sayings are true symbols that
open up the depths to the discerning eye.

Take for example this remark which I used as a motto for my paper on
symbols:

> Every man's condition is a solution in hieroglyphic to those inquiries he
> would put. He acts it as life, before he apprehends it as truth.[110]

---

[110] Emerson, "Nature," p. 3.

If he had written nothing else, those two sentences would demonstrate that Emerson had a profound understanding of the objective psyche and the stages of development the ego must pass through to reach awareness of it. He is telling us that we live out unconsciously a myth or an archetype long before we can relate to it objectively. If we would have answers to our life questions, we must examine ourselves, how we live and what we are. The fruits of years of analysis are distilled in these two sentences.

Emerson describes clearly what Jung has termed the collective unconscious or objective psyche. He opens his essay on "History" with this statement:

> There is one mind common to all individual men. Every man is an inlet to the same and to all of the same. . . . What Plato has thought, he may think; what a saint has felt, he may feel; what at any time has befallen any man, he can understand. Who hath access to this universal mind is a party to all that is or can be done, for this is the only and sovereign agent.[111]

Again, in the essay, "Nominalist and Realist":

> I am very much struck in literature by the appearance that one person wrote all the books; as if the editor of a journal planted his body of reporters in different parts of the field of action, and relieved some by others from time to time; but there is such equality and identity both of judgment and point of view in the narrative that it is plainly the work of one all-seeing, all-hearing gentleman.[112]

Emerson's term for the objective psyche is *Over-Soul*. In his essay by this title, he states that the ego's feeling of lack can itself be seen as evidence of the fullness which is missing: "What is the universal sense of want and ignorance, but the fine innuendo by which the soul makes its enormous claim?"[113] He recognizes unambiguously the essential nature of the objective psyche, namely, that it is objective or autonomous in relation to the ego:

---

[111] Emerson, "History," p. 123.

[112] Emerson, "Nominalist and Realist," p. 439.

[113] Emerson, "Over-Soul," p. 261.

When I watch that flowing river which, out of regions I see not, pours for a season its streams into me, I see that I am a pensioner; not a cause but a surprised spectator of this ethereal water; that I desire and look up and put myself in the attitude of reception, but from some alien energy the visions come.[114]

If anyone doubts that Emerson had a practical, working awareness of how the unconscious operates and obtrudes itself on the conscious personality, let him read the following passage. The psychological sophistication of the twentieth century has nothing to teach him here:

If we consider what happens in conversation, in reveries, in remorse, in times of passion, in surprises, in the instructions of dreams . . . we shall catch many hints that will broaden and lighten into knowledge of the secret of nature.[115]

He also understood the mechanism of projection. At a time when he was pondering the accusations of atheism that were being made against him, he wrote the following comment in his journal: "It is plain from all the noise that there is atheism somewhere; the only question is now, Which is the atheist?"[116] The process of withdrawing an anima projection is described in his poem, "Give All to Love." The poem urges that a man submit completely to his love for a woman; but when she wants to leave him he must freely let her go because:

> Though thou loved her as thyself,
> As a self of purer clay,
> Though her parting dims the day,
> Stealing grace from all alive;
> Heartily know,
> When half-gods go,
> The gods arrive.[117]

Emerson perceived the central suprapersonal source of psychic en-

---

[114] Ibid., p. 262.
[115] Ibid., p. 263.
[116] Perry, *Journals*, p. 138.
[117] Emerson, p. 775.

ergy, the Self. What he describes in the following passage as soul could be translated as Self and would be an absolutely accurate psychological description:

> All goes to show that the soul in man is not an organ, but animates and exercises all the organs; is not a function . . . is not a faculty, but a light; is not the intellect or the will, but the master of the intellect and the will; is the background of our being, in which they lie—an immensity not possessed and that cannot be possessed. From within or from behind, a light shines through us upon things and makes us aware that we are nothing, but the light is all. . . . What we commonly call man. . . . Him we do not respect, but the soul whose organ he is, would he let it appear through his action, would make our knees bend.[118]

As would be expected from a man with such openness to the unconscious, Emerson had a keen appreciation of the transformative power of symbolism and the process of analogical thinking. He demonstrates symbolic understanding in his first published essay, "Nature," where he says:

> Every natural fact is a symbol of some spiritual fact. Every appearance in nature corresponds to some state of the mind, and that state of the mind can only be described by presenting that natural appearance as its picture. . . . It is easily seen that there is nothing lucky or capricious in these analogies, but that they are constant, and pervade nature. These are not the dreams of a few poets, here and there, but man is an analogist. . . .[119]

Emerson sees the origins of language as evidence of the pristine, natural function of the psyche. All expression begins as imagery:

> savages . . . converse in figures. As we go back in history, language becomes more picturesque, until its infancy, when it is all poetry. . . . The same symbols are found to make the original elements of all languages[120]

> The moment our discourse rises above the ground line of familiar facts and is inflamed with passion or exalted by thought, it clothes itself in im-

---

[118] Emerson, "Over-Soul," p. 263.

[119] Emerson, "Nature," p. 15.

[120] Ibid., p. 16.

ages. . . . good writing and brilliant discourse are perpetual allegories.[121]

Emerson's thorough understanding of symbolism and the unconscious enabled him to appreciate in a quite modern way those twin phenomena, myths and dreams. About myths, he wrote:

> The beautiful fables of the Greeks, being proper creations of the imagination and not of the fancy, are universal verities. What a range of meanings and what perpetual pertinence. . . ![122]

And again:

> This voice of fable has in it somewhat divine. It came from thought above the will of the writer. That is the best part of each writer which has nothing private in it; that which he does not knows; that which flowed out of his constitution and not from his too active invention. . . .[123]

About dreams, he has this to say:

> A dream may let us deeper into the secret of nature than a hundred concerted experiments.[124]

> [In dreams] often we see ourselves in masquerade—the droll disguise only magnifying and enhancing a real element and forcing it on our distant notice. . . .[125]

> Our dreams are the sequel of our waking knowledge. The visions of the night bear some proportion to the visions of the day. . . . We see our evil affections embodied in bad physiognomies. . . . "My children," said an old man to his boys scared by a figure in the dark entry, "My children, you will never see anything worse than yourselves.". . . in dreams . . . every man sees himself in colossal, without knowing that it is himself.[126]

Every deep encounter with the unconscious brings up the problem of opposites. Emerson was very familiar with the relation between the op-

---

[121] Ibid., p. 17.
[122] Emerson, "History," p. 138.
[123] Emerson, "Compensation," p. 178.
[124] Emerson, "Nature," p. 37.
[125] Emerson, "Over-Soul," p. 263.
[126] Emerson, "Spiritual Laws," p. 199.

posites and wrote eloquently on this subject. He devoted his whole essay, "Compensation," to a discussion of the opposites and their interplay. He knew about *enantiodromia,* the law by which an extreme or one-sided position inevitably constellates its opposite. He began his essay on "Compensation" with these lines of verse:

> The wings of Time are black and white,
> Pied with morning and with night.
> Mountain tall and ocean deep
> Trembling balance duly keep.[127]

He also had a vision of the unity of the Self that lies behind and reconciles the conflict of the opposites. This is evident in the following lines from the poem, "Brahma," which owes something to his reading of the then recently translated Hindu scriptures:

> If the red slayer think he slays,
>   Or if the slain think he is slain,
> They know not well the subtle ways
>   I keep, and pass, and turn again.
>
> Far or forgot to me is near;
>   Shadow and sunlight are the same;
> The vanished gods to me appear;
>   And one to me are shame and fame.
>
> They reckon ill who leave me out;
>   When me they fly, I am the wings;
> I am the doubter and the doubt,
>   And I the hymn the Brahmin sings.[128]

These passages go to show that Emerson had a keen intuitive perception of the opposites and of the need for them to be balanced and reconciled. Nonetheless, his life and writings convey the distinct impression that Emerson himself was one-sided. We have already noted his depreciation of extraversion and of the sensation function. In general, he

[127] Emerson, "Compensation," p. 170.
[128] Emerson, *Writings*, p. 809.

stands for spirit and is largely opposed to matter. He reveals this bias particularly in his essay, "Prudence," where he makes it evident that sensuality is his unassimilated shadow: "Genius is always ascetic. . . . Appetite shows to the finer souls as a disease. . . ."[129] Again, in his essay, "The Poet":

> Painters, poets, musicians and actors have been more than others wont to lead a life of pleasure and indulgence. . . . as it was an emancipation not into the heavens but into the freedom of baser places, they were punished for that advantage they won, by a dissipation and deterioration.[130]

Melville recognized this defect in Emerson and made the following notation in his copy of *Essays* after the above-quoted passage:

> No, no, no.—Titian—did he deteriorate? Byron?—Did he.—Mr. E. is horribly narrow here. He has his Dardanelles for his every Marmora.—But he keeps nobly on, for all that![131]

The clearest evidence that Emerson did not achieve a reconciliation of opposites within himself is his endorsement of the doctrine of *privatio boni*. In his address to the Harvard Divinity School, he stated:

> Good is positive. Evil is merely privative, not absolute: it is like cold, which is the privation of heat. All evil is so much death or nonentity. Benevolence is absolute and real.[132]

In fairness to Emerson, it must be mentioned that he uttered these words at the age of thirty-five. His view may have changed in later years, although I am aware of no clear evidence to indicate such a change.

In spite of his failure to realize the insight in his personal life, in the abstract Emerson saw clearly and described beautifully the majestic, compensating interplay between the opposites. His introverted vision also caused him to encounter that central psychic image, the mandala. This image appears in his essay, "Circles." Here he called the circle "the

---

[129] Emerson, "Prudence," p. 243.

[130] Emerson, "The Poet," p. 333.

[131] J. Leyda, *The Melville Log*, vol. 2 (New York: Harcourt, Brace & Co., 1951), p. 649.

[132] Emerson, "An Address," p. 69.

highest emblem in the cipher of the world" and attributed to Augustine that magnificent description of God as a circle whose center is everywhere and whose circumference is nowhere.

Emerson had a profound sense of the fact that the psyche creates the events that befall it. Listen to these penetrating insights from *The Conduct of Life*:

> The secret of the world is the tie between person and event . . . the soul contains the event that shall befall it. . . . The event is the print of your form. . . .
>
> Events grow on the same stem with persons. . . .
>
> Each creature puts forth from itself its own condition and sphere, as the slug sweats out its slimy house on the pear leaf. . . .
>
> A man will see his character emitted in the events that seem to meet, but which exude from and accompany him. . . .
>
> there are no contingencies. . . . Law rules throughout existence. . . .[133]

Emerson would have felt completely at home with the concept of synchronicity. He was obviously familiar with the phenomenon. For instance, he speaks of certain kinds of people who:

> are made up of rhyme, coincidence, omen, periodicity, and presage; they meet the person they seek; what their companion prepares to say to them, they first say to him; and a hundred signs apprise them of what is about to befall.[134]

Surely, Emerson as an intuitive type must have had his own share of this type of experience.

Perhaps of all of Emerson's doctrines, Jungians will be most responsive to his plea for the realization of the whole man. In several places, he speaks eloquently of the fragmented man, the one who is no more than a hypertrophied, specialized function. Emerson discovered for himself the old Gnostic image of the *Anthropos*, the original whole man. He judged

---

[133] Ralph Waldo Emerson, *The Conduct of Life* (New York: Doubleday & Co., no date), pp. 29ff.

[134] Ibid., p. 33.

individuals by comparing them with the complete original and found them only pitiful fragments.

There is One Man—present to all particular men partially, or through one faculty . . . [but] you must take the whole society to find the whole man. . . . Unfortunately, this original unit, this fountain of power has been distributed to multitudes, has been so minutely subdivided and peddled out, that it is spilled into drops, and cannot be gathered. The state of society is one in which the members have suffered amputation from the trunk, and strut about so many walking monsters—a good finger, a neck, a stomach, an elbow, but never a man.[135]

In another place, a similar idea is expressed:

Among the multitude of scholars and authors we feel no hallowing presence; we are sensible of a knack and skill rather than of inspiration; they have a light and know not whence it comes and call it their own; their talent is some exaggerated faculty, some overgrown member, so that their strength is a disease. In these instances the intellectual gifts do not make the impression of virtue, but almost of vice. . . .[136]

Or take the following passage, which concludes with a beautiful description of the persona-identified man:

Great men or men of great gifts you shall easily find, but symmetrical men never. . . . All persons exist to society by some shining trait of beauty or utility which they have. We borrow the proportions of the man from that one fine feature, and finish the portrait symmetrically; which is false, for the rest of his body is small or deformed. I observe a person who makes a good public appearance, and conclude thence the perfection of his private character, on which this is based; but he has no private character. He is a graceful cloak or lay figure for holidays.[137]

In these passages, Emerson is foreshadowing Jung's theory of the function types and is urging that the ego relate to the Self, the wholeness of man, rather than identify narrowly with a single specialized function.

---

[135] Emerson, "American Scholar," p. 46.

[136] Emerson, "Over-Soul," p. 273.

[137] Emerson, "Nominalist and Realist," p. 436.

In Emerson's day the social pressure toward specialization had only begun; today it has reached the extreme. What was true then is doubly true now, and Emerson's plea to rediscover the whole man carries for us the greatest urgency.

Not only did Emerson emphasize the scattered, fragmented aspect of human life, he also attempted to make definite suggestions as to how the individual could be healed and made whole. All of these suggestions center around the need for greater individual consciousness. He always saw the problem as residing in the individual himself. He scorned the projection device that will try to correct others while leaving oneself unchanged: "All men plume themselves on the improvement of society, and no man improves."[138] The individual must be transformed and his soul redeemed through self-awareness:

> The problem of restoring to the world original and eternal beauty is solved by the redemption of the soul. The ruin or the blank that we see when we look at nature, is in our own eye. The axis of vision is not coincident with the axis of things, and so they appear not transparent but opaque. The reason why the world lacks unity, and lies broken and in heaps, is because man is disunited with himself.[139]

The goal is for the individual to be a whole person, not an anonymous statistic in the collective mass:

> Is it not the chief disgrace in the world, not to be an unit; not to be reckoned one character; not to yield that peculiar fruit which each man was created to bear, but to be reckoned in the gross, in the hundred, or the thousand, of the party, the section, to which we belong. . . ?[140]

In spite of the comments of some of his critics, Emerson was not advocating inflated egoism or irresponsible freedom. He knew as well as Nietzsche that, "Many a one hath cast away his final worth when he hath cast away his servitude."[141] He was urging loyalty to the inner authority

---

[138] Emerson, "Self-Reliance," p. 166.

[139] Emerson, "Nature," p. 41.

[140] Emerson, "American Scholar," p. 63.

[141] Friedrich Nietzsche, *Thus Spake Zarathustra*, part 1, chap. 17. [See transla-

which could replace reliance on projected collective and conventional authority:

> The populace think that your rejection of popular standards is a rejection of all standard. . . . But the law of consciousness abides. There are two confessionals, in one or the other of which we must be shriven. You may fulfil your round of duties by clearing yourself in the *direct*, or in the *reflex* way. . . . I have my own stern claims and perfect circle. It denies the name of duty to many offices that are called duties. But if I can discharge its debts it enables me to dispense with the popular code. If any one imagines that this law is lax, let him keep its commandment one day.[142]

As we have seen, Emerson had his defects. As is usually the case, they were the defects of his virtues. Let those who have equaled his accomplishments criticize him for his deficiencies. We cannot expect everything from a single man. Like the great men he described, he also existed for society by one "shining trait." His great accomplishment was the superlative development of introverted intuition and the embodiment of his intuitive insights in striking and enduring phrases. He was a psychologist in the broad sense because his subject was the universal mind. And his writings have taken their place among the treasures of human culture as a particularly eloquent expression of that universal mind. They thus properly become another text, another document of the soul, to be examined and assimilated by modern psychology.

There is an *ecclesia spiritualis*. In the process of assimilating the old culture to the new psychology, we discover again and again colleagues of the spirit. Emerson was such a colleague. He was a dedicated forerunner of the new world view that is only now beginning to reach its full emergence. The essence of this new view is well expressed by another colleague of the spirit, Teilhard de Chardin:

> The work of human works . . . [is] to establish, in and by means of each one of us, an absolutely original centre in which the universe reflects itself

---

tion by R. J. Hollingdale (Middlesex: Penguin Books, 1961), p. 89.—Eds.]
[142] Emerson, "Self-Reliance," p. 161.

in a unique and inimitable way."[143]

This statement could have been written by Emerson. It expresses precisely his own view. In fact, all men who speak from within the living experience of the psyche say essentially the same thing. As Emerson has said, teachers are of two kinds: "one class speak *from within*, or from experience, as parties and possessors of the fact; and the other class *from without*, as spectators merely. . . ."[144] Emerson is one of the teachers from within. He knew the reality of the psyche and the riches it contains. His writings are an eloquent witness to that fact.

Review of C. G. Jung, *Nietzsche's 'Zarathustra': Notes of the Seminar Given in 1934-1939*. Ed. James L. Jarrett. 2 vols. (Princeton: Princeton University Press, 1988) [145]
Edward F. Edinger

The publication of Jung's *Nietzsche's "Zarathustra"* provides an occasion to consider his very important relation to Nietzsche.

Friedrich Nietzsche (1844-1900) was a brilliant nineteenth-century philosopher, poet, and prophet. In cultural history he is the harbinger of the twentieth century and the first truly "modern man." Although the son of a Protestant pastor, Nietzsche was a violent critic of Christianity and, in his later years, identified himself explicitly with the Antichrist. At the age of forty-four, he had an abrupt mental breakdown and was confined to an asylum, where he was diagnosed as having general paresis, a syphilitic brain disease. He died twelve years later.

Nietzsche's masterwork is *Thus Spake Zarathustra*, a stunning prose poem in which the ancient Persian prophet, Zarathustra, returns to earth, proclaims a devastating critique of contemporary man, and announces a

---

[143] Pierre Teilhard de Chardin, *The Phenomenon of Man* (New York: Harper Torchbooks, 1961), p. 261.

[144] Emerson, "Over-Soul," p. 272.

[145] This review was first published in *Psychological Perspectives* 20, no. 1 (Spring-Summer 1989), pp. 173ff.—Eds.

new morality. Most of this work was written in a state of inspiration. Nietzsche himself describes the state:

> Has anyone at the end of the nineteenth century a clear idea of what poets of strong ages have called *inspiration*? If not, I will describe it. If one had the slightest residue of superstition left in one's system, one could hardly reject altogether the idea that one is merely incarnation, merely mouthpiece, merely a medium of overpowering forces. The concept of revelation—in the sense that suddenly, with indescribable certainty and subtlety, something becomes *visible*, audible, something that shakes one to the last depths and throws one down—that merely describes the facts. One hears, one does not seek; one accepts, one does not ask who gives; like lightning, a thought flashes up, with necessity, without hesitation regarding its form—I never had any choice.
>
> A rapture whose tremendous tension occasionally discharges itself in a flood of tears—now the pace quickens involuntarily, now it becomes slow; one is altogether beside oneself, with the distinct consciousness of subtle shudders and of one's skin creeping down to one's toes; a depth of happiness in which even what is most painful and gloomy does not seem something opposite but rather conditioned, provoked, a *necessary* color in such a superabundance of light; an instinct for rhythmic relationships that arches over wide spaces of forms—length, the need for a rhythm with wide arches, is almost the measure of the force of inspiration, a kind of compensation for its pressure and tension.
>
> Everything happens involuntarily in the highest degree but as in a gale of a feeling of freedom, of absoluteness, of power, of divinity. The involuntariness of image and metaphor is strangest of all: one no longer has any notion of what is an image or a metaphor: everything offers itself as the nearest, most obvious, simplest expression. It actually seems, to allude to something Zarathustra says, as if the things themselves approached and offered themselves as metaphors ("Here all things come caressingly to your discourse and flatter you; for they want to ride on your back. On every metaphor you ride to every truth. . . . Here the words and word-shrines of all being open up before you; here all being wishes to become word, all becoming wishes to learn from you how to speak").
>
> This is *my* experience of inspiration: I do not doubt that one has to go back thousands of years in order to find anyone who could say to me, "It's

mine as well."[146]

This ecstatic state of mind gave birth to *Thus Spake Zarathustra*. It poured directly out of the unconscious; the book is an amazing psychological document. Zarathustra announces a whole new world view, which, in truth, is the harbinger of depth psychology. The way in which Nietzsche describes the collective shadow of modern man is breathtaking. The book abounds in brilliant psychological truths, but it also contains subtle, very dangerous poison. As Jung tells us, it is "morbid." This is because its transcendent insights have not been assimilated by the whole man; they have not been humanized, but rather are a product of inflation. Nevertheless, the insights are so profound and so relevant to Jung's own discoveries that, in the midst of his encounter with the unconscious (winter of 1914-15), Jung "studied it very carefully and made a lot of annotations" (391). The Zarathustra Seminar is the ripe fruit of that careful study presented twenty years later.

Jung's first encounter with Nietzsche's *Zarathustra* occurred while he was in medical school in 1898. In *Memories, Dreams, Reflections*, he says that at first he was held back from reading Nietzsche "by a secret fear that I might perhaps be like him. Perhaps—who knows?—he had had inner experiences, insights which he had unfortunately attempted to talk about, and had found that no one understood him." Jung continues:

> In spite of these trepidations I was curious, and finally resolved to read him. *Thoughts Out of Season* was the first volume that fell into my hands. I was carried away by enthusiasm, and soon afterward read *Thus Spake Zarathustra*. This, like Goethe's *Faust*, was a tremendous experience for me. *Zarathustra* was Nietzsche's *Faust*, his No. 2, and my No. 2 now corresponded to *Zarathustra*—though this was rather like comparing a molehill with Mount Blanc. And Zarathustra—there could be no doubt about it—was morbid. Was my No. 2 also morbid? This possibility filled me with a terror which for a long time I refused to admit, but the idea cropped up again and again at inopportune moments, throwing me into a cold sweat, so that in the end I was forced to reflect on myself. Nietzsche had

---

[146] Friedrich Nietzsche, "Ecce Homo," in *Basic Writings of Nietzsche*, trans. Walter Kaufmann (New York: Modern Library, 1968), pp. 756f.

discovered his No. 2 only late in life, when he was already past middle age, whereas I had known mine ever since boyhood. Nietzsche had spoken naively and incautiously about his *arrheton*, this thing not to be named, as though it were quite in order. But I had noticed in time that this only leads to trouble. He was so brilliant that he was able to come to Basel as a professor when still a young man, not suspecting what lay ahead of him. Because of his very brilliance he should have noticed in time that something was amiss. That, I thought, was his morbid misunderstanding: that he fearlessly and unsuspectingly let his No. 2 loose upon a world that knew and understood nothing about such things. He was moved by the childish hope of finding people who would be able to share his ecstasies and could grasp his "transvaluation of all values." But he found only educated Philistines—tragi-comically, he was one himself. Like the rest of them, he did not understand himself when he fell head first into the unutterable mystery and wanted to sing its praises to the dull, godforsaken masses. That was the reason for the bombastic language, the piling up of metaphors, the hymnlike raptures—all a vain attempt to catch the ear of a world which had sold its soul for a mass of disconnected facts. And he fell—tightrope-walker that he proclaimed himself to be—into depths far beyond himself.[147]

It is evident from this account that the twenty-three-year-old Jung was frightened by his first encounter with Nietzsche's *Zarathustra*.

From the perspective of 100 years, we can now understand Nietzsche to have been the first depth psychologist. As Jung puts it: "It is only the tragedies of Goethe's *Faust* and Nietzsche's *Zarathustra* which mark the first glimmerings of a break-through of total experience in our Western hemisphere."[148] But Goethe did not *live* Faust's experience of Mephistopheles the way Nietzsche *lived* his experience of Zarathustra. Nietzsche is perhaps the first Western man to have experienced a psychological encounter with the Self—and he perished in that encounter. How could it have been otherwise, since he was the first to tread this unknown region and thus was ignorant of its dangers? We depth psychologists owe an immense debt to Nietzsche, the pioneer. Jung learned from

[147] Jung, *Memories, Dreams, Reflections,* pp. 102f.
[148] Jung, *Psychology and Religion, CW* 11, par. 905.

his experience; without Nietzsche's example to warn him, Jung's encounter with the unconscious also might have been fatal.

Nietzsche's mistake was that his ego identified with the emerging Self—the "total experience"—personified by the Wise Old Man, Zarathustra. As Jung tells us:

> The way in which [Nietzsche] wrote it is most remarkable. He himself made a verse about it. He said: *"Da wurde eins zu zwei und Zarathustra ging an mir vorbei,"* which means: "Then one became two and Zarathustra passed by me," meaning that Zarathustra then became manifest as a second personality in himself. That would show that he had himself a pretty clear notion that he was not identical with Zarathustra. But how could he help assuming such an identity in those days when there was no psychology? Nobody would then have dared to take the idea of a personification seriously, or even of an independent autonomous spiritual agency. Eighteen eighty-three was the time of the blooming of materialistic philosophy. So he had to identify with Zarathustra in spite of the fact that he felt, as this verse proves, a definite difference between himself and the old wise man.[149]

It is this inflated identification of ego with Self that makes Nietzsche's Zarathustra "morbid" and dangerous for the psychologically naïve. Jung expresses this point explicitly:

> But *I* call it a mistake that he ever published *Zarathustra*. That is a book which ought not to be published; it should be reserved for people who have undergone a very careful training in the psychology of the unconscious. Only then, having given evidence of not being overthrown by what the unconscious occasionally says, should people have access to the book. For in *Zarathustra* we have to deal with a partial revelation of the unconscious. It is full of inspiration, of the immediate manifestation of the unconscious, and therefore should be read with due preparation, with due knowledge of the style and the intentions of the unconscious. If a man reads *Zarathustra* unprepared, with all the naïve presuppositions of our actual civilization, he must necessarily draw wrong conclusions as to the meaning of the "Superman," "the Blond Beast," "the Pale Criminal," and

---

[149] Jung, *Nietzsche's "Zarathustra,"* pp. 9f.

so on. And such people will surely draw such conclusions as murder-for-the-sake-of-the-cause. Many suicides have felt themselves justified by *Zarathustra*—as any damned nonsense can be justified by *Zarathustra*. So it is generally assumed that Nietzsche is at the bottom of a whole host of evils on account of his immoral teaching, while as a matter of fact, Nietzsche himself and his teaching are exceedingly moral, but only to people who really understand how to read it.

You see, it all depends upon what level one speaks from—whether one is talking on the level of the ordinary understanding or of an extraordinary understanding. Whatever you say on the normal level is understood by all the people who are on that level, but if you say something which really comes from a level underneath as *if* it belonged to the normal level, then it will be misunderstood. People will not realize that it comes from the layer below, and that in order to really understand it they themselves should be below. Of course that is very difficult, because we never reckon with such levels, but in dealing with a product like *Zarathustra*, we must consider this question.[150]

In spite of this criticism, Jung adds in another place: "We always must recognize, however, that we would not know what we know today if Nietzsche had not lived. Nietzsche has taught us a lot."[151]

Jung acknowledges that his central concept of the Self owes something to Nietzsche (p. 391). Although this concept originally derives from the Upanishads, it probably recommended itself to Jung through his reading of *Zarathustra*. In Part 1, Section 4, "On the Despisers of the Body," Nietzsche writes this about the Self:

Behind your thoughts and feelings, my brother, there stands a mighty ruler, an unknown sage—whose name is self. In your body he dwells; he is your body. . . . Your self laughs at your ego and at its bold leaps. "What are these leaps and flights of thought to me?" it says to itself. "A detour to my end. I am the leading strings of the ego and the prompter of its concepts."[152]

---

[150] Ibid., pp. 475f.
[151] Ibid., p. 544.
[152] Kaufmann, *Basic Writings*.

Zarathustra does not represent Nietzsche's first encounter with the Self. In a posthumously published autobiographical work (probably not known to Jung), Nietzsche informs us that his encounter with the Self (Personality No. 2) began at the tender age of 12:

> Of all the books in the Bible, First Samuel, especially in the opening passages, made the profoundest impression on me. In a way, it may be responsible for an important spiritual element in my life. It is where the Lord three times wakes the infant prophet in his sleep, and Samuel three times mistakes the heavenly voice for the voice of Eli asleep near him in the temple. Convinced, after the third time, that his prodigy is being called to higher services than those available to him in the house of sacrifices, Eli proceeds to instruct him in the ways of prophecy. I had no Eli (not even a Schopenhauer) when a similar visitation darkened the opening days of my adolescence. I was all of twelve when the Lord broke in on me in all His glory, a glaring fusion of the portrait of Abraham, Moses, and the Young Jesus in our family Bible. In His second visitation He came to me not physically but in a shudder of consciousness in which good and evil both clamored before the gates of my soul for equal mastery. The third time He seized me in front of my house in the grasp of a terrible wind. I recognized the agency of a divine force because it was in that moment that I conceived of the Trinity as God the Father, God the Son, and God the Devil. . . . I replaced Samuel with Zarathustra . . . .[153]

Nietzsche's awareness of Personality No. 2 thus began almost as early as Jung's. These particular revelations, with their emphasis on the opposition that exists within the deity, indicate that the Self in its modern phenomenology had been constellated in Nietzsche. The core issue for him became the Christ-Antichrist polarity. While consciously siding with Antichrist, he unconsciously identified with Christ; thus, in his insanity, he signed some of his letters, "The Crucified One." Either way, Nietzsche lived his life out of a profoundly religious attitude. As Jung writes:

---

[153] Friedrich Nietzsche, *My Sister and I*, trans. Oscar Levy (New York: Bridgehead Books, 1951), p. 184. Although this work has been dismissed by Walter Kaufmann as fraudulent, it is clearly authentic.

The tragedy of *Zarathustra* is that, because his God died, Nietzsche him-self became a god; and this happened because he was no atheist. He was of too positive a nature to tolerate the urban neurosis of atheism. It seems dangerous for such a man to assert that "God is dead": he instantly became the victim of inflation.[154]

Although Jung's emphasis on Nietzsche's pathological inflation is necessary and appropriate, it does not quite do justice to Nietzsche's per-sonal accomplishment. Nietzsche is a heroic martyr for the cause of emerging depth psychology. If one reads him carefully, one gets hints that he deliberately chose the way of inflation in order to learn what lies on the other side. Although he was pushed over the brink of psychosis by syphilitic brain damage, in some sense it also seems he chose it. In his posthumous autobiography he wrote:

The legend-makers saw Empedocles plunging into the belching flames of Aetna, but this fate was reserved not for the great pre-Socratic but for me alone. Having been separated from the love of my life [Lou Salome], the love that made me human, I made my desperate plunge into the fires of madness, hoping like Zarathustra to snatch faith in myself by going out of my mind and entering a higher region of sanity—the sanity of the raving lunatic, the normal madness of the damned![155]

In the same work, Nietzsche wrote these moving words from his room in the madhouse:

Is my honor lost because women have betrayed me to weakness, or I have betrayed my own strength, seeking the power of true knowledge which alone can save us from approaching Doom? Am I completely damned be-cause I am crushed beneath the Athenian dead on the plain of Marathon? Let Demosthenes, the eloquent defender of Athenian honor, deliver his fu-neral oration over me: "No, you have not failed, Friedrich Nietzsche! There are noble defeats as there are noble deaths—and you have died no-bly. *No, you have not failed!* I swear it by the dead on the plain of Mara-thon.

I swear it.

[154] Jung, "Psychology and Religion," *Psychology and Religion, CW* 11, par. 142.
[155] Nietzsche, *My Sister and I*, p. 114.

I swear it![156]

With Nietzsche's autobiography available, we can now see his life in its entirety as a noble tragedy—an heroic sacrifice which inaugurated the age of depth psychology and first brought the Greater Personality to the awareness of modern man. Jung writes as much:

> Nietzsche always reminds me of those criminals or prisoners of war who were chosen to represent the gods, in Mexico and also in Babylonia. They were allowed every freedom until the sun went down, and then they were sacrificed to the gods. . . . That is Nietzsche all over, being entirely instrumental, a figure on the chess board, giving us a living account through his confession of his experiences. It is an unrealized and undigested experience, but of course with all the advantages and all the virtues of an immediate and living experience.[157]

Jung's massive seminar on Nietzsche's Zarathustra defies any attempt at summary. This magisterial enterprise, done *ex tempore*, demonstrates to any perceptive reader Jung's millennial magnitude. This work belongs chiefly to the future; I fear that only a handful of contemporaries will be able to follow where it leads.

As Jung tells us, Nietzsche's Zarathustra has a "double bottom."[158] Its basic content is a revelation for modern man of the transpersonal Self, represented by the figure of Zarathustra. This message is sound and profound. However, it is transmitted through the frail and sometimes morbid ego of the man, Nietzsche. The consequence is that Zarathustra's message is contaminated and distorted by Nietzsche's intermittent identification with the Self. Jung's task is to separate Nietzsche from Zarathustra and to recover the purity of the original revelation. In the process, Jung provides an exhaustive analysis of Nietzsche's atheistic inflation and his failure to integrate the shadow. Since Nietzsche is the first modern man, this analysis is relevant to us all—to the extent that we claim to be modern.

---

[156] Ibid., pp. 244f.

[157] Jung, *Nietzsche's "Zarathustra,"* p. 1147.

[158] Ibid., p. 830.

We owe Professor James L. Jarrett, the editor, considerable gratitude for his willingness to undertake this gargantuan project. He provides a helpful introduction and numerous footnotes. Unfortunately, the text is marred by a large number of typographical and editorial errors.[159]

Review of C. G. Jung, *Psychology and Alchemy*, volume 12 of *The Collected Works of C. G. Jung*, Trans. R. F. C. Hull. Bollingen Series XX (New York: Pantheon Books, 1953). [160]
Edward F. Edinger

This is the first volume to be published in an 18-volume English edition of *The Collected Works of C. G. Jung*. It is the first English translation of *Psychologie und Alchemie,* originally published in 1944. Other volumes of the collected works published to date (July, 1954) include: *Two Essays on Analytical Psychology* (Volume 7) and *The Practice of Psychotherapy* (Volume 16).

Psychology and Alchemy is a major work of the author's later years. Its subject matter represents Jung's great interest in mythological, religious, and alchemical symbolism and their relationship to depth psychology. It is a difficult book for the average scientifically-trained doctor, delving as it does into obscure medieval alchemical treatises and ancient Gnostic doctrines. A previous knowledge of Jung's psychological theories is assumed, and without this knowledge much of the book may be incomprehensible.

The central theme is the alchemical opus and its correspondence to the course of events experienced in a deep psychological analysis. This correspondence is illustrated by a series of dreams from a patient undergoing psychotherapy. These dreams often showed a remarkable similarity to the imagery used by the alchemists in describing the procedure for the

---

[159] A list of 49 substantive "Corrections" was found in Edinger's private papers—Eds.

[160] This review was first published in the *American Journal of Psychiatry,* vol. 111 (November 1954), p. 395.—Eds.

transformation of matter. It is Jung's view that the conscientious alchemists—leaving out the quacks and charlatans—in attempting to transform base matter into gold, the elixir of life, or the Philosophers' Stone were actually projecting into matter their own unconscious process of personality transformation. In other words, the psychic process of transformation or sublimation of primitive, infantile personality traits was seen as a chemical process; and the alchemist attempted to transform in his retort an original "black substance" *(nigredo*—often filth or feces) into something of supreme value. Jung has this to say:

> Strictly speaking, projection is never made; it happens, it is simply there. In the darkness of anything external to me I find, without recognizing it as such, an interior or psychic life that is my own. . . . while working on his chemical experiments the operator had certain psychic experiences which appeared to him as the particular behavior of the chemical process. Since it was a question of projection, he was naturally unconscious of the fact that the experience had nothing to do with matter itself. . . . He experienced his projection as a property of matter; but what he was in reality experiencing was his own unconscious. (par. 346)

The implications of this viewpoint are considerable. If the parallels between the alchemical transformation process and modern dream symbolism are valid, they mean that there is an inherent unconscious drive towards personality development with the goal symbolized by the elixir of life or the perfect, incorruptible substance. This process could then be considered an archetypal pattern of human development. Awareness of this drive towards transformation within himself could be of considerable assistance to the patient who is struggling with his own primitive and infantile traits. These latter dark and unpleasant aspects of personality are considered by Jung to correspond to the *nigredo* or *massa confusa,* which was the raw material the alchemists attempted to transform. The transformation process is also a kind of redemption of inferior matter, and the alchemists considered it in this light. They alluded to the analogy of Christ's redemption of human sins in describing their work. However, their attitude was fundamentally heretical, because the individual alchemist took upon himself the task of redemption—whereas the Church maintained that Christ had already accomplished this task for all mankind and that every believer could share the fruits of His redemption by means of faith. The alchemists thus represent the beginning of a new step in the development of human consciousness—namely, the awareness that redemption or development of personality is not automatically accomplished by faith in a divine figure but is a task requiring arduous conscious effort. It is to this task—in projected form—that many sincere alchemists devoted a lifetime of work.

Jung has found that showing patients the similarities between their dreams and alchemical or religious symbolism has definite therapeutic effect. This so-called method of amplification makes the patient aware, by means of symbolical parallels, that his problems are not unique but rather are basically the problems of all humanity. This procedure often frees the neurotic from his self-imposed seclusion and strengthens his efforts to bring about his own inner transformation.

Although this is a difficult book, the reviewer believes it is a very important one. Jung has opened up a totally new field for psychological exploration. As often happens to a pioneer, adequate recognition of his accomplishment may be posthumous.

Review of C. G. Jung, *Mysterium Coniunctionis: An Inquiry into the Separation and Synthesis of Psychic Opposites in Alchemy*, volume 14 of *The Collected Works of C. G. Jung.* Trans. R. F. C. Hull. Bollingen Series XX. Princeton: Princeton University Press, 1963. [161]

Edward F. Edinger

This magnificent final volume concludes Jung's researches into the psychology of the unconscious and, in particular, into the psychological implications of alchemy. In the concluding paragraph Jung tells us the purpose that alchemy has served for him:

We can see today that the entire alchemical procedure for uniting the op-

---

[161] This review was first published in *The Journal of Analytical Psychology* 10, no. 2 (July 1965): pp. 92f.—Eds.

posites which I have described in the foregoing, could just as well represent the individuation process of a single individual, though with the not
unimportant difference that no single individual ever attains to the richness
and scope of the alchemical symbolism. This has the advantage of having
been built up through the centuries, whereas the individual in his short life
has at his disposal only a limited amount of experience and limited powers
of portrayal. . . . No case in my experience is comprehensive enough to
show all the aspects in such detail that it could be regarded as paradig-
matic. . . . Alchemy, therefore, has performed for me the great and invaluable service of providing material in which my experience could find suf-
ficient room, and has thereby made it possible for me to describe the individuation process at least in its essential aspects. (par. 792)

Jung's breadth of view, which is one of the glories of this work, will
undoubtedly be a stumbling block for many. What for him is only "suffi-
cient room," for others of less scope will be a disorienting vastness of
depth in which they are lost. Also, the strict empirical-descriptive method
to which Jung holds will be a problem to those who need the security of
containment in well-ordered theoretical constructions no matter how narrowly based or premature they may be. From such critics will come the
familiar epithets of dismissal. Jung has answered them in advance:

The difficulty for my critics seems to be that they are unable to accept the
concept of psychic reality. A psychic process is something that really exists, and a psychic content is as real as a plant or animal. . . . It is perfectly
true that one can play metaphysics with psychic facts. . . . But the ideas
themselves are not metaphysical; they are empirically verifiable phenomena that are the proper subject of the scientific method. (par. 651)

Nevertheless, what Jung has to convey is so truly original and so far
ranging in its implications that I suspect that this book will be a real challenge even to those most psychologically sophisticated. What he here
presents in rich and documented detail can perhaps best be described as
an anatomy of the objective psyche. As with all anatomy books, it is not
easy reading. It requires that the reader bring to it an empirical experience of psychic images analogous to the dissection that must accompany
the study of anatomy. In my own case, those parts of the book that dealt
with images I have encountered in myself or in my patients were illumi-

nating; whereas the discussion of images to which I could bring no first-hand experience remained somewhat vague and abstract.

Jung's so-called allusive style is very evident in this book. Image is piled upon image, parallels and analogies branch out and intertwine in all directions until the reader feels caught in a labyrinthine network. Repeatedly, while reading, I found that I had lost my way and was obliged to retrace my footsteps until I could pick up the path some pages back.

This is no fault of Jung. The nature of the subject requires the approach he uses. The analogical method is the only way into the unconscious. The allusive style is the natural style of the unconscious itself, and the one we must use if we are to fathom the meaning of dreams and other unconscious products. The only alternative is to apply a preconceived theory. But, besides violating scientific empiricism, this method is sterile because it allows one to extract no more meaning from an image than that which he has already put into it. There is no enlargement of consciousness. Jung's style is deliberate, an integral part of his method.

The content of this book defies any attempt at a brief review. Broadly speaking, it is a treasury of images pertaining to the individual's discovery of the Self. Jung's primary commitment was always to the maximum development of the individual personality. His discoveries demonstrated that such development requires a conscious relationship to the archetypal images within. As he writes:

> Only the living presence of the eternal images can lend the human psyche
> a dignity which makes it morally possible for a man to stand by his own
> soul, and be convinced that it is worth his while to persevere with it. (par.
> 511)

This book, together with many of Jung's later writings, documents the "eternal images." It remains the task of each individual, according to his capacities, to realize their living presence. By word and example Jung has done all that is humanly possible to promote such a realization. *Mysterium Coniunctionis* is a splendid capstone to the life work of a master spirit.

"Consciousness without Peer." A Review of Marie-Louise von Franz. *C. G. Jung: His Myth in Our Time*. Trans. William H. Kennedy (New York: Putnam's Sons, for the C. G. Jung Foundation for Analytical Psychology, 1975). [162]

Edward F. Edinger

The magnitude of Jung's life and work has not yet dawned on the world. Even some of his followers are reluctant to acknowledge his true dimensions. He is the carrier of a consciousness so magisterial that it has no peer. Quite understandably did he complain in a late unpublished letter that "I am practically alone. There are a few who understand this and that, but almost nobody that sees the whole."[163]

There can be no question of a critical evaluation of Jung's work at present for the simple reason that no one exists who is competent to judge it. Let a man appear who has gone deeper than Jung and has seen the psyche more comprehensively than he has—to his judgments I shall listen with respect. But so far such a man is not to be found. Jung thus becomes a kind of touchstone. Our reactions to him reveal the nature of ourselves. In my view, he embodies the highest level of consciousness yet achieved by humanity, and the extent to which one realizes this act is a measure of his awareness of psychic reality. Valid books on Jung at present, therefore, cannot be critical or evaluative. They must explicate, exemplify, and mediate the canon Jung has left us. This is the nature of Dr. von Franz's latest book, *C. G. Jung: His Myth in Our Time*.

Like the Philosophers' Stone, the highly individuated personality has the power to replicate himself. By a kind of psychological genetics he generates a family tree—a multiple series of filiations—which reproduce his essence for generations. Dr. von Franz is an example of this phenomenon. She is a true spiritual daughter of Jung, a carrier of the pure Jungian elixir, and the next best thing to Jung himself. And so it is with this book. We are given a distilled essence of Jung's life and work which

---

[162] This review was first published in *Psychological Perspectives* 7, no. 1 (Spring 1976), pp. 106ff. See below, note 195.—Eds.

[163] From a letter to Eugene Rolfe dated November 13, 1960.

is rich, complex, and profound as only Jung can be. The only occasion for disappointment is that the reader who is well versed in Jung's writings, especially *Memories, Dreams, Reflections*, will find most of the material already familiar to him. However, in compensation, there are precious gems of new information scattered throughout the book. For instance, we are told that Jung once said, "Everything I have written has a double bottom (4)." Again, when he was once asked how he could live with the knowledge he had recorded in *Answer to Job*, he replied, "I live in my deepest hell, and from there I cannot fall any further." (174)

The author organizes her presentation around the major guiding images that underlay Jung's opus. A chapter is devoted to each of the following: "The Underground God," "The Storm Lantern," "The Physician," "Mirror-Symmetry and the Polarity of the Psyche," "The Journey to the Beyond," "The Anthropos," "The Mandala," "Coincidentia Oppositorum," "Man's Morning Knowledge and Evening Knowledge," "Mercurius," "The Philosophers' Stone," "Breakthrough to the Unus Mundus," "Individual and Society," "Le Cri de Merlin."

What most interests me about this book are the implications of its title. What is Jung's myth? What is its relevance for our time? Dr. von Franz approaches these questions obliquely, chiefly through description of Jung's ideas. Where specific answers are offered, it is with quotations from Jung. The issue is faced most squarely in the chapter entitled "Coincidentia Oppositorum," in which *Answer to Job* is discussed. The high point of this chapter is a quotation from *Memories* (somewhat fuller than von Franz uses) as follows:

> The unavoidable internal contradictions in the image of a Creator-god can be reconciled in the unity and wholeness of the self as the *coniunctio oppositorum* of the alchemists or as a *unio mystica*. In the experience of the self, it is no longer the opposites "God" and "man" that are reconciled, as it was before, but rather the opposites within the God-image itself. That is the meaning of divine service, of the service that man can render to God, that light may emerge from the darkness, that the Creator may become conscious of His creation, and man conscious of himself.
>
> That is the goal, or one goal, which fits man meaningfully into the scheme of creation, and at the same time confers meaning upon it. It is an

explanatory myth which has slowly taken shape within me in the course of the decades. It is a goal I can acknowledge and esteem, and which therefore satisfies me. (173f.)[164]

This quotation should be put beside another one from *Memories*:

Man's task is . . . to become conscious of the contents that press upward from the unconscious. Neither should he persist in his unconsciousness, nor remain identical with the unconscious elements of his being, thus evading his destiny, which is to create more and more consciousness. As far as we can discern, the sole purpose of human existence is to kindle a light in the darkness of mere being. It may even be assumed that just as the unconscious affects us, so the increase in our consciousness affects the unconscious.[165]

These two quotations convey the essence of Jung's myth for our time. It is elaborated more fully in *Answer to Job*, which von Franz tells us is the only one of Jung's works with which he was completely satisfied. (161) A new myth can regenerate a society, and this may prove to be the function of Jung's myth for Western civilization. It offers a sound new container to hold the precious life-essence of meaning which has been spilled during the breaking of the vessels of traditional religion.

In this new myth, man is perceived as a necessary partner of God. *Consciousness*, whose only carrier is the individual, is the supreme value, goal, and meaning of the universe. It has groped its way blindly out of the boundless chaos and laboriously fashioned a vessel to contain it—the individual self and its spatio-temporal incarnation, the human ego. The ego, in turn, after a long series of mistakes, presumptions, and grandiosities, with torturous slowness, backslidings, and perversities, gradually learns its purpose for being—to be the carrier of cosmogonic consciousness. The mythless ones who encounter this new myth and are gripped by its *numen* will be drafted into its service and will go to make up a new *Ecclesia Spiritualis*.

---

[164] See Jung, *Memories, Dreams, Reflections*, p. 338, for the full quotation.
[165] Ibid., p. 326.

Eleanor Bertine: A Memorial[166]
Edward F. Edinger

I knew Eleanor Bertine first as the friend and partner of my analyst, Esther Harding. She was the kindly, open-faced woman who occupied the adjoining consulting room and who would smile when she saw me occasionally in the waiting room. Later, I knew her as my control analyst who supervised my first efforts at psychotherapy. And still later I knew her as a professional colleague.

What first impressed me was the clarity and agility of her mind. She had an unusual capacity to recognize the essential issues in a situation and to give them concise expression. As I got to know her better, another quality stood out even more prominently, the quality of integrity. Although she was capable of taking quite firm positions, if questioned, she was always willing to examine the matter openly in a mutual quest for the objective truth.

She was a sturdy, highly responsible woman, with a profound sense of duty which was, at times, almost austere. She was also capable of great gentleness. I recall, for instance, that during my supervision with her she told me several times that Jung had told her she should react more to her patients. Finally, I caught on and asked if she meant to suggest that I should react more to my patients. Yes, that was her meaning. But she had been so exceedingly gentle that I had almost missed the point.

Eleanor Bertine was a pioneer. She was one of that scant handful of people who first brought Analytical psychology to America, and of whom all but one has now fallen. More than once she remarked on the difficulty of those early years—the loneliness, the professional isolation, how much she would have given for supervised analysis and the training aids which are now available to young analysts. The pioneer is the first to enter the unknown region. Those that follow have the immense advantage of having the new area already roughly mapped out. But the pioneer

---

[166] This tribute was first published in *Spring 1968,* pp. 5ff. The author had read it at the Memorial Meeting for Dr. Bertine, New York City, March 11, 1968.— Eds.

meets the unknown without mediation. For him the first problem is survival. Eleanor Bertine once confessed that she was almost swamped in those early years. But she did survive. And we who came after are immensely indebted to her and to her pioneer colleagues for drawing the first charts of the wilderness and smoothing our way.

Not only did she survive, but she also became a woman of extraordinary human quality whom I feel privileged to have known. She was one of those rare people "who saw life steadily and saw it whole."

Funerals and memorial services are for the survivors. We need help to experience the impact and to assimilate the meaning of a death. The dead, presumably, are beyond the reach of our praise or blame; but we the living need memorial meetings such as this. In the case of Eleanor Bertine this is especially true. She is dead. We know that with our minds. But the manner of her going was so gradual, so ambiguous, that who can say when, precisely, she left us? We have lost a beloved friend or an esteemed colleague. But the impact of that loss upon us has been blurred by the excruciatingly slow and drawn-out process through which it happened. We are in danger of missing the full intensity of our experience. Let us not allow that to happen.

For those who knew Eleanor Bertine as a therapist, their source of help and understanding is gone forever. And such a source is a rare thing to find in this world.

For those who knew her as a beloved friend and partner in relationship, their love has been orphaned and will surely not find another such as she.

For those who knew her as one of the "older ones"—to be relied upon for guidance and for that comfortable feeling that there is someone wise and stable in the background—their source of borrowed wisdom and security is gone. And they must find whatever they can within themselves.

And, finally, for those who are themselves close to her in years of life, there must be the realization that their own allotted time is short.

Death has a way of jarring us back to essentials, reminding us of the simple facts that we have but one life to live and all that matters is how to live it. The primordial image of the judgment of the soul at death comes up to haunt us; and we ask ourselves anxiously if we could say as confidently as the apostle Paul: "I have fought the good fight, I have finished the race, I have kept the faith." (2 Timothy 4:7)

No one may pass judgment on the life of another. But speaking for myself and what Eleanor Bertine means to me, I believe that Eleanor Bertine kept faith with her own life hypothesis, the quest for consciousness. She spent her life as an advance skirmisher in the battle for a new level of human consciousness, and she died in the midst of that battle. When that battle is won, in the words of Matthew Arnold,

> Let the victors when they come,
> When the forts of folly fall,
> Find [her] body by the wall[167]

M. Esther Harding: 1888-1971[168]
Edward F. Edinger

Esther Harding died in London on May 4, 1971, at the age of 82. She was the dean of Analytical psychology in America, and her death marks the end of an era for Analytical psychology in this country. It can be said of her, more truly than of any other person, that she brought Jungian psychology to America. She committed herself to this task with great personal sacrifice; and, in a lifetime of effort, she succeeded.

With the advent of Jung, something truly new has appeared. Through his discovery of the reality of the psyche and of individuation as the process by which the individual realizes that reality, Jung has brought to

---

[167] From Matthew Arnold, "The Last Word," (1867), in *The Norton Anthology of English Literature*, vol. 2, pp. 1053f. [Edinger alters the poem's last line, from "find thy body by the wall."—Eds.]

[168] This memorial tribute was first published in *Spring 1972*. The author had read it at a Memorial Meeting for Dr. Harding held on October 22, 1971, New York, sponsored by the Analytical Psychology Club of New York, the New York Association for Analytical Psychology, and the C. G. Jung Foundation for Analytical Psychology.—Eds.

birth a wholly new view of man and the world. This new view seems nothing less than the inauguration of a new aeon. Esther Harding was one of the first, and one of the few, fully to realize this fact. As a result, she was called to an arduous lifetime vocation.

Her calling grew out of a personal crisis. As a young physician she had a major psychological upheaval which led her eventually to see Jung in Zürich. While working with Jung, she had a dream which in essence was this: She was floundering helplessly in the open sea and had almost lost hope when Jung appears in a large, sturdy ship in the guise of Noah. Offering his hand, he helps her aboard.

As the dream implies, Esther Harding's encounter with Jung was decisive and lifesaving. Consequently, the rock on which she built her life was her relationship to Jung and Jungian psychology. The ship, which was her own salvation, she learned to operate; and, with it, she in turn rescued many castaways. Her experience can be considered as exemplary of Jung's effect on his whole age. He has brought a redemptive viewpoint to an age floundering in spiritual chaos.

Esther Harding was British. I do not know the reasons for her decision to come to America, but I know that it was difficult. She experienced at first hand the uprooting effects of immigration, which are part of the ancestral heritage of all Americans. She once told me that many times in those early years when she consulted the *I Ching,* she would get hexagram 56, "The Wanderer." As the text says, "A wanderer has no fixed abode; his home is the road." "Strange lands and separation are the wanderer's lot." This was part of the price for performing her work in America.

Esther Harding was a woman with a stern sense of duty. She saw herself as performing a most serious and important function, and she gave the utmost devotion to the fulfillment of that task. Although she would never have used these words, I use them in their most earnest and authentic sense. She was a priestess of the new dispensation, and she paid the heavy personal price that such a role imposes.

Left to right: Barbara Hannah, M. Esther Harding, Marie-Louise von Franz (about 1960)

Figure 12. Three Jungian pioneers.

She was a wise woman, a stalwart woman, indeed a whole woman, one who evoked respect more often than love and suffered for that fact. We here pay tribute to a rich and creative personality, one who has contributed much to her fellow man and, highest praise of all, one whose life is a credit to her master's teaching.

In Memory of Marie-Louise von Franz (1915-1998) [169]
Edward F. Edinger

It is a sad task for me to write farewell remarks about Marie-Louise von Franz. Next to Jung himself, she has exemplified for me what individuation is and what it means to be conscious. I first met her in the fifties when she would come to New York to give seminars on such things as fairy tales and the "Sapentia Dei" in the *Aurora Consurgens*. With the exception of Jung, I probably learned more about the psyche from her than from any other person. I was impressed by her brilliant intellect, her erudition, her uncanny intuition, and—later—by her profoundly human responses to feeling issues of depth. As I got to know her better, it was her total personality that had the greatest impact—the magnitude of her consciousness.

"Individuation" and "consciousness" are the goals of Jungian psychology, but they are very hard to define. Given our competitive instincts, it is even difficult to acknowledge these accomplishments when we encounter them in others. At present we have no reliable way to measure objectively the magnitude of an individual's consciousness. And yet, clearly, differences in size of consciousness do exist. In my judgment, Jung's level of consciousness was and is without peer. After his death, Dr. von Franz took over for me that premier position among the living. Her relation to Jung was extraordinary. She was his true spiritual daughter. Although thoroughly her own person and in no sense identified with him, she submitted herself to the full impact of Jung's magisterial

---

[169] This tribute in memory of Dr. von Franz was first published in *The Journal of Analytical Psychology* 43, no. 3 (July 1998), p. 411.—Eds.

consciousness and allowed herself to be transformed by it. Like the Philosophers' Stone, "Jungian consciousness" underwent a multiplication and reproduced itself in her. As a result, she took on Jung's most important quality, a profound commitment to the transpersonal Self.

Our understanding of the collective unconscious teaches us that the collective psyche is a continuum connecting all the members of our species. Given this fact, it seems likely that those carriers of a large consciousness serve an "Atlas function," supporting the world of collective consciousness and assuring the continuity of civilization. When one of these "great ones" dies, the psychic continuum is torn, exposing us to eruptions from the depths.

> Then, behold, the veil of the temple was torn in two from top to bottom; and
>
> the earth quaked, and the rocks were split, and the graves were opened. . . ."

(Mat. 27:51-52; NKJB)

In my view, Dr. Von Franz's consciousness was of this order. Her death has torn a hole in the world's psyche. It is a dangerous gap that will be hard to fill.

PART V

INDIVIDUAL AND SOCIETY

Individuation: A Myth for Modern Man[170]
Edward F. Edinger

I am going to talk to you tonight about some rather deep and abstruse material. What I hope to be able to do is to introduce you to, and perhaps mediate for you, some major matters that concerned Jung in his last years. And, of course, the more one studies Jung, the more one realizes that the further along one goes with his life work, the harder it is to follow him. The vast majority of people can follow Jung's thinking up to 1912, let's say. A smaller number can follow him up to maybe 1920, when *Psychological Types* came out. After that, it gets very difficult. And after 1950—well, for most people, forget it.

But that is the material I am going to attempt to introduce to you, at least in some brief fashion. In those last years, Jung was concerned with relating his discoveries concerning the nature of the individual psyche to the overall development of the collective Western psyche—in its whole historical culture and development. The major book in which he engages this matter is entitled *Aion*, published originally in German in 1951.

We know from the work of historians and anthropologists that in order for a human society to remain alive and soundly functioning, it requires a central operative myth that conveys a religious way of life to the individual members of that society. It is generally recognized by thoughtful people that Western society no longer has a living myth—and that is a very dangerous state of affairs. On the other hand, when danger comes to mind, I think of the lines of Hölderlin, which Jung was fond of quoting:

---

[170] This essay was first published in *Psychological Perspectives* 39 (Summer 1999): pp. 19ff. The author had delivered it as a lecture to The Friends of Jung in San Diego, California, January, 1988.—Eds.

"Where danger is / Grows also the rescuing power." I think that idea is illustrated by the appearance of Jung at this particular stage in the history of Western society; because the historical spirit that has brought us to our current dangerous state of mythlessness has also brought us the work of Jung. His ideas have created the possibility of a whole new myth, a whole new world view or life attitude, which gives us an opportunity to replace or revivify our lost myth.

Jung penetrated to a deeper level of the psyche than did Freud. Jung discovered what he called the collective unconscious, also termed the objective psyche or the archetypal psyche. In his practical work with patients, he came to realize that most patients over the age of thirty-five, on the verge of the second half of life, did not achieve a real cure unless they found a religious attitude toward life. Now this religious attitude, of course, had nothing to do with allegiance to a creed. Jung has given a very nice definition of religion as the attitude peculiar to a consciousness that has been changed by the experience of the *numinosum*. In other words, religion is the consequence of an *experience*.

Without going into details, we might describe the *numinosum* as the religion-creating archetype in the psyche. It is the God-mage which, if one has a living experience of it, generates the religious attitude just by virtue of the experience. You don't have to have faith, you don't have to strain or sacrifice your intellect, or your doubts, or anything else. If you have the living experience, that is the demonstration. Modern people, in increasing numbers, are obliged to seek this original experience because we have lost the orientation provided by the traditional religions. Since we have lost our sense of being contained in this old myth, we are in urgent need of a new one. This is what I am going to talk about—what I call "the myth for modern man."

Jung gives a very explicit description of "modern man" in *Civilization in Transition*:

> The man we call modern, the man who is aware of the immediate present, is by no means the average man. . . .
>
> The man who has attained consciousness of the present is solitary. The "modern" man has at all times been so, for every step towards fuller con-

sciousness removes him further from his original, purely animal *participation mystique* with the herd, from submersion in the common unconsciousness. Every step forward means tearing oneself loose from the maternal womb of unconsciousness in which the mass of men dwells. Even in a civilized community the people who form, psychologically speaking, the lowest stratum live in a state of unconsciousness little different from that of primitives. Those of the succeeding strata live on a level of consciousness which corresponds to the beginnings of human culture, while those of the highest stratum have a consciousness that reflects the life of the last few centuries. Only the man who is modern in our meaning of the term really lives in the present; he alone has a present-day consciousness, and he alone finds that the ways of life on those earlier levels have begun to pall upon him. The values and strivings of those past worlds no longer interest him, save from the historical standpoint. Thus he becomes "unhistorical" in the deepest sense and has estranged himself from the mass of men who live entirely within the bounds of tradition. Indeed, he is completely modern only when he has come to the very edge of the world, leaving behind him all that has been discarded and outgrown, and acknowledging that he stands before the Nothing out of which All may grow.

. . . . An honest admission of modernity means voluntarily declaring oneself bankrupt, taking the vows of poverty and chastity in a new sense—and, what is still more painful—renouncing the halo of sanctity which history bestows. To be "unhistorical" is the Promethean sin, and in this sense the modern man is sinful. A higher level of consciousness is like a burden of guilt. But, as I have said, only the man who has outgrown the stages of consciousness belonging to the past. . . can achieve full consciousness of the present. To do this, he must be sound and proficient in the best sense. . . . It is these qualities which enable him to gain the next highest level of consciousness.[171]

You will note that Jung called man "unhistorical." This means that we are no longer contained in a tradition. That is, our individual identities are no longer propped up by unconscious containment in a religious, cultural, or ethnic identification. We are alone, and we are without a myth.

---

[171] Jung, "The Spiritual Problem of Modern Man," *Civilization in Transition, CW* 10, pars. 149ff.

When this stage of affairs happens to a large number of people, it creates a problem for society as a whole. It is very interesting that the Christian myth has presaged this state of affairs. Jung talks about this in *Aion*. Here he points out that the Christian myth has built into itself an idea of an *enantiodromia* which means, turning into the opposite: high turning into low, cold turning into hot, and so on. Christian myth has built into it this idea of an enantiodromia, as evidenced by the fact that it predicts that the figure of Christ will be followed by his opposite—Satan, the Antichrist. Concerning this, Jung writes in *Aion*:

> The dechristianization of our world, the Luciferian development of science and technology, and the frightful material and moral destruction left behind by the Second World War have been compared more than once with the *eschatological* events foretold in the New Testament. These, as we know, are concerned with the coming of the Antichrist. . . . The Apocalypse is full of expectations of terrible things that will take place at the end of time, before the marriage of the Lamb. This shows plainly that the *anima christiana* has a sure knowledge not only of the existence of an adversary but also of his future usurpation of power.[172]

In considerable detail, Jung discusses the whole psychological phenomenon of Antichrist following the image of Christ in the Christian aeon that is now coming to an end. According to astrological symbolism, the Christian aeon corresponds to the Age of Pisces, because during this two-thousand-year period the spring point of the sun has been moving through the constellation of Pisces. This constellation consists of two fishes, one positioned vertically and the other, horizontally. Christ has been identified with the vertical fish and the Antichrist with the horizontal one. It is a matter of astronomical fact that the spring point entered the horizontal fish about the sixteenth century, the time of the Reformation and the Renaissance. And with these movements in consciousness "comes that spirit which culminates in the modern age," that is, the spirit of the Antichrist.[173]

---

[172] Jung, *Aion*, *CW* 9ii, par. 68.
[173] Ibid., par. 149.

Now, it is very interesting that precisely at this time—let's say, 1500 A.D.—the legend of Faust arose. This legend belongs to the same symbolism as that of the Antichrist. According to this legend, Dr. Faust, a very learned physician, becomes bored with his empty life and invokes and communicates with the devil—selling his soul to the devil in return for magical knowledge, leisure, and power. Among other things, he is granted the power to evoke the figures of Greek mythology, including Helen of Troy; the devil permits him to have Helen of Troy as his paramour. Finally, after a certain period of time, Faust must pay the piper (like his cousin Don Juan), and he is dragged into hell by the devil. That is the basic story. It is quite remarkable that during the past five hundred years, this story has been told again and again and again in poetry, prose, and music. One scholar, E. M. Butler, has written a book, *The Fortunes of Faust*, describing in detail fifty different versions of Faust.[174] And there are a lot more than that. Probably the most notable versions are Christopher Marlow's *Doctor Faustus* (1592), Goethe's *Faust* (1808, 1832), and—in modern times—Thomas Mann's novel, *Dr. Faustus* (1947), which was based on the life of Nietzsche.

Behind the Christian myth stands the figure of the historical Jesus of Nazareth. And, similarly, behind the Faust myth stands the historical figure of Dr. John Faustus. There *was* a historical Faust; he is not just a legend. He lived from approximately 1480 to 1540; and, though not much is known about him, there is definite historical evidence that he lived. He was a personal acquaintance of the Protestant reformer, Melanchthon, who, we are informed, believed in the reality of Faustus' powers. He is said to have died during a demonstration of flying, which he was putting on for a royal audience. Very shortly after his death, legendary material so quickly obscured his biography that, as with Christ, we cannot see much of the historical Faust. But I think it is highly significant that the historical Faust was a contemporary of the following people: Martin Luther, the first reformer of the Catholic Church; Leonardo de Vinci, the greatest artist of the Renaissance; Paracelsus, the great alchemist-

---

[174] E. M. Butler, *The Fortunes of Faust* (Cambridge: Cambridge University Press, 1979).

apothecary physician; Columbus, the first European to discover America; Erasmus, the great humanist scholar who was the first to make the New Testament available in Greek; Copernicus, the discoverer of the Copernican view of the solar system; Vesalius, the great anatomist; and Machiavelli, the pioneer of objective statecraft. All these extraordinary men were contemporaries of John Faustus. And, hence, all of them partake, in one way or the other, of the Faustian legend.

Looking back to the sixteenth century, what we can say now, what we can see happened, was that the God-image fell out of heaven into the human psyche. In the course of that fall—out of its metaphysical status and into the status of human psychological experience, in the course of that movement from heaven to earth—the God-image underwent an *enantiodromia,* turning from Christ into Antichrist, turning from Christ to Faust, so to speak. This course of events was predicted long ago in the Book of Revelation, where we read: "Woe to the inhabiters of the earth and of the sea! For the devil is come down unto you, having great wrath, because he knoweth that he hath but a short time" (Rev. 12:12; King James version).

From the standpoint of Jungian psychology, this transformation from Christ to Antichrist/Faust is what happened in the sixteenth century. Of course, the men of the Renaissance, and the Reformation, and the scientific revolution—the artists, the scholars, the scientists, explorers, and reformers—certainly did not consider their experience devilish or deriving from Antichrist. Certainly not. They all thought of themselves as good Christians excited by the expansion of human knowledge—certainly, that excitement was perfectly compatible with containment in the Christian religion. But they were wrong; *history* proved them wrong. Things looked different form the standpoint of the unconscious. What the unconscious does at this time is throw up, like a compensating dream, the Faust legend. And the Faust legend informs us that what is really going on are dealings with the devil, dealings with Antichrist. However, nobody noticed what had happened until about the nineteenth century, when a few sensitive souls began to realize that something was seriously wrong in the Western psyche.

For instance, Wordsworth, at the beginning of the century, confesses in one of his poems to feeling a forlornness and a yearning for the pagan world. He, indeed, did try to deal with the lost Christian myth by a regression to pagan nature worship. At the age of thirty-seven, he writes the poem, "The World Is Too Much with Us":

> The world is too much with us: late and soon,
> Getting and spending, we lay waste our powers;
> Little we see in Nature that is ours;
> We have given our hearts away, a sordid boon!
> This Sea that bears her bosom to the moon,
> The winds that will be howling at all hours,
> And are up-gathered now like sleeping flowers,
> For this, for everything, we are out of tune;
> It moves us not.—Great God! I'd rather be
> A Pagan suckled in a creed outworn;
> So might I, standing on this pleasant lea,
> Have glimpses that would make me less forlorn;
> Have sight of Proteus rising from the sea;
> Or hear old Triton blow his wreathed horn.[175]

In this poem, Wordsworth disregards the Judeo-Christian myth entirely. Its loss is the real reason for his "forlorn" condition. The worldly preoccupation with "getting and spending" is only a symptom of the lost God and is itself a consequence of scientific materialism. As one nineteenth critic, Mark Rutherford, put it: Wordsworth substituted "a new and living spirit for the old deity, once alive, but gradually hardened into an idol."[176] However, Wordsworth's "new and living spirit" is actually a regression to pagan nature worship and not a solution to the problem.

Another sensitive poetic soul of the nineteenth century, Matthew Arnold, was the son of the pious schoolmaster at Rugby, Thomas Arnold. In his youth he wrote a classic nineteenth-century lament for our lost re-

---

[175] William Wordsworth, *The Poetical Works of Wordsworth* (London: Oxford University Press, 1961).

[176] Basil Willey, "William Wordsworth," in *The Encyclopedia Britannica*, 15th edition (Chicago: H. H. Benton, Publisher, 1974).

ligious myth. I want to read that lament to you. "Dover Beach" is really a threnody to the lost god.[177] It was written in 1851, at age twenty-nine:

> The sea is calm tonight.
> The tide is full, the moon lies fair
> Upon the straits—on the French coast the light
> Gleams and is gone; the cliffs of England stand.
> Glimmering and vast, out in the tranquil bay.
> Come to the window, sweet is the night air!
> Only, from the long line of spray
> Where the sea meets the moon-blanched land.
> Listen! You hear the grating roar
> Of pebbles which the waves draw back, and fling,
> At their return, up the high strand,
> Begin, and cease, and then again begin,
> With tremulous cadence slow, and bring
> The eternal note of sadness in.
>
> Sophocles long ago
> Heard it on the Aegean, and it brought
> Into his mind the turbid ebb and flow
> Of human misery; we
> Find also in the sound a thought,
> Hearing it by this distant northern sea.
>
> The Sea of Faith
> Was once, too, at the full, and round earth's shore
> Lay like the folds of a bright girdle furled.
> But now I only hear
> Its melancholy, long, withdrawing roar,
> Retreating, to the breath
> Of the night wind, down the vast edges drear
> And naked shingles of the world.
>
> Ah, love, let us be true
> To one another! For the world, which seems
> To lie before us like a land of dreams,

---

[177] Matthew Arnold, *The Oxford Authors* (New York: Oxford University Press, 1986).

So various, so beautiful, so new,
Hath really neither joy, nor love, nor light,
Nor certitude, nor peace, nor help for pain;
And we are here as on a darkling plain
Swept with confused alarms of struggle and flight,
Where ignorant armies clash by night.

This retreating "Sea of Faith" of which he speaks is the Judeo-Christian myth, which was no longer serving to contain the advanced minds of the nineteenth century. And like orphans who have lost their mother, they are ejected into the cold cruel world where there is no "joy, nor love, nor light, / Nor certitude, nor peace, nor help for pain." It is quite interesting that the only hope Arnold offers is that a personal love relationship might carry the meaning of the lost connection with God. In fact, he wrote this poem on his honeymoon! But we know that a personal relationship cannot stand up under the burden of such excessive weight as that expectation carries. It cannot be a substitute for the God-image; it would break under the load.

This psychological truism is illustrated humorously by a parody on "Dover Beach" written by Anthony Hecht and published in 1967, exactly one hundred years after "Dover Beach." This poem [entitled "The Dover Bitch: A Criticism of Life"] shows us what the twentieth century has done to the nineteenth-century's lament for the lost God:

So there stood Matthew Arnold and this girl
With the cliffs of England crumbling away behind them
And he said to her, "Try to be true to me,
And I'll do the same for you, for things are bad
All over, etc., etc. . . ."[178]

This poem provides not only humorous respite but also illustrates how impossible it is for a personal love relationship to carry the weight of the God.

Matthew Arnold is out of fashion now, but many young lovers of my

[178] Anthony Hecht, "The Dover Bitch: A Criticism of Life," in *Collected Earlier Poems* (New York: Alfred A. Knopf, 1992).

generation and the generation preceding mine recited "Dover Beach" to each other in utmost seriousness. This solution to the problem of the lost myth did not work, just as Wordsworth's solution did not work. It is significant how the poem ends: "And we are here as on a darkling plain / Swept with confused alarms of struggle and flight, / Where ignorant armies clash by night." That is a strikingly dramatic image of the activated opposites: "ignorant armies clash by night." This is the problem that confronts those who have lost their containing myth, because the activated God-image appears as a pair of opposites when it first comes into human experience. So when Mephistopheles confronted Faust, he opened up the problem of opposites—just as the serpent in the Garden of Eden opened up the problem of opposites for Adam and Eve when it lured them into eating of the tree of the knowledge of good and evil. That is the consciousness of the opposites that comes from eating that fruit.

Later in the nineteenth century, Nietzsche nailed down this psychological fact in his work, *Thus Spake Zarathustra* (written in 1883), where he announced unequivocally that God is dead. Jung says:

> When Nietzsche said that "God is dead," he uttered a truth which is valid for the greater part of Europe. People were influenced by it not because he said so, but because it stated a widespread psychological fact. The consequences were not long delayed: after the fog of –isms, the catastrophe.[179]

Now, in the twentieth century, it has become an open secret that God is, indeed, dead. This is no intellectualism. It is a terrifying psychic fact for an increasing number of individuals.

Let me summarize my historical observations to this point. About 1500 A.D. the God-image fell out of heaven into the human psyche. In other words, it was withdrawn from metaphysical projection and became available for direct conscious experience. This event had a two-fold effect. On the one hand, it greatly increased the energy available to the individual ego, promoting investigation of previously forbidden areas; on the other hand, it had the delayed effect of alienating the ego from its transpersonal connection, from its sense of having divine guidance. This,

---

[179] Jung, "Psychology and Religion," *Psychology and Religion, CW* 11, par. 145.

then, led to the collective experience of being orphaned in a meaningless universe. This double effect—increased energy and power for the ego, linked to a lost relation to God—creates a psychological state of either inflation or despair. The collective view is that the last five hundred years have been a time of great progress and advancement; and so they have. But, as indicated by myth and legend, the unconscious characterized this period by the advent of Antichrist, the diabolical Faustian man. The realization of our lost and desperate condition began to dawn in the nineteenth century and reached major proportions in the twentieth century.

It is in this historical setting that the advent of Jung occurred with his discovery of the process of individuation. What had been going on in the collective psyche since 1500 A.D.—the descent of the God-image into empirical man—finally reached full individual consciousness in C. G. Jung. This achievement occurred during his confrontation with the unconscious (beginning on December 12, 1913, and lasting until 1918), which enabled him to discover empirically the collective unconscious. As he tells us in his autobiography, *Memories, Dreams, Reflections*, it followed his realization that he had no myth. This experience was his first step in the discovery of his new myth. We can now realize that what happened to Jung is typical: namely, that the discovery of a new myth, or the revitalization of an old one, requires that the individual have a direct experience of the collective unconscious. That is what will do the job. However, there is a hitch, because such experience is dangerous. It can destroy as well as heal. A direct experience of the collective unconscious opens up the opposites, which can tear apart the individual—unless imagery emerges that unites them, the imagery of the Self. It is the discovery of those images that unite the opposites that constitutes the process of individuation.

Individuation is the process whereby the ego encounters the Self, the inner God-image, and establishes a living relationship to it. When that happens, the lost God-image is rediscovered within. The word Jung uses for the inner God-image is "Self," with a capital "S." This very word indicates what a highly ambiguous endeavor individuation is, because *self* reminds us of *selfishness*, of *self-centered* narcissism; it reminds us of solipsistic megalomania. It does not emit a very good odor in contemporary usage. Our apprehension is only increased when we learn that Jung describes individuation as the continuing incarnation of God. In talking about that, he quotes Christ saying in John 10:34, "I said, you are gods." This sounds like pretty dangerous doctrine. In fact, it sounds very similar to Faust's experiment with the devil. Here was Faust, initially a good man, exposing himself to evil and opening himself to the experience of the opposites. So he becomes the prototype of a modern consciousness that sets forth on that dangerous journey of individuation. The story of Faust is an image of what we do when we take the unconscious seriously. Jung puts it in very stark terms in *Psychology and Alchemy*:

> There have always been people who, not satisfied with the dominants of conscious life, set forth—under cover and by devious paths, to their destruction or salvation—to seek direct experience of the eternal roots, and, following the lure of the restless unconscious psyche, find themselves in the wilderness where, like Jesus, they come up against the son of darkness. . . . [180]

The obvious danger in this operation is that the ego will identify with the Self and succumb to an atheistical inflation. In fact, this is a very grave danger for the modern psyche. The contrary danger is that of alienation, a state of disconnection from the Self, causing despair. That is really just the other side of the coin from inflation. Between this Scylla and Charybdis lies the possibility of individuation in which the ego consciously connects with the Self but does not identify with it. This is easier said than done!

An encounter with the Self leads immediately to the problem of the opposites, which exposes one to severe inner conflict. If one can endure the conflict of the activated opposites, the unconscious will generate symbols of what we call the *Coniunctio*—symbols of reconciliation. This is what happens in the Faust legend. In Goethe's version, for instance, in Part One we have the union of Faust and Gretchen, and in Part Two we

---

[180] Jung, *Psychology and Alchemy, CW* 12, par. 41.

have the union of Faust and Helen of Troy, an archetypal figure. In a letter Jung wrote concerning this matter, he said:

> I have devoted a special work to this problem—*Mysterium Coniunctionis.*
> . . . It contains everything that forms the historical background—so far as
> this is alchemical—of *Faust.* These roots go very deep and seem to me to
> explain much of the numinous effect that emanates from Goethe's "main
> work."[181]

We can see that Jung's masterwork, *Mysterium Coniunctionis*, can be considered as the culmination of the Faust legend, and Jung himself can be considered as the ultimate Faustian man. *Mysterium Coniunctionis* provides an exhaustive discussion of the symbolism of the *Coniunctio* in alchemy and related material. In Jung's later years, he viewed the symbolic image of the union of opposites to be crucial to the healing of the modern psyche. That is why he gave such great efforts to the elaboration of this image. The mystery of the *Coniunctio* is the mystery of individuation itself. It poses the terrible question: How can the individual consciously experience the opposites without being torn apart by them? It answers this question by means of symbolic imagery expressing the Self in its capacity as reconciler of opposites.

I have been talking about historical factors. Now, let's talk about how the opposites impinge upon the individual. Certainly, the most crucial and terrifying pair of opposites is that of good and evil. The very survival of the ego depends on how it relates to this matter. In order to survive, the ego must experience itself as more good than bad. This explains the creation of what we call the shadow in childhood, in the early phase of psychological development. The young ego can tolerate very little experience of its own badness without succumbing to demoralization. This accounts for the universal phenomenon we see all around us: the phenomenon that obliges us to locate evil. Whenever something evil happens, its cause or blame—the responsibility for it, if at all possible—must be *located.* Somebody must carry the burden of that evil. With the maturation of the ego in the process of individuation, this changes some-

---

[181] Jung, *Letters*, vol. 2, p. 246.

what. The individual becomes able—a little bit, anyway; I do not want to be overly optimistic in this regard—to take on the task of being the carrier of evil rather than having to locate it outside himself or herself for personal survival. Another way of putting it: one becomes capable of carrying the opposites and, to that extent, is thereby promoting the *Coniunctio* as far as the collective psyche is concerned.

In the early phase of developing this capacity to recognize the opposites, we have what might be called the "pendulum phase." During this phase, the individual is cast back and forth between differing moods of guilty inferiority and unworthiness on the one hand, and of optimistic well-being, confidence, and personal worth on the other hand. It is as though he or she encounters darkness and lightness, one after the other. Jung makes a quite remarkable statement about this phase:

> The one-after-another is the bearable prelude to the deeper knowledge of the side-by-side, for this is an incomparably more difficult problem. Again, the view that good and evil are spiritual forces outside us, and that man is caught in the conflict between them, is more bearable by far than the insight that the opposites are the ineradicable and indispensable preconditions of all psychic life, so much so that life itself is guilt.[182]

This may help you understand why *Mysterium Coniunctionis* is not a very popular book! The quotation gives us some idea of what a grave matter it is to really consider, seriously, the problem of the opposites.

I think it can be fairly stated that understanding the opposites is the key to the psyche. Once you become familiar with the phenomenon of the opposites, you will see it everywhere. The operation of the opposites in the collective psyche is exposed to view *everywhere*. Every war, every contest between groups, every dispute between political factions, even every game is an expression of the opposites striving towards a *coniunctio*. So, whenever we fall into an identification with one side of a pair of warring groups or factions, we lose the possibility of carrying the opposites. At such times, then, we locate the enemy, the contrary, the opposites, the evil, on the outside and—in the course of that exteriorization of

---

[182] Jung, *Mysterium Coniunctionis*, *CW* 14, par. 206.

one half of oneself—each becomes a mass person. Jung puts it this way:

> If the subjective consciousness prefers the ideas and opinions of collective consciousness and identifies with them, then the contents of the collective unconscious are repressed. . . . And the more highly charged the collective consciousness, the more the ego forfeits its practical importance. It is, as it were, absorbed by the opinions and tendencies of collective consciousness, and the result of that is the mass man, the ever-ready victim of some wretched "ism." The ego keeps its integrity only if it does not identify with one of the opposites, and if it understands how to hold the balance between them. This is possible only if it remains conscious of both at once.[183]

Let's carry it a step further. How can you become conscious of the opposites, assuming that you aren't to start with? Where are the opposites to be found? I can make a very specific suggestion. You will find the opposites by examining carefully whatever you love or hate. Long ago, Socrates said, "The unexamined life is not worth living." That is a very apt motto for the process of individuation. *We find the opposites by examining carefully whatever we love or hate.* This is an exceedingly difficult procedure, because the inclination to *examine* does not usually accompany the passions of love and hate. But it is in our loves and our hates that the opposites reside. The very first sentence of *Mysterium Coniunctionis* reads: "The factors which come together in the coniunctio are conceived as opposites, either confronting one another in enmity or attracting one another in love" (par. 1). So, the *Coniunctio* as an archetype is operating every bit as much in fights as it is in loves. Those are the two ways unconscious *Coniunctio* energies express themselves—by hatred and attractions. Whenever we take an urge to love or hate too concretely, the *Coniunctio* is exteriorized, which thereby destroys the possibility of a conscious experience of the *Coniunctio*. If we are gripped by a strong attraction or repulsion to a person or thing, we should reflect on it.

In *The Practice of Psychotherapy*, Jung says:

> Unless we prefer to be made fools of by our illusions, we shall, by care-

---

[183] Jung, "On the Nature of the Psyche," in *The Structure and Dynamics of the Psyche, CW* 8, par. 425.

fully analyzing every fascination, extract from it a portion of our own personality, like a quintessence, and slowly come to recognize that we meet ourselves time and again in a thousand disguises on the path of life.[184]

Similarly, our passionate antipathies must be subjected to full analytic scrutiny. We must ask ourselves: Who do I hate? Which groups or factions do I fight against? Whoever or whatever they are, they are part of *me*. I am bound to that which I hate, as surely as I am bound to that which I love. Psychologically, the important thing is *where one's libido is lodged*, not whether one is for or against a given thing. If you pursue such reflections diligently, you will gradually collect your scattered psyche from the outer world—like the dismembered body of Osiris. It is this kind of work, which is the work of individuation, that creates the *Coniunctio* and, in the process, promotes a net increase of consciousness in the world.

The world is torn asunder by the strife between the opposites, a state of affairs that has grown progressively worse in the past five hundred years. This strife between the opposites is what Jung calls the wretched "isms." Emerson says, "All men plume themselves on the improvement of society, and no man improves." As Jung puts it in "The Undiscovered Self": "If the individual is not truly regenerated in spirit, society cannot be either, for society is the sum total of individuals in need of redemption" (par. 536). Jung makes this suggestion:

> If only a world-wide consciousness could arise that all division and all fission are due to the splitting of opposites in the psyche, then we should know where to begin. . . . What does lie within our reach is the change in individuals who have, or create for themselves, an opportunity to influence others of like mind. I do not mean by persuading or preaching—I am thinking, rather, of the well known fact that anyone who has insight into his own actions, and has thus found access to the unconscious, involuntarily exercises an influence on his environment[185]

These individuals with insight into their "own actions" are the ones

---

[184] Jung, "The Psychology of the Transference," in *The Practice of Psychotherapy, CW* 16, par. 534.

[185] Jung, *Civilization in Transition, CW* 10, pars. 575, 583.

who, to a greater or lesser extent, have experienced the *coniunctio*. They are the ones who are aware of the fact that the opposites make up the psyche itself and, therefore, make up *one's own psyche*. Therefore, they become carriers of the opposites rather than exteriorizers of the opposites. According to the standpoint of Jungian psychology, if society is to be redeemed, it will be done through the cumulative effect of such individuals. The idea is that when enough individuals can carry the consciousness of wholeness, the world itself will become whole.

Figure 13. Edward F. Edinger (1992).

The Question of a Jungian Community[186]
Edward F. Edinger

Do the two words, "Jungian" and "community" truly go together, or are they so separate in their implications that they generate a paradox? That's the question that I'm entertaining this evening. I'm sure you all know how concerned Jung was that individuals discriminate themselves from the state of *participation mystique* with the collectivity. That was a major issue with Jung that he emphasized repeatedly. And he repeatedly told us how dangerous group psychology can be for the existence of the individual. He discusses this concern in that long marvelous paragraph 240 in *Two Essays on Analytical Psychology*. Let me read you portions of that to give you the flavor. This is Jung speaking:

> For the development of personality, then, strict differentiation from the collective psyche is absolutely necessary. . . . [If a person is identified] with the collective psyche he will infallibly try to force the demands of his unconscious upon others, for identity with the collective psyche always brings with it a feeling of universal validity—"godlikeness"—which completely ignores all differences in the personal psyche of his fellows.

And a little later:

> It is a notorious fact that the morality of society as a whole is in inverse ratio to its size; for the greater the aggregation of individuals, the more the individual factors are blotted out, and with them morality, which rests entirely on the moral sense of the individual and the freedom necessary for this. Hence every man is, in a certain sense, unconsciously a worse man when he is in society than when acting alone; for he is carried by society and to that extent relieved of his individual responsibility. Any large company composed of wholly admirable persons has the morality and intelligence of an unwieldy, stupid, and violent animal.[187]

Of course, human beings are social animals and cannot live without

---

[186] This essay was first published in *Psychological Perspectives* 48, no. 1 (2005): 37-47. This was Dr. Edinger's last public lecture presented to the C. G. Jung Foundation of New York on September 12, 1995.—Eds.

[187] Jung, *Two Essays on Analytical Psychology, CW* 7, par. 240.

society. And so we read in another place where Jung writes:

> If, then, man cannot exist without society, neither can he exist without oxygen, water, albumen, fat and so forth. Like these, society is one of the necessary conditions of his existence. It would be ludicrous to maintain that man lives in order to breathe air. It is equally ludicrous to say that the individual exists for society. "Society" is nothing more than a term, a concept for the symbiosis of a group of human beings. A concept is not a carrier of life. The sole and natural carrier of life is the individual, and that is so throughout nature.[188]

Now, that last thought was written in 1941. At the end of his life, Jung had this to say in *Memories, Dreams, Reflections*:

> All collective identities, such as membership in organizations, support of "isms," and so on, interfere with the fulfillment of this task [of individuation]. Such collective identities are crutches for the lame, shields for the timid, beds for the lazy, nurseries for the irresponsible; but they are equally shelters for the poor and weak, a home port for the shipwrecked, the bosom of a family for orphans, a land of promise for disillusioned vagrants and weary pilgrims, a herd and a safe fold for lost sheep, and a mother providing nourishment and growth. It would therefore be wrong to regard this intermediary stage as a trap; on the contrary, for a long time to come it will represent the only possible form of existence for the individual, who nowadays seems more than ever threatened by anonymity.[189]

Well, that's quite a statement. But I think, if we're honest, we'll all admit that we're all to some extent lame, timid, lazy, shipwrecked, orphans, weary pilgrims, and lost sheep. And that means we all need containment and the warm embrace of some embodiment of the Mother archetype. But the problem, then, is to reconcile this inevitable need with the maximum individuation of which we are capable. That's where we encounter the question of a "Jungian community."

As I reflected on this question of community, I realized there are really several different kinds of community. First of all, there is what we might call the "primary community." That would be the organic commu-

[188] Jung, *The Practice of Psychotherapy, CW* 16, pars. 223f.
[189] Jung, *Memories, Dreams, Reflections,* pp. 342f.

nities that are rooted in our biology, our inheritance, and the earth out of which we are born. And these primary organic communities would include the family, the tribe, the ethnic group, and the geographical and national group that one has been born into. Those are all organic and rooted very deeply in the depths of the psyche.

Then, there are "secondary communities." One kind of secondary community would be what we could call "functional" communities. I'm thinking here of associations that are based on mutual interest or occupation—such as guilds, or unions, or professional associations, political causes, hobbies, and various interests that generate communities—that serve as functional communities. And then I think there's another kind of secondary community that I would call "religious" or "ideological" communities—and these would be based on shared religious experience or shared world views that are basic and central to one's life. These would include churches, and religious-philosophical societies or groupings, or perhaps groupings around a charismatic figure. An antique example, I think, would be the Pythagorean brotherhood of ancient Greece. That would be a religious community that is secondary in the sense that it's not rooted in biology or innate birth circumstances, but it develops secondarily.

Now Jung is quite concerned with the fact that the individuals need to be born *out* of their condition of identity and containment: first of all, from their organic community—from their family, and tribe, and ethnic groupings. And then they need to be born *out* of identity from their secondary functional communities, as well. Because, as Jung sees it, the individual is far more than a social or communal unit. The center of transpersonal identity—which we call the Self—needs to be discovered within the psyche of the individual, rather than being projected onto the community. So long as the latter pertains, the community is the carrier of the Self, and individuals—in so far as they are identified with the community—are irresponsible. The image that I like to use is that of a fish swimming in a pond. I often speak of a Zen koan that asks the question, "Who discovered water?" And the answer to the question is, "Not the fish." That particular little story has considerable relevance for psychologists and analysts, you see, because initially we all live like fish swimming around in the unconscious quite blissfully, unaware of the medium that surrounds us. And as long as we're in that state, the science of psychology cannot exist. Who's going to ask what's the nature of water in such a situation? Water would not have been distinguished as a separate entity from one's being. But, if one is a lungfish, then it's one's destiny to get out of the water; because as one starts losing gills and develops lungs, one is about to suffocate in that water. Unless the lungfish climbs out onto dry land and into the atmosphere, it will perish. And when it's out, then the lungfish discovers, "Oh, where I was back there, that's water!" These are the issues that one must engage when confronting our topic.

Now it's certainly true that developmental potential varies considerably with different individuals. In fact, it can be said that modern society contains among its many members representatives of all levels of historical development. And there are only a very few people that are constructed so as to be available for the most modern level of development. For some, their life goal is fulfilled if they can just find a comfortable pond to swim in and achieve a comfortable containment. But, for others, it's a psychic death to remain in such a pond, and they have to rebel and become schismatics of one kind or another. And then there are still others who achieve greater individuation, who are able—having left the pond—to recognize the nature of water. They can return to the pond consciously, so to speak, and make their connections with the occupants of the pond on a conscious and individual basis rather than on a collective basis.

Now, the question is: How do these reflections apply to the "Jungian community" here in New York City? That's the question I'm addressing. I understand that you have five separate organizations represented here. You have the New York Association of Analytical Psychology (NYAAP)—the professional organization of colleagues who share a craft. And, then, there's the Jung Institute, which is a professional organization for purposes of training. Those two are functional organizations. Then we have the Jung Foundation which is a promotional organization, the purpose of which is the advocacy of Jungian psychology to the public and whose membership is largely lay, I believe, although many do have some analytic experience. Then there's the Archive for Research in Archetypal Symbolism (ARAS)—a scholarly project that is, I would say, not explicitly Jungian but has a somewhat larger context than Jungian. It is really a spin-off of Jungian psychology, and it seeks the attention of the larger artistic and academic community. And, finally, there's the Analytical Psychology Club. Now it's here, in the Analytical Psychology Club, that I think we have the prospects of having a real Jungian community.

It's an interesting phenomenon that Analytical Psychology Clubs started springing up all around after the beginning of Jungian analysis. Patients and ex-patients felt the need for mutual fellowship. And it was a kind of spontaneous phenomenon that generated the psychology clubs—first in Zürich and then in other places. It was an original phenomenon that did not have to do with ulterior professional motives. It stemmed from inner individual needs and was not a matter of professional expediency. And I think it's interesting to reflect on this phenomenon and ask ourselves, "What does it mean?" People that have required the help of plumbers don't form "Plumbing Clubs." People who have suffered heart attacks or some other illness usually don't form "Heart Attack Clubs" or "Cancer Clubs"—although that is starting to change. I realize there are advocacy groups emerging for certain diseases; and Alcoholics Anonymous is the original example of these. But they're not quite the same thing as Psychology Clubs. These advocacies don't come to celebrate their shared experience of cancer, for instance. It's different. We may be able to find some parallels with the APC's, but they are really significantly different from these other groupings. And it brings up the question: Why is it that encounter with Jungian psychology—and especially the experience of personal analysis—tends to generate clubs?

You know, Jungian psychology is a science; Jung has always maintained that vigorously. But it is a unique science, because it's the science of the psyche. And when one has a living experience of this science, it has much more profound effects than experience of the physical sciences have—things like geology, or physics, or astronomy. They may have clubs, astronomy and geography clubs and things like that, but they're not of the same nature as an Analytical Psychology Club. And that's because a depth experience of the psyche generates reactions that we really have to call "religious." Jung writes about this in a letter:

> All science is merely a tool and not an end in itself. Analytical psychology only helps us find the way to the religious experience that makes us whole. It is not this experience itself, nor does it bring it about. But we do know that Analytical psychology teaches us that *attitude* which meets a transcendent reality halfway.[190]

It is an encounter with this transcendent reality that we call the *numinosum*. And in another place, Jung says that for him "the term 'religion' designates the attitude peculiar to a consciousness which has been changed by experience of the *numinosum*."[191] So the people that have the inclination to form Analytical Psychology Clubs have shared something of this experience, and we know that the experience of the *numinosum* has an isolating effect on the individual. It sets the person apart, because the experience is essentially incommunicable. If one attempts to communicate it, at least in its concrete particulars, one is sure to be misunderstood—almost certainly if you start blabbing about it. So, in such a situation, to find other people who have had similar experiences and who understand that experience in the same psychological terms—that creates the basis for a genuine organic group, a real brotherhood or sisterhood. That's because bonds of comradeship are forged by having a shared experience, especially an intense emotional experience.

A good example of this phenomenon is the comradeship that is born out of war experiences. And the same thing applies to those, on the one hand, who have made the trip to the "Underworld" and have gazed into the "Abyss" or, on the other hand, who have felt the great flow of "Grace" that can come from the depths at moments of the greatest need.

If they had the further mutual experience of finding their way through

---

[190] Jung, *Letters*, vol. 2, p. 264; italics Jung's.

[191] Jung, "Psychology and Religion," *Psychology and Religion, CW* 11, par. 9.

that darkness of the unconscious with the help that Jung's road map of the region has provided, then such people will be further linked by their love for Jung whose help they recognize and whose help in many cases may have been life saving. And it's out of such mutual experiences that a psychic brotherhood and sisterhood is generated. It's a kind of *ecclesia spiritualis*, a "spiritual church," which I think is the sound psychological basis for a genuine "Jungian community."

Now, in the past, such experiences might have been assimilated into the symbolism of the prevailing religion, or occasionally they might have generated a new religion or a schismatic sect of some kind. And that, of course, still happens today. But the great difference now is that we have a depth psychology that can understand these experiences, not in metaphysical terms, but in psychological terms that are appropriate to the modern mind. You see, the numinous experience is an encounter with the archetypal transpersonal psyche which is collective and not individual. And, as we know, it's vitally important that the ego not identify with these collective contents; rather, they must be recognized as belonging to our species and not to the individual. If individuals have that realization, then they achieve a conscious organic connection to humanity as a whole and recover the original unconscious connection that they had to grow out of—like the lungfish did. They recover that original connection, but now on a conscious level.

This means, then, that the experience of the collective archetypes— providing one doesn't identify with them—promotes a new conscious relationship with others and with the outer collective. And, indeed, it's been truly said that object love is the extraverted aspect of individuation; it becomes the "glue" that can hold the new community together. For those who have had this depth experience in Jungian analysis, the personal figure of Jung looms very large; because ultimately we recognize that he is the agent who has made our experience possible—*and* made it understandable so that it could be assimilated. And inevitably the experience of such depths generates a profound love for Jung, a profound object love. In fact, I think I can estimate roughly the depth of an individual's experience of the psyche by knowing his or her attitude toward

Jung. The deeper the experience one has had, the greater the appreciation of Jung, as a general rule. There are certain people who criticize me, saying that I idealize Jung and that I may even have a residual transference on Jung. I disagree with those reductive interpretations, because I consider my attitude as objectively appropriate, not subjectively distorted.

I consider what I feel toward Jung to be object love born out of an accurate perception of objective value. That, of course, can't be proved; and one might say, "So who's right?" Certainly, all sorts of dubious things have taken place in the name of "love." And yet it does remain the most powerful force on earth—it is the apotheosis of what we call libido. Each individual must decide whether a given phenomenon is object love or subjectively distorted transference of some kind or other. We're all on our own in that regard; each has to make an individual judgment about each phenomenon that's presented. I know no better test to put to such questions than the biblical saying, "By their fruits you shall know them." Only authentic psychic realities bear ultimately positive fruit.

A phenomenon somewhat analogous to Analytical Psychology Clubs occurred in antiquity with the Pythagorean brotherhood. Pythagoras was associated with the discovery of certain properties of numbers, and great numinosity was attached to those discoveries. Numbers were felt to reveal the mysterious depths of the universe—and accompanying this shared numinous experience a religious brotherhood developed. Plato mentions Pythagoras in *The Republic* (10.600b), as Burnet writes:

> We are told. . . that he won the affections [*agapē*, "love"] of his followers in an unusual degree [literally, "won their enduring love"] by teaching them a "way of life," which was still called Pythagorean.[192]

That's what we call charisma: love and loyalty generated for the person who shows us the way to the experience of the transpersonal. Now, unfortunately, with many modern examples the individual granted charisma becomes identified with it. Then it gets contaminated with an ego power motive that ultimately can have quite damaging effects both on

---

[192] John Burnet, *Early Greek Philosophy* (London: A. & C. Black, 1930, 4th edition), 85. Edinger's glosses.

the individual and those others who are associated with that person. But that apparently was not the case with Pythagoras. I think the Pythagorean brotherhood is just one example of the general tendency for a fellowship group to gather around a shared experience of the transpersonal which then generates a sacred community—and even occasionally it may grow into a full-scale church.

In conclusion, we can certainly say that the quality of any group depends on the quality of the individuals that make it up. And it's usually the case that the group will function no better than its lowest common denominator, unless it is blessed with unusually effective leadership. Now, in the case of Jungian psychology groups, the whole question is the level of analysis, personal analysis, that the individuals that make up the group have had. You see, everything depends on the degree of self-knowledge of individuals: the individual's personal immediate experience and understanding of the basic aspects of the psyche that we speak of as the shadow, the animus, anima, and the Self.

It does seem today that what's called "Jungian psychology" is more popular than ever. But, unfortunately, it's often largely an intellectual inflation that plays abstractly with Jung's discoveries as concepts rather than encountering them as living realities in themselves. And what we most need, therefore, are better analyzed individuals. The quality of the group that such individuals make up will then take care of itself if the individuals that compose the group are sufficiently conscious. Let me end with a quote from Jung from *Mysterium Coniunctionis*:

> If the projected conflict is to be healed, it must return into the psyche of the individual, where it had its unconscious beginnings. He must celebrate a Last Supper with himself, and eat his own flesh and drink his own blood, which means that he must recognize and accept the other in himself. . . . Is this perhaps the meaning of Christ's teaching, that each must bear his own cross? For if you have to endure yourself, how will you be able to rend others also?[193]

---

[193] Jung, *Mysterium Coniunctionis*, *CW* 14, par. 512.

Postscript

Let me add a "postscript." It is something Jung said in an informal meeting on October, 1937, while visiting New York City. In fact, he made this remark just a few blocks from where we are tonight. It can be read today in *C. G. Jung Speaking*:

> People sometimes call me a religious leader. I am not that. I have no message, no mission; I attempt only to understand. We are philosophers in the old sense of the word, lovers of wisdom. That avoids the sometimes questionable company of those who offer a religion.[194]

Well, that's what he said in 1937. But on November 13, 1960, he wrote this in a letter to Eugene Rolfe which can be found in his book, *Encounter with Jung*:

> I have failed in my foremost task: to open people's eyes to the fact that man has a soul and there is a buried treasure in the field and that our religion and philosophy are in a lamentable state.[195]

In 1937, Jung didn't have a message. But here he seems to feel that he did have a little bit of a message, of some kind or other. I often meditate on this particular passage; I take it as a personal challenge to comfort Jung in that moment of distress he was expressing there. It may be that a few people's eyes are, indeed, being opened to the fact "that man has a soul and there is a buried treasure in the field and that our religion and philosophy are in a lamentable state."

---

[194] McGuire and Hull, eds., *C. G. Jung Speaking*, 98.

[195] Eugene Rolfe, *Encounter with Jung* (Boston: Sigo Press, 1989), p. 158.

PART VI

INTERVIEWS

Edward F. Edinger in Conversation with David Serbin[196]

My meeting with Dr. Edinger took place at a leisurely hour of Saturday morning, December 11, 1982, when I visited his hillside home in the canyon. His greeting was warm and cordial as he ushered me into a book-lined study. On the wall of the study, photographs of Jung, Lincoln, and Emerson were prominently displayed, as three men influential in Edinger's life. Once we were seated and settled, Dr. Edinger expressed his curiosity about how our interview would evolve. He appeared to me a soft-spoken, private man, but his eyes seemed to shine with quiet anticipation as my questions began.

How did your interest in Jungian psychology begin? Was there a significant experience that happened to you, or a dream? Or had you always been interested in it?

I think I can answer that best by giving a little review of what my life had been up to the point of encountering Jung. In retrospect, many things take on an import that were not recognized at the time. In my boyhood, I had a very important experience of having what I can only call a love affair with chemistry. I was absolutely gripped by chemistry, chemical compounds and chemical procedures. I had a home laboratory, and I spent a lot of time in it. I was fascinated by chemical processes and the transformations that took place. Only in retrospect did I realize that what I was really interested in was the alchemical dimension of chemistry. But, at the time, it was quite literally matter itself, so that I really had a personal experience of what the alchemists experienced.

---

[196] David Serbin was a long-time member of the Analytical Psychology Club of Los Angeles and conducted this interview for that organization's *Bulletin* (January-March 1983). A reprinted shorter version appeared in *Psychological Perspectives* 14, no. 2 (Fall 1983), pp. 162ff.—Eds.

So I thought I would be a chemist. Of course, I did other things in school, too, but I went to college as a chemistry major intending to be a chemist, a professor of chemistry. But in college I encountered some particularly good zoology professors, and my interest began to shift to biological science. That led naturally into medicine.

I wasn't so interested in healing people. I was interested in understanding life, and the highest form of life was man. Therefore, I needed to go to medical school to study the biology of the human being. There, I was exposed to the usual psychiatric training, which had no mention of Jung at all. It was of no interest to me, so I didn't give psychiatry a second thought in medical school. I opted for internal medicine and took an internship in that. Then, to fulfill my military requirement, I spent two years as an army medical officer—largely, in the Panama Canal Zone.

I went through a crucial period of reorientation then because I was very dissatisfied, I discovered, with the practice of medicine. It just seemed to miss the point. There was a very big, "So what?" about everything I did, in terms of physical medicine. That was, of course, because I hadn't found my own way; and, therefore, everything I did had a meaningless quality to it. It was during that period that I first made the discovery of Jung, from reading.

It just happened, as an accident?

I won't say "accident." I don't use that word very often. I'm not even sure I believe in accidents. I can't even remember how it happened precisely, but I believe I first heard of Jung in reading—what's his name?— Philip Wylie. I don't know whether you know Wylie, he really belongs to another age. There is a particular book I had in mind, *Generation of Vipers*. He had some contact with Jung and was quite taken by Jungian psychology, although he's more remembered as a social commentator, an acerbic, disputatious, rebellious man. He was the one who debunked "Momism."

Anyway, my entrance to Jung was, thus, kind of through the back door, since it was through this somewhat wild and iconoclastic Philip Wylie. That led me to some of [Jung's] works available then. However, it didn't have an immediate effect of leading to a commitment. That took a while—a couple of more years after I got out of the army, did some more work in internal medicine. My dissatisfaction with my condition sort of incubated.

Do you mean with the condition of the work you were doing—it seemed meaningless to you?

Yes, my psychological condition, my state of "lostness." Until one morning; it was in October of 1950. I woke with the conviction, "You must become a Jungian analyst!" And I proceeded to do that.

It sort of dawned on you one morning.

That's right.

I'm impressed by your ability to translate Jung's concepts into terms that people can relate to more easily, perhaps. It would seem you are a thinking type. Could you elaborate on your typology?

Oh, yes. Naturally, I've thought a good bit about it. I think each reasonably well-developed person has two good functions. He has a good judgment, or rational, function; and he has a good perception function. The rational/judgment functions are thinking and feeling. The perception functions are sensation and intuition. So along the line, I think I've always had good thinking, good sensation. I'm not sure what I would put first. And I don't think it's necessary to put one first. But they've both been good functions. Probably, rule of thumb, the way to tell what the superior function is, is to start with the inferior function. That's always the easiest one to locate. In my early life, I'd say probably feeling was my most inferior function, and by that criterion thinking would then have been the original superior function.

Anyway, thinking and sensation are my two functions that are best developed. That probably accounts for my relative ability to concretize and present psychological material in some kind of understandable form. The majority of Jungian analysts have intuition as their perceptive function. So I think sensation is a help there.

Your writings seem primarily to deal with spiritual aspects of Jungian psychology—as opposed to, for example, the feeling function, the anima. Is that your primary interest—the spiritual aspect—or is it that you feel this is the most important thing needing elucidation at this particular point in history?

I don't think I'm chiefly interested in the spiritual dimension. At least, not as I understand the term "spiritual." I think what I'm interested in is the transpersonal dimension, which is not the same as spiritual. It belongs to another category of understanding. That is my chief concern: how the ego can relate in a consistent, ongoing way with the transpersonal, archetypal dimensions of the psyche.

In your writings you talk about the need for us to deal with God's dark side. And it seems to me that the society in which we live is becoming darker and darker. You mention in one of your lectures, I think, that the development of the psyche was a matter of life and death. In the film, "Matter of Heart," Jung apparently had some very negative visions near the end of his life.[197] Marie-Louise von Franz spoke of the existence of some notes he had written, but she was very reluctant to study these notes. So I wonder how you feel personally about the outlook for our society. Where are we headed? Are we coming more and more under God's "dark" side?

That brings up very, very important matters indeed. First if all, I'd like to refer to the fact that—as Jung has taught us to realize—the whole outer manifestation of human society and collective functioning is a summa-

---

[197] *Matter of Heart: The Extraordinary Journey of C. G. Jung into the Soul of Man,* DVD, directed by Mark Whitney (1985; New York: Kino on Video, 2001).

tion of all the psychology of the individuals that go to make up the human race. And, secondly, all that remains unconscious in those "X" number of individuals manifests itself externally in the history of the race. It lives itself out in an exteriorized way.

These are exceedingly important realizations to have—how the history and political phenomena of the human race derive from the total sum of all the individual human psyches that make up the human race.

With that preface, what I see going on is a massive exteriorization of an unconscious process going on in a multitude of individuals. What is unconscious lives itself out in the political life of the planet. And the process is just awesome in its proportions. It seems absolutely inevitable that immense turmoil, convulsive movements, and eruptions of chaos in vast proportions are in the making so far as the political-historical aspect of mankind is concerned. That, I think, will dwarf the upheaval that took place at the beginning of the Christian era with the gradual disintegration of the Roman Empire. That was small potatoes by comparison to what will happen this time. However, I think that's bearable, and I'll tell you why I think it's bearable.

In the first place, I want to concentrate on the individual, because the individual is the one that carries all life. That's why I made the preface that what we see in the collective exterior is just a summation of the unconscious state of individuals. So far as the individual is concerned— each one who is able—is obliged to witness whatever unfolds. Each individual has only one life to be responsible for, his own. He has only one death to endure. So that, strictly speaking—if there is a vast destruction—that's no harder on the individual than enduring his single death, however he comes to it, you see.

But what makes it so awesome is the psychological effect of witnessing a huge catastrophe of immense quantitative proportions. When one has a standpoint, a realization of what it means and what's going on— that tends to make it more bearable.

What I understand is going on is that we are going through the birth throes of a new world view. And it's perfectly evident to me that Jung has been the first perceiver, the first *depth* perceiver in full measure of what the new world view is to be. He's really brought it to birth single-handedly—first of all, by virtue of his psychological experience. He had the experience, he's had the enlargement of consciousness that five or six hundred years from now will be the norm of the upper educated crust of society, in my opinion.

Five or six hundred years, you say?

Yes.

So he was that far ahead of his time.

Yes, yes. I'm just speaking in terms of my best judgment. It's very fallible. But this is how I perceive things, anyway. What is perfectly clear to me is that Jung is so far ahead of everybody else on earth that it can't even be perceived. It's not even recognized, not even by Jungians.

Do you mean the extent of his consciousness is what is not recognized?

That's right. I do mean that. It's there in his writings to be seen, to the extent one's able to perceive it. I feel I can perceive it just a little bit, and there's a lot more that I can't yet. I see all around me that the same thing is true of everybody else. It's this realization that makes—for me, anyway—the coming turmoil and upheaval at least abstractly bearable. I don't know if I can bear it in the concrete because I haven't experienced it yet. But the beginning is at least being able to bear it in the abstract. I am so impressed by the power, the potency, and the versatile adaptability of the dynamic of life—biological life—that I don't doubt life will survive the worst possible catastrophes. I don't doubt that human life will survive, because whatever the catastrophe is, it will be done by agents of life to life. I can detect a purposefulness that can make whatever short-range chaos and turmoil we have to go through bearable.

Do you feel that there's any possibility that because Jung was so far ahead of his time his teachings might get lost?

Get lost? You know how I feel about that. I don't believe that any authentic psychological accomplishment can get lost. I believe the psyche has a reality. It operates in a relatively invisible sphere, and the achievements of that dimension have a reality that *can't* get lost. They are facts, and there may be nobody around to pick up that fact for a while, maybe a long while. But he did live. He did perform his task. To use his own phrase, he did win through to the "Resurrection Body." In other words, he's left a "glorified" psychic body—a psychic reality— deposited in the collective psyche that is *there*. It is indestructible. That's a very agreeable thing for me to remind myself of.

In one of your articles you discuss the teachings of Jesus. In particular, you quote statements about loving your enemies—and "do not resist one who is evil, but if anyone strikes you on the right cheek, turn to him the other also, and if anyone would sue you and take your coat, let him have your cloak as well."[198]
What is meant here, you indicate, is a certain inner attitude toward the unconscious. Specifically, if we turn a kind face toward the unconscious, it will hopefully respond in kind. But what about those unconscious forces that are truly or intrinsically demonic? I'm thinking of a Jung quote to the effect that it is truly horrifying to gaze into the face of absolute Evil. And if we "love" our enemies, if we approach these demonic forces that way, can we transform them?

This is a difficult matter to deal with abstractly or in general. The word "acceptance" might be more helpful in talking about dark realities, rather than "love." Some of the facts that go to make up the foundation of psychic existence are very dark facts indeed. But they are facts and, therefore, must be accepted—as facts are accepted. You don't have to like them. But it's advisable to accept reality, both physical and psychic real-

---

[198] See Edinger, "Christ as Paradigm of the Individuating Ego," in *Ego and Archetype,* p. 142.

ity, as one discovers it. One's much more likely, then, to make an adaptation that will work if he accepts facts as they are. Evil is one of the facts of psychic existence.

Do you think in this country there's a possibility of some sort of revolution taking place? Unemployment keeps rising. Men and women don't seem to be getting along very well, families are breaking apart, the media have unbelievable power.

Well, I'm interested in the psychology of America, its history and its collective symbolic course. You know, from the beginning, a lot of individuation images have been built into the American experience. It started out with the colonists. They projected onto America the "Promised Land." They thought of themselves as a new version of the Israelites that would inhabit the Promised Land. And, indeed, it took some such symbolism to make them sturdy enough to be able to endure the hardships of the sea crossings and the settlements in this completely unfurnished wilderness. The mythological dimension had to be constellated in a very powerful way in order for them to survive.

There's a fine book on that subject that I recommend to anybody who's interested in it: *The Puritan Origins of the American Self,* by Sacvan Bercovitch. It's a Yale University Press paperback.[199]

But starting with the very beginning, individuation symbolism was activated. Then, it's as though the conflict of the opposites, which is an important feature of that symbolism, came to a head at the time of the Civil War. There's been no civil war in history quite like the American one, which really split the nation right down the middle. I see that very much as part of the individuation symbolism.

The whole process of the gradual freeing of the black population, first of all from slavery and subsequently, gradually, from inferior status— that all belongs to the symbolism of the assimilation of the shadow. Furthermore, our function as a melting pot, in which people from all nations

---

[199] Sacvan Bercovitch, *The Puritan Origins of the American Self* (New Haven: Yale University Press, 1975).

of the earth have had a chance to come and merge in the melting pot and create a new race—that's unique in human history. There's nothing like it. I don't think there's any significant nation on earth that doesn't have an ethnic community and representation in America. We really are a grand alchemical retort that is attempting to forge into a unity all the various strains, nationalities, and races of the world. Now, wouldn't you expect such an enterprise to be rather tumultuous? I would.

So you ask, "Might there be a revolution?" Well, there's already been two. I'm calling the Civil War a revolution. It's a revolution in the sense of a tumultuous uprising transition. I think the psychological history of America is a kind of continuous revolution—in the sense of the individuation and assimilation of shadow symbolism I'm talking about.

But now we can't confine ourselves to the vessel of the nation; that's too small a container. Now the vessel must be the planet, the whole world. Now the crucial polarization is between Russia and America. It's similar to the split that took place at the time of the Roman Empire, which split the eastern and western divisions of the Empire and the Church. Now they are polarized for some kind of reunion. So what we're witnessing is the prelude of a *Coniunctio*, a conjunction of the Western psyche, the healing of the split between East and West that happened in its early years. And that new *coniunctio* will take place one way or another. Mutual destruction is also *coniunctio*.

So it could go one way or the other.

Yeah, either way, in the short term. What will come about is a *coniunctio* in the long term. That's how I see it. The intense preoccupation, competition, and hostility between Russia and America remind me of what Jung tells us: the important thing is not whether one is for or against a given matter, but what one is preoccupied with, what one talks about. This intense preoccupation of Russia with America, and America with Russia—that's part of a "love dance," in the long sense. I often think when I see two wrestlers embracing in a ring, that would be distasteful to me. I'd think: Why do they want to do that? Each trying to overcome the other.

They're in a state of hostility, apparently. And yet the image that they're creating is an image of embrace. See how the opposites turn into each other? It's the same on a grand scale when two nations are at war with each other. Consciously, they are in a state of enmity, and each wants to destroy the other. Unconsciously, they're in a state of mutual embrace.

You mention that in one of your articles discussing a series of dreams that a patient had before he died. He had a dream about two people in a boxing ring, only it seemed like a dance.[200]

That's right.

Turning to another area, did you see the film, Matter of Heart?[201]

Yes, I did.

What was your impression if it?

Oh, a lot of impressions. A lot. I think you'd have to be more specific. Your question reminds me of what patients sometimes ask me. They say: "What do you think of me?" (mutual laughter) Oh, my, that's too big a question!

Well, as far as the film—I asked several people—most of them thought it didn't have a point of view. They liked it yet had a hard time figuring out what it was really about. I'll rephrase the question. Could the film have been made better?

You see, my general principle in reacting to people and to efforts and enterprises is to react to what a person *is*, or what a thing *is*, rather than what it isn't. So, what this film *is*, is a compilation, a synthesis of a vast

---

[200] Edinger, *Ego and Archetype*, p. 209.
[201] See above, note 197.

amount of interview data—that's been condensed and ordered in a certain way to give one a kind of manageable meal, possible to digest. It's one particular way of condensing and ordering a vast amount of data. I keep thinking of it as a meal. I found it very nourishing.

In other words, you're not evaluating as a filmmaker would.

Not at all. I'm not a filmmaker. I think of it just in terms of its content.

You've stated in one article, "In my experience, the basis of almost all psychological problems is an unsatisfactory relation to one's urge to individuality. And the healing process often involves an acceptance of what is commonly called selfish, power-seeking, or auto-erotic. The majority of patients in psychotherapy need to learn how to be more effectively selfish and more effective in the use of their own personal power."[202] Are you referring here to our willingness to relate to and develop our inferior function, or are you referring to our willingness to relate to our shadow side?

Not the inferior function, no. I'm referring to attitudes about the ego, its dynamism. This usually comes under the category of power motivation. That's how it's usually spoken of. There's a long historical tradition. The emergence of Christianity was a major factor in this tradition but not the only one. The same thing applies in the tradition of Stoical philosophy, so it isn't confined to Christianity. But there's a long historical tradition to depreciate concrete, particular ego existence in order to establish a better relation to the spiritual pole of being. And the concrete way this tradition has often expressed itself has been to build up a dissociation within the individual concerning his inclinations. This is very complex, and it can't be dealt with adequately in just a few words. What I had in mind in what you quoted was Jung's whole standpoint in introducing another level of recognition and acceptance of the individual. It's a

---

[202] Edinger, *Ego and Archetype,* p. 160.

whole new world view, and it requires a reevaluating of much that had been rejected by the earlier one-sidedly spiritual world view. So in that sense, it does involve what you inquired about—going into the shadow, what had previously been repressed as shadow.

The Christian virtues are real virtues and authentic values, but the trouble with them and the way they're usually lived out is that they are pretenses rather than reality. Practically everybody—I do it all the time—practically everybody lives as though he's better than he is. He lives as though he's more considerate, more loving, more generous, more unselfish than the facts of his psychology warrant. In other words, it's as though he distributes checks to various people written on an overdrawn bank account, on a psychic bank account that doesn't have anything in it—under the guise of being a kind, loving, considerate, related person. It's not virtue to sham virtue. It's much more authentically virtuous to be what one *is*. And it also, then, has the great advantage of allowing one to carry his own weight. Because if he does *not* acknowledge what he is, then by an unconscious process he transmits to his environment around him the task of carrying the weight that he won't carry for himself. I assure you that's what happens. So, those are some of the thoughts I have in mind behind that remark you quoted.

Are you Jewish?

No. But you asked me a question and I want to answer it, because I think it is important. I want to take this opportunity to respond to it. If I were asked what my religious allegiance or conviction is, this is what I would probably answer. I think this is important to our whole collective religious problem. I would answer that I am one-third Jewish, one-third Catholic, one-third Protestant, and one-third secular humanist. These are the four major religious viewpoints in the Western psyche. It's because practically everybody identifies himself with just one that we have all the contention among the various factions. I put it in that wry form of four "thirds" because it fits the symbolism of "three and four" and the kind of miraculous quality you have to have to squeeze "four" into what started out as "three." But that's a picture, as I see it, of the collective psyche of Western civilization. It's made up of four factions. And I think anyone who is trying to go the full way with Jung will try to achieve something of that same combination.

But as far as your background is concerned . . .

As far as background is concerned—which I'm not responsible for—my background is fundamentalist Protestantism.

When you say you're not responsible for it . . .

My parents gave me my background. I'm not responsible for that. I'm responsible for what I *do* with it, but not for having it.

Looking at Jung's upbringing as a Christian, I've often wondered—you see, I'm Jewish—I've wondered if some of the problems that Jung and Freud had with each other might have had to do with their religious background. Is that a possibility?

I don't think so. I think Freud had some trouble with Jung on the basis of his own Jewishness. Because Freud didn't accept his Jewishness. He projected onto Jung anti-Semitic tendencies that Jung didn't have. As I see it, Freud projected some of his own attitude towards his Jewishness onto Jung. So it caused a problem between them in that respect. I don't think it caused a problem from Jung's standpoint. He has made it clear what his problem with Freud was: Freud wouldn't give him room enough in their relationship to realize what he had to do.

Have you worked with Jung?

I have done no analysis with Jung. I've met him and talked to him briefly on a couple of occasions, which I'm grateful for, but I've had no analytic work with him.

What was your impression of him as a man?

The impression was of "bigness." First of all, he was a big man physically. That was my first realization when I met him. Then, of course, his capacity to be so totally present and to talk about what is most relevant. It took me some years before I realized that what I talked about with Jung was, indeed, the most relevant thing for me to talk about. But that was part of his "bigness," part of his breadth of perception. He could so see the reality of things that he could immediately engage them.

You mean you'd be talking to him about what seemed an off-the-cuff thing, yet it would turn out to be the appropriate thing at that moment.

Well, the full realization of how the subjects were indeed the central things—that's dawned on me more and more during the years since.

There's just time remaining for a few more questions. Could you tell us something about the personal life that lies behind your writing and your thinking? Like what kinds of hobbies or interests do you have?

I'm not sure that would be relevant. I think I need a different kind of question.

For example, you once gave a talk. And a Jungian analyst introduced you by saying, "Welcome to Los Angeles. We'd like to get to know you as our neighbor, as our friend." It sounded like she was drawing a distinction between "you" that is presented through your writing and thinking and the "you" as a person.

I don't make any such distinction. You ask me about various activities or contexts, what objects or what circumstances I seek out to live my life in—but the life is all one piece. I don't think it tells you anything significant just for me to tell you that I'm interested in the game of chess. Or that I play the recorder.

They're interesting.

But they don't tell you anything about *me*. If I were to enlarge upon this and say, "You now, the game of chess has a very interesting archetypal background. Let me tell you about it"—pretty soon I'd be giving another lecture. That's what I'd do, that's what I am, that's what goes on in my head. Or, when playing the recorder, I'm thinking what's the connection between the vibrating column of air and the sequence of notes that goes into my ear and grips my heart, and can squeeze it, and makes tears come to my eyes. How does that happen? What's going on? I don't think the actions are the important things. They're just the incidents, so to speak.

So it would be similar to Jung saying in his autobiography that he considered his outward life "singularly" unimportant?

I guess it would, now that you put it. It would correspond that way, uh-huh.

Do you mind if I ask a question about my personal process?

You can always ask questions. I don't promise to answer them (smilingly), but you're free to ask.

I've been doing a fair amount of work with sandtrays, and in one of your articles, you discussed a dream with a frog in it. In my sandtrays, frogs come up a lot. They seem to function as some sort of transpersonal force that holds all the disparate elements in my sandtray together. Would you discuss the symbolism of the frog?

I think it's in *The Visions Seminars*, that Jung has a very nice section on the symbolism of the frog.[203] One of the things he talks about there is that the frog is a diminutive animal version of man. There's something about

---

[203] Jung, *Visions: Notes of the Seminar Given in 1930-1934*, 2 vols., ed. Claire Douglas (Princeton: Bollingen Series XCIX, Princeton University Press, 1997).

the frog and its form that is very similar to the human being. So we get a glimpse of another aspect of ourselves through the imagery of the frog. And, of course, the big feature of the life of the frog is the total transformation it undergoes from its aqueous condition as a tadpole to its developing lungs and living on dry land. It undergoes this total change. So, it's an image of the evolutionary process that has been retained within the lifetime of a single organism, you see, which has moved from the original state of living in water to developing lungs and living on dry land.

I use that image often, as a matter of fact, in my analytic work. It's the image of the fish that one day starts moving out of the water onto dry land. It's the image of the evolutionary process that we are products of. If one is a fish that's destined to live on dry land, you've got lungs starting to develop. It gets harder and harder to live in water, because you need air. Water's too thick. If you're a fish that's developing lungs, then it's a matter of life or death for you to get out of the soup of "participation mystique" that fish live in as they swim around in their pond. You have to go into the more rarified atmosphere of air because you're a lung creature. On the contrary, if you're a fish forever, you'd better stay put—safely contained in whatever collective identities amount to your pond. On the other hand, if you're meant to evolve further, if you're a lung fish, then you have to get out of that pond in order to realize yourself. Now, all this comes out of the "frog," because the frog's life cycle goes through both stages.

I have just one more question. You mentioned earlier that Jung was five or six hundred years ahead of his time and that a lot of Jungians have not yet grasped the significance of his awareness. What about the man on the street? I think you mention somewhere that because organized religion doesn't work anymore, we have to find the transpersonal values within ourselves. And we have all these people walking around who have lost their faith in organized religion; it seems highly doubtful that they could relate to Jungian psychology. So what happens to them? Where do they go?

I don't know. You see, you're asking me a collective question. I don't have any response to collective questions. If you present me with *one* particular man on the street, that would be a different story. But I don't have a general answer. If you brought me one particular man, I *might* be able to get him back into his particular religious tradition that he came out of, with some new understanding of it. At least, we'd have a shot at it.

I see what you mean. I have a tendency to talk in generalities sometimes. Do you have anything else you'd like to say?

Nothing else comes to mind. Seems to me I've said an awful lot! I was interested to see just what *would* come out. It's very interesting what has.

Yes, extremely interesting. And I thank you very much.

The Psyche and Global Unrest
An Interview with *In Touch*[204]

From Somalia to Bosnia, from Northern Ireland to India, from numerous Latin American nations to Near and Far Eastern lands, the globe is blistering with national, religious and political adversaries, now in the late twentieth century. That there is something dangerous, something destructive in the collective energies motivating these wide-ranging antagonisms seems obvious enough.

For some illumination on the psychic processes behind these demonic energies, In Touch *turned to Edward F. Edinger, whose recent interviews and published texts have clearly indicated an analytic intelligence at work on just such issues. . . .*

One knows from your recent interviews, both on tape and in print, that you are concerned with the disturbing political, social, and religious

---

[204] This interview was conducted for *In Touch*, the newsletter of the Centerpoint Educational Center, 1993. Dr. Edinger helped design the first Centerpoint courses.—Eds.

events of these days. That's a big and serious subject, of course, but it would be interesting to hear what you have to say about these highly collective phenomena.

I do keep an eye on what is going on in the collective psyche and how the opposites are going to play themselves out on the world stage.

I want to quote you something, a passage in Jung's *Answer to Job*. Here's the sentence. It's actually not the total sentence Jung uses, but it's the part that I feel opens up a whole universe if we can understand it. It says: "The *imago Dei* pervades the whole human sphere and makes mankind its involuntary exponent."[205] Now what that tells us is that the sum total of human history, of which current political events are a portion, that sum total is the biography of God. So that's what we are seeing played out on the world stage in history and in current events. If one really grasps that psychological reality, then the panorama that opens before you—as we witness what's going on in the world—is seen from the depth dimension of the collective psyche. That's the perspective I have in mind when I say that I think that Islam is the rising entity on the world stage. When Jung died it still looked as though the *coniunctio* energies in the collective realm were going to play themselves out between the U.S. and the Soviet Union. But that conflict of opposites has shifted abruptly.

Jung is supposed to have said that eventually the conflict would not be between Russia and America but between the East and the West.

.

That's certainly the way it's shaping up, although Islam isn't really the East, because it's had a foot in the Western door for some centuries in the past, hasn't it? Anyway, when he wrote *The Undiscovered Self* in 1957, he was naturally thinking chiefly about the USSR and the United States.[206]

---

[205] Jung, *Psychology and Religion, CW 11*, par. 660.

[206] Jung, *Civilization in Transition, CW 10*.

Do you see Islam as primarily a negative energy or more as a mixture of both positive and negative elements?

I think of the opposites as equal, basically. Look at what the Islamic fundamentalists say about the West, their critique of the West. You know we get the truest appraisal of ourselves by listening to our enemies. My policy is to listen more to my enemies than to my friends when I'm interested in self-knowledge. Because your enemies aren't interested in flattering you, they're interested in finding your weaknesses and magnifying them. And the great virtue of Islam is that they're contained within a living religion. I'm talking about the fundamentalists now. The defect, of course, is that it's a primitive, undifferentiated sort of thing. They share many things in common with our own Christian fundamentalism. But Christian fundamentalism doesn't have the world-wide movement that Islamic fundamentalism has. They're God-oriented. Their terrorism is not out of personal motivation, it's out of a transpersonal motivation. That goes all the way back to the tradition of the Assassins. You know that word, "assassin," is cognate with the word, "hashish." Nine centuries ago certain Muslim sects would get themselves high on hashish and then go about their task of assassination, always for the glory of Allah. So it was a religious phenomenon. They've got just what we in the West lack. We're caught in an atheistic neurosis, an inflated neurosis, of our decaying society.

Do you then envision a further decay, a continuing decay?

Oh, absolutely. We're seeing the beginning of it with the break-up, the fragmentation, of the Soviet Union. You know, in one of my books I start out by quoting Yeats' poem, "The Second Coming." It's all there, in a couple of stanzas. It's all there, every bit of it. Let me read it to you because it's so relevant to what I'm talking about. I quote it on page 10 of *The Creation of Consciousness.* I preface it by saying, "The loss of a central myth brings about a truly apocalyptic condition, and this is the state of modern man. Our poets have long recognized this fact. Yeats gave it stark expression in his poem, 'The Second Coming.'" Then I quote it:

> Turning and turning in the widening gyre
> The falcon cannot hear the falconer;
> Things fall apart; the centre cannot hold;
> Mere anarchy is loosed upon the world,
> The blood-dimmed tide is loosed, and everywhere
> The ceremony of innocence is drowned;
> The best lack all conviction, while the worst
> Are full of passionate intensity.
>
> Surely some revelation is at hand;
> Surely the Second Coming is at hand.
> The Second Coming! Hardly are those words out
> When a vast image out of *Spiritus Mundi*
> Troubles my sight: somewhere in sands of the desert
> A shape with lion body and the head of a man,
> A gaze blank and pitiless as the sun,
> Is moving its slow thighs, while all about it
> Reel shadows of the indignant desert birds.
> The darkness drops again; but now I know
> That twenty centuries of stony sleep
> Were vexed to nightmare by a rocking cradle,
> And what rough beast, its hour come round at last,
> Slouches towards Bethlehem to be born?

That's a familiar poem. And there's a lot there.

It's all there, and we're watching that scenario live itself out. Every day I ponder this question. I have a quotation from Jung's letters that I'm reflecting on constantly. It was written in April of 1955 to Victor White. Jung says,

> Just as Job lifted his voice, so that everybody could hear him, I have come to the conclusion that I had better risk my skin and do my worst or best to shake the unconsciousness of my contemporaries rather than allow my laxity to let things drift toward the impending world catastrophe.[207]

---

[207] Jung, *Letters,* vol. 2, p. 239.

Now, the question is, if one is in the position of Cassandra, as I feel I am and as Jung certainly was—one who can see how things are going to be, but nobody believes you—what's one's responsibility or what can one do under those circumstances? Unless I come up with a better one, so far my best answer is: speak as best I'm able to those that will come after.

I speak a little bit about this subject in Part 3 of that video interview ["An American Jungian," included in this book]. What I say there is that the best thing I know to do is to bear witness to—to mediate and bring into visibility, as best I am capable—what Jung has to say in his later work, especially *Answer to Job*. Because the time of troubles is in the wings. The evidence of it is obvious, if you have any eyes to see, and there are going to be terrible troubles.

We get a glimpse of it in what's going on in Bosnia right now, you see. Ghastly! Absolutely ghastly! And when that level of disorder hits the West as a whole, the depth and magnitude of suffering is just unimaginable. And the question will be, in order to keep their sanity, what will people do? Well, the vast majority will regress to more primitive modes of functioning. We'll see a great resurgence of authoritarianism and a religious regression to fundamentalisms of all kinds. But for those that have enough consciousness to recognize such movements as primitive and atavistic, they won't be able to ascribe to that; and they'll be in the position Yeats speaks of. They will be the best who have lost all conviction, you see, while the worst are full of their passionate intensity. And the best will have lost all conviction.

But *Answer to Job* provides the best with a new level of conviction that may be just reachable to them if they are powerfully prodded by their suffering and by the immediacy of their suffering to try to understand the meaning of what's happening to them. You see, they will be psychologically demoralized if they can't find the events meaningful—and secularism doesn't provide that sense of meaning. It's missing the transpersonal dimension. And my thought, anyway, is that just possibly, under those circumstances, some kind of saving remnant might find *Answer to Job* and the other works of Jung as life-saving.

What you propose, then, is to speak wherever possible.

To speak and to write.

To communicate.

I don't have the libido now to put any more books together. But, wonder of wonders, just as that has happened, people have popped up here and there who want to edit some of my taped course material into books. Joan Blackmer is working on my "Mysterium" lectures. She's one example. Another example is Deborah Wesley who had edited my Greek mythology material, and it's going to be published by Shambhala next year. Another example is a course I have entitled, "The New God-Image," a study of Jung's key letters concerning the evolution of the Western God-image. That's going to be published by Chiron next year. And Lawrence Jaffe put together my course on *Answer to Job*, and that came out as *Transformation of the God-Image*. It's just miraculous to me that just as my energy waned, people showed up who had the interest in doing that.

.

Do you see contemporary events, such as Bosnia, as being related to the Revelation material?

Oh, absolutely. It's all part of the Apocalypse. It's all there, definitely.

Does the end of this aeon have any relevance here, too?

Jung talks about that in *Aion*.[208] I've given a year's course on *Aion*, and that's being worked on and made into a book. It's amazing how much there is, because I have done quite a bit of teaching here. It's all on tape, it's available to be worked over. *Aion* is the other great work that yields so many insights in terms of the international political situation. And in answer to your question, it's a decided "yes." It's all part of the Antichrist phenomenon that has manifested in the last five hundred years.

---

[208] Jung, *Aion, CW* 9ii.

You know, the Faust legend started five hundred years ago. The legendary Dr. Faustus is thought to have lived between 1480 and 1540. Fifteen hundred is the rough date when the God-image fell out of heaven into the human psyche. When it fell, it manifested as Lucifer—it reversed its polarity. So that's what we've been witnessing the last five hundred years.

.

Does AIDS have anything to do with the Antichrist phenomenon?

The AIDS phenomenon? Yes, it's another example of the apocalyptic. The fundamentalist Christians see it as a plague sent by God for lascivious behavior. Now, if one can translate that primitive concretism into the element of psychological truth it contains, then I think the nature of the virus reveals the "sin"—in quotation marks—the psychological sin that it's the avenger of. The virus is a totally new kind of virus that has the capacity to penetrate that part of our physiology which determines, when something enters our system, whether it's "I" or "not-I"—whether it belongs to the organism or whether it's foreign to the organism. If it's foreign, it attacks it, rejects it. That's how the immune system works to protect us from diseases of all kinds. And that immune system is what modern medicine has to break down in order to put in transplants, to graft in a new kidney or a new heart. It has first to feed medicine to the organism that kills the immune system so that it won't reject the alien organism. I'm against medical transplantation on psychological grounds. That is something the inflated modern scientific ego, of course, wouldn't pay any attention to at all.

Anyway, the AIDS virus does the same thing that certain medications do for allowing transplants. There are a lot of legends going around that the AIDS virus escaped from some research laboratory. I doubt that is factually true, but it's got a mythical reality to it—it's got a symbolic reality. It's the AIDS virus that breaks down our basic mechanism that preserves and protects individuality. It would reduce everybody to the basic common denomination of virus; that's about as low a living form as you can get.

I see it as part of the grand phenomenon of loosening. Every word in that poem of Yeats is significant. He uses the word "loosed" twice. The Greek word for that is *lyo*. We get the words "lysis" and "analysis" from it. It's a grand *solutio*, that's what it is. It pertains to the symbolism of that alchemical operation, which I talk about in one of my chapters in *Anatomy of the Psyche*. That is what's being promoted on the grand scale of the AIDS virus. Now it would be very interesting, indeed, to have a chance to see what dreams are coming out with in regard to the patients with AIDS or with the HIV virus. My partner Dianne has worked with an HIV-positive man. She's got some very remarkable material. She doesn't feel able to put it into any shape yet; the time may come when she will. She worked with him some years ago now; he's still healthy, miracle of miracles! Anyway, it's material like that which I think will give us some hint as to what the unconscious itself says about it. I haven't had any direct experience with AIDS patients. But I'm on the lookout for depth material. What people have talked about so far regarding AIDS has been very superficial stuff.

.

It's such a highly collective phenomenon. It looks like an invasion of the collective psyche into the lives of individuals.

Exactly. That's a good way of putting it. That is what it is.

.

So what is it up to?

You could think of it as a grand *solutio*, one process in the making of the Philosophers' Stone, you see. But it's not a very pleasant process when you're in the midst of it.

.

Do you have any reaction to the increasing use of visual imagery in education, news reporting, entertainment, etc.? Is there any particular significance in that?

I'm sure there is. I'm more aware of the negative aspect of it than I am of the positive aspects. What alarms me most is the fate of books. There are a lot of people in the know who assure us that books are on the way out, that we're going to get everything from our computer screens before long. I'm not sure things are going to last long enough for it to go too far. So I think that will be a moot point anyway. But certainly the technology is marvelous and wonderful, absolutely wonderful. But everything depends on the nature of the individuals using it, doesn't it?

Among other things, we have those recent tapes of yours, and they're available to a wide audience.
.
Exactly. It's wonderful that we also have Jung in motion pictures, and these have been transferred to tape. That's marvelous.

Concerning your recent tapes, I've found that some people are rather disturbed by tape number three [of "An American Jungian"], which I suppose is understandable.

Oh, I'm very interested to hear that. Tell me what kind of reactions they have had.

Principally, they seem disturbed by the idea of what you call "continuing incarnation." Is that your term or Jung's?
.
That's Jung's term, absolutely.

Some find this very problematic to deal with because they feel that you are equating Jung with God, and that bothers them. Or equating Jung with Jesus at any rate.

Okay, there's a certain level of truth to that. You see, that's what "continuing incarnation" means. It means that Christ was a paradigm, the first-born of a whole family of brothers. That's even stated explicitly in the New Testament. And that's what Jung is talking about. But it's dangerous doctrine, you see, because it sounds like inflation. I never argue about these matters at all. When that sort of remark is made, I'll acknowledge, "Yes, you've got a valid point there. Anyone who dared to write *Answer to Job* is in danger of trespassing on divine territory. And I very much appreciate your worry about that." I wouldn't dispute it at all. Because the way I understand such reactions, they indicate where the individual is; and I don't want to push an individual off some standing position that he's found that allows him to survive in the tumult of existence. I have no desire to do that at all. But, here and there, there will be an individual for whom such way of seeing opens up meanings that help him find himself—rather than lose himself. That's the only person I'm interested in talking to.

Are there any of the realities of Analytical psychology which can be adequately communicated outside of analysis?

Well, they're operative everywhere. But the trouble is that all the psychological realities that Jungian psychology deals with, that we see in the outer world, go by different names for ordinary people and are assumed to have different etiologies by most people. For instance, just as a little example, I very much wish (it's a kind of fantasy of mine) that in the medical practice of the future, when a person is admitted to the hospital—at the same time that a medical history is taken, and a physical exam is taken, and various blood tests and X-rays are taken—at the same time, he would routinely be questioned about dreams that the individual thought might conceivably be relevant to his illness. Now, that's just a little thing, and it could very easily be brought about. But it's impossible—totally out of the question. It's so alien to the scientific orthodoxy that it would be laughed right out of the room. You see? So that's why we are left with the one-to-one setting. There isn't any other setting that can communicate what we have to point to.

You're familiar, of course, with von Franz's book, On Dreams and Death.[209]

---

[209] Marie-Louise von Franz, *On Dreams and Death*, trans. Emmanuel Xipolitas Kennedy and Vernon Brooks (Boston: Shambhala, 1986).

Yes, I am.

And you may know that she and Emmanuel Kennedy are collecting what they call "death dreams" in an effort to see what the psyche may have to say about post-mortal existence. Do you have a personal perspective on what is frequently referred to as "the Beyond"?

What is very clear is that when someone psychologically close dies, it tears open an opening into the deeper layers of the unconscious—out of which, then, come dreams of a depth which ordinarily don't come to an individual. That's very clear. I've seen that happen again and again. Many of those dreams have the deceased as a major figure, showing the deceased person in certain circumstances. Now it's always impossible to be able to know definitely whether the figure of the deceased person refers to an objective existence in the Beyond or whether it may refer to the effects of the deceased person and his death on the dreamer. It's impossible to know that. We can't know it. Certainly many of the dreams carry with them a conviction of objectivity that tells us that they have a psychological objectivity at least.

I came across an interesting book a while back. This book was published in England. The author is Arthur Guirdham, and the title is *The Cathars and Reincarnation*. Let me read part of the jacket blurb: "The record of a woman who through dreams and impressions in waking consciousness remembers her life in the 13th century . . . . A story of reincarnation. . . . . The woman was a heretic, a Cathar, in France in the 13th century. . . . She was able to place accurately family and social relationships."[210] The author is a psychiatrist, although he did not do any treatment of her in the conventional sense of the word. Now it turned out in the course of his study of this case that he reached the conclusion that he also is reincarnated from that time past. The reason I'm bringing this up is that this woman whose case is described had been a practicing Catholic who was excommunicated before she ever saw the psychiatrist. Now

---

[210] Arthur Guirdham, *The Cathars and Reincarnation* (Welling-borough, UK: Turnstone Press, 1982).

we don't know, we don't have a good enough case history to know, what the details of the excommunication were. But that makes a connection right away, you see, with heresy.

Now here's the kind of hypothesis I'm inclined to entertain as an alternative to the straightforward simplistic notion of reincarnation. I'm inclined to think that reincarnation imagery derives from a situation in which the modern current individual has had an archetypal experience which reaches a depth that constellates a certain archetype that has historical analogues. That person is, in effect, reincarnating an archetypal role or an archetypal reality which makes him or her a brother or sister to other historical individuals who have incarnated that same archetypal constellation or role. In this case, we have a practicing Catholic who had a close relation to the Church. And then—for reasons that are not very clear—she fell afoul of the Church and was excommunicated and fell into the same relation to the Church that the ancient Cathars did, constellating thereby that archetypal pattern of things which would make her sort of symbolically a "reincarnation" of the Cathars. This could then set into motion synchronistic phenomena—that we don't understand completely at all—that I think could explain some of the events that are described in this book. Now, I'm not sure how clear I made that, because it's a kind of subtle idea.

Now, this is all in response to your question about the Beyond. As I mentioned in *The Creation of Consciousness*, I have a hypothesis about it. But that's all it is, a hypothesis. And the hypothesis is that whatever an individual has authentically and consciously integrated into his totality—into his unique existential totality—that is added as an increment to the archetypal collective psyche at his death. And that this is one of the ways the collective unconscious evolves, that it grows and enlarges and differentiates.

As to the state of the personal ego, I really don't have anything to say. I don't know. You know Jung recommends, as a good idea for old people, that they fantasize what the afterlife will be. I indulge in that activity. I don't know whether this fantasy is original or whether it's derived from all of the mythological, legendary symbolism that has accreted to me through my years or not, but I find myself having some of the same kind of fantasies as legends talk about. Legends talk about resting in Abraham's bosom, things like that, joining the company of the saints. I don't think in those terms, but I fantasy in terms of joining with Jung, with my dead son, that sort of thing. But that's fantasy. Certainly, what von Franz is doing is the hard work of laying out the data as we can accumulate them. What is clear is that a living, conscious connection to the archetypal psyche puts a friendly face on death and the Beyond. Death is the goal of life, and to reach one's goal is an occasion for celebration.

Figure 14. Edward F. Edinger (1922-1998).

PART VII

THE MEMORIAL SERVICE[211]

PROGRAM

In Memory
Edward F. Edinger
December 13, 1922—July 17, 1998
Pierce Brothers Westwood Village Chapel
July 26, 1998
2:00 PM

Music (recorded)
"Quia Respexit Humilitatem,"
from *Magnificat* by Johann Sebastian Bach

Introductory Comments

DONALD SLOGGY, OFFICIANT:[212]

On behalf of the families, I want to welcome and thank everyone for coming, some from very near and some from very far, just as Ed's life touched both near and far.

We have gathered here on this day to honor, to lament, to remember, and to celebrate our dear colleague, mentor, and friend, Edward F. Edinger, and to sing this great old warrior on over to the other side. We are here to recall once more how the Power of the World lived and moved

---

[211] We are particularly grateful to the Edward F. Edinger Memorial participants for allowing their words to appear here. They spoke not with the intention of publication but to honor Ed. In print, their heartfelt remarks continue to do so.—Eds.

[212] Donald Sloggy is a Jungian analyst with a practice in Santa Monica, California.

through this man to do its work and how this man, Edward F. Edinger, accepted that task and tethered himself to that Power. He hitched himself to that wagon to work utterly in service of it, so that "God's secret intentions" might find voice and expression, and so that those deep stirrings in the human soul which so yearn to be incarnated in this world might find such lucid and living expression.

Edward Edinger offered his life that the Divine Opposites might find a living vessel through which to reconcile and incarnate. It is fitting that we begin with a selection from Bach's *Magnificat*, something Edward requested. It is Mary's song of praise upon learning she is pregnant with the Deity. In fact, Mary has offered herself to incarnate the Deity, she has accepted her fate and feels very blessed. She says, "My soul doth magnify the Lord." I think that in addition to its great beauty, I believe this song and passage was special to Edward because he, too, felt blessed and honored that his life and his vocation were filled with such deep meaning and purpose. And I suspect that he, too, felt deeply blessed by God.

Central to Edward's calling was the life and work of C. G. Jung, born on this day, July 26, 1875, 123 years ago. We could exclaim, "What a coincidence!" But, as an elder once said to me, "Coincidence? It's a lazy word, and it doesn't explain the half of it." What I do know is that Ed was really the first person to clearly articulate who Jung was—an "epochal man"—and Jung's consequent place in history. That is a profound act which has not been realized yet. What Jung discovered, and Ed devoted his life to, was the living psyche and its innate and sacred urge to realize itself in human consciousness. That we honor Edward Edinger's passing on this day that Jung was born feels very fitting and, in fact, most meaningful.

It is still far too early to realize that we have just witnessed the passing of a giant from our midst. Edward is one of the substantial and illuminating spirits of our time; and, with his leaving, there is a noticeable dimming of the light. His life has been like a sunrise. He has been a bringer of light, and his words have illuminated the dark places of our individual lives and the twilight of this time in which we live. He is what the American Indian prophet, Black Elk, called a "word sender." "The earth is like a garden, and over it his words go like rain, making it green. And after his words have passed, the memory of them will stand long in the west like a flaming rainbow."

And now his red sun has sunk at last, into the hills of gold, and peace to this old warrior of whom it has been told . . . and you, dear Edward, will wear the starry crown. Oh, Lord, show us the way.

Most of us know Ed as a Jungian analyst, as a teacher, a mentor, a writer, and how his deep and introverting Eros tethered itself in service to the stream of eternal images. That same Eros also moved deeply with his family and friends and in his own personal life. And I think we can get a glimpse of that as his family and friends share some of their thoughts and reflections.

Remarks from the Family

CLARA JENDROWSKI[213]

Hello, my name is Clara; I'm Ed's daughter. The flowers on the casket are from his grandsons—Nicholas, who is ten years old, and Alexander, who is four. They couldn't be here today. But I was talking with Nicholas the other day about his favorite memories of Grandpa. He talked about grandpa teaching him chess and giving him a chess set of his own. And with a big smile, he mentioned Grandpa's gifts. Grandpa gave great gifts. Just like he always knew what to say, he always knew what to give as a gift. Nicholas also talked about learning about stars and planets from his grandpa. I, as well, have memories as a child looking at the sky through a telescope with Dad.

One of my earliest memories of my dad is when I was four or five years old. Usually, I would spend the last hour or so before my bedtime downstairs with Dad watching TV or something. During this time, I'd try my hardest to fall asleep. Because if I succeeded, Dad would carry me upstairs and tuck me in bed. My first thought when I woke up in the

---

[213] Clara Jendrowski is Dr. Edinger's daughter who resides in Lockport, New York.

morning was, "Could I remember going to bed the night before?" If I couldn't, then I knew Dad had carried me sleeping up to bed and tucked me in. And that made me very happy.

In recent years, Dad "carried" me up still. When life would get crazy and out of kilter, as it is wont to do, my dad was the one I would turn to to get me back my balance. His words of wisdom, his caring and love for me, were invaluable to me. I enjoyed talking with my dad so very much. He was fascinating as well as incredibly funny, and very sweet. Being, as he called me, a chip off the old block, I enjoyed many hours of psychological conversations with Dad as well. I'm going to really miss those talks, really miss my dad.

JOHN CORDIC (SPEAKING ALSO FOR CLAUDIA CORDIC AND NANETTE CORDIC TEVROW)[214]

I'm thankful for the chance to share a few thoughts and feelings for my sisters, Nanette and Claudia, and for myself about our dear Edward. Having Ed become part of our family for the past twenty years has meant more than we can say. What he's given us can't really be expressed in words but rather in the way we live our lives. He had such a thorough grasp of what is real and important that there's almost no end to where a few words of remembrance can go. Luckily, I'm not longwinded.

What follows here are just a few precious memories. When I close my eyes and think of Ed I can't help but smile, a broad easy smile. Ed was so true to himself that you couldn't help but feel a little inspired being with him. I guess we all know that he didn't thrive on social occasions, but you'd never see him fail in one either. For me, it was a subtle wit that shone in those situations. Often, we'd see Ed at lunches or dinners my sisters and mother would prepare. On other family events he'd bring a tiny flask of scotch. And while my sisters would insist that he didn't need to bring his own drink, Ed would say, "Well, one must be prepared." (laughter) Once with my sisters, and mother, and fiancée around the table, he said to me, "You know, John, I'm a bit overwhelmed surrounded

---

[214] John Cordic, Claudia Cordic, and Nannette Cordic Tevrow are the children of Dianne Cordic, Ed's partner. They reside in the greater Los Angeles area.

by all these beautiful women. I'm glad to have another fellow around." I also was glad. Once, years ago, my mother inquired about my romantic life. Edward looked up at his plate and said, "Tell her she can't ask you those kinds of questions." (laughter). He *was* very funny.

As the years have gone by, we've gained a confidence from him. I can almost hear him say, "This is me, these are my values, and don't attempt to meddle." Sometimes during a conflict, I can think to myself, "What would Ed do?" And it seems he would say, "Seek the truth, mitigate, and stand fast by your position."

My sister Nanette said something very beautiful about Ed. She said that "it's nice to be with someone with whom you don't feel compelled to keep up conversation. It was easy to be with Ed and just be quiet." Nanette said, "It could feel like the quiet of the very early morning and that, while he's left our earth, she can still feel his quiet and stillness."

I think he's given us an ability to get to the core of things. It's a relief in the chaos of today to look at the essence of things and take what portion is good and move onward. His absolute clarity—and what in life he has been willing and not willing to give his time to—has proved an invaluable example. It's also a comfort to think that he wasted little time in life. I think what touches me deepest is that such a disciplined and practical man could take journeys to such mysterious places.

But he *was* a practical man. I want to relay a little story here that my sisters and I remember well. We were gathered at the house on Roscomare in the back yard where there's a steep hill that's covered with ivy. So this afternoon, we're sitting around having lunch, when suddenly this huge deer, about four or five feet high, came walking right down about twenty feet away from us and started eating at the ivy. Ed ducked into his study and reappeared with an air pellet rifle—a kind of harmless little deal—but no sooner was he out the door than he got off a shot, and the deer darted off and ran up the hill. We were looking around, this was almost a vision, and my sisters and I expected to get some kind of deep analysis. But Edward just looked and said, "Right in the flank." (laughter) We laughed; he got the humor in that. So, among other things, Ed was a good shot.

My sister Claudia's favorite memories of Ed are of time spent paging through art books. His interest in art was never intellectual or aesthetic or academic but rather human and spiritual. She said that on the rare occasion she saw something in an image that he didn't he would get very enthusiastic but always give it back by way of saying, "Oh, look what that says about you, that you would see that." And Claudia said that—since he loved to teach—once she got him talking about how the psyche expressed itself in an image, she knew that she was going to get another hour or two of time with him.

Much of what we've gained from Edward has come through our mother. I know the thing that we love most about Ed is the happiness that he brought her. They were true soul mates.

Music (recorded)
"Air" from *Suite No. 3 in D* by Johann Sebastian Bach

Remarks from Colleagues

PAMELA POWER[215]

Ed Edinger was my analyst, my mentor, my colleague, and my dear friend. I met him in 1972 at a conference and was immediately impressed by him. I wanted to work with him in analysis, and I did so a few years later. I began to understand the fateful dimension of my connection to him a few years into my analysis when I brought him a dream of which he took particular notice. That dream portrayed an encounter between the ego and the amoral destructive aspect of the deeper unconscious—the dark side of God. For Ed, this encounter within the individual psyche plays a crucial role in the transformation of the collective God-image. I, too, became drawn into this issue as my analysis proceeded. Ed was profoundly affected by Jung's seminal work on this matter, *Answer to Job*,

---

[215] Pamela Power, Ph.D., is a Jungian analyst practicing in Santa Monica, California.

saying that Jung's statement, "Whoever knows God has an affect on him," to be the single most important statement in that book. Knowing that the best and worst of human nature belong to and originate from the same paradoxical entity became a central motif for Ed's lectures, teaching seminars, and books.

For Ed, this knowing was not intellectual or conceptual knowledge. It was knowledge gained from painful, personal experience. He wrote in *The Creation of Consciousness* that one must be "willing to risk a conscious encounter with his primitive affects in the faith that they are capable of transformation." And "the primitive, desirous aspect of the transpersonal psyche collides with the spiritual principle of restraint and . . . [one] becomes a living crucible for the transformation of God." Ed made it his life task to elucidate this far-reaching visionary aspect of Jung's work.

Ed had keen insight into the psychological meaning behind current catastrophic world events. He was a down-to-earth, no-nonsense man who knew and expressed his view that the task of confronting and humanizing the demonic forces unleashed in the world at this time could only be accomplished in the individual psyche. As he said in *Science of the Soul*: "One individual at a time. It's not done collectively, not done in committee. It's done one lonely individual at a time who has the experience of divine ambiguity—and in the process of that experience penetrates it with human consciousness which transforms it."

Ed did not hesitate in public or private to express his high regard for and opinion of Jung. During one of my last meetings with him, we were discussing deprecating attacks on Jung and, in particular, the tendency to interpret Jung's personal psychology—"As if they could," he remarked. He was loyal to Jung. And he said to me, "I make it personal to Jung because although we know it means being loyal to the psyche, that way of putting it is so abstract that it lets one do anything. Being loyal to Jung, it pins one down."

Above all, Ed valued what he called "Jungian consciousness," by which he meant a profound commitment to the transpersonal Self and a willingness to be a vessel for containing, transforming, and reconciling the divine opposites. Ed wasn't perfect, and he knew it. He lived as fully from his limitations as from his extraordinary talents. He lived true to his values no matter what anyone thought about it—and this impressed me greatly. I'll always remember when I struggled and with difficulty was able to remain true to my values. At those times, Ed would say to me, "It's getting lonely, isn't it?"

DEBORAH WESLEY[216]

In one of C. S. Lewis' fantasy novels, the narrator meets the guiding spirit of another planet and discovers that this being—although it seems to be standing vertically—is at the same time not really at right angles to the floor of the room. Yet he feels not that the being itself is aslant but that the floor of his room is no longer horizontal. It seems to have heeled up like the deck of a ship, and the being itself seems to be at the true vertical. This is a good metaphor for a good many of my experiences with Edward Edinger. You could say it's what one feels when the smaller viewpoint meets the broader.

In 1993, I was thrilled at the opportunity to edit Ed's lectures on Jung's work, *Aion*, for publication as a book. Preparing a manuscript from those taped lectures and readying Ed's sketchy diagrams of the material took many months of work—both by myself and by Thorton Ladd who redrew many of the diagrams from his own highly visual perspective. In time, the wheels ground, and the first copies of the book arrived. Such excitement! Then, such dismay. Through a mix-up at the printer, several pages of illustrations had large errors in them. Thornton and I were both anguished at the spoiling of this important work, and we finally decided to underwrite the expenses of having the book reprinted in the correct form. Tremblingly, I telephoned Ed to confess the disaster and to tell him of our decision to have the book reprinted. His reaction was unperturbed and immediate: "No, I don't think you should do that." He went on to say that a work like *Aion* which deals in large part with the relationship between good and evil is bound to attract the dark forces. If

---

[216] Deborah Wesley, Ph.D., is a Jungian analyst living in Los Angeles.

we tried to have it reprinted to produce a perfect copy, other errors would then show up in it. We should see what had happened as a part of the nature of the text itself.

What has been even more surprising and touching to me was Ed's reaction to the offers of help that began to come forth from Ed's colleagues. When some years ago, his illness left him without the energy to prepare his work for publication, he seemed moved and genuinely surprised that people would be eager to help him. But so they have been, and his books continue to appear—some comfort to us in our loss and a treasury that will outlive us all.

GILDA FRANTZ[217]

There is a wonderful feeling in this room on this occasion as there is a sense of depth and beauty present. I was going to tell you something about Edward Edinger that very few people know. And then I had a dream. So my challenge is: Do I still tell you this private thing that only a few people know about Edward Edinger? The part of me that says "yes" is going to tell you the private little thing; then I will tell you the dream.

Edward Edinger liked to jitterbug (laughter). I have seen him do this on only two or three occasions. I often felt that if the moment was right, the music was right, and his mood was right, he'd actually like to jitterbug—the lindy hop, as I remember.

I had this dream just before I woke up this morning:

> I'm in a modern art gallery, and I see a friend speaking on the telephone. I hear her telling Ed about each of the paintings in the gallery. And she is strolling from one to the other as if to give him a sense of the entire exhibit. I, the dreamer, am amazed that she's speaking with him. And in the way of dreams I can see him talking on the phone to her. He is the Ed that I remember from the late 60s and the early 70s, in his prime, well, and alive. And I wake up.

An invitation from Kieffer Frantz brought Ed to California.[218] His rela-

---

[217] Gilda Frantz is a Jungian analyst practicing in Santa Monica, California.

[218] The reference is to Gilda's husband, Kieffer Frantz, M.D., also a Jungian analyst, now deceased.

tionship with Dianne kept him here. His coming into the Jungian world of Northern and Southern California is an amazing story of being called and answering that call. By saying "yes" to that invitation, he changed the course of his life and perhaps many of the lives in this room as well. He certainly affected mine. I knew Ed first as a friend, then as a colleague, and then as an analyst and teacher.

I once asked him how he discovered the idea of representing the alchemical stages in a diagrammatic form. He replied that he was inspired by a contemporary painting in an art gallery—probably, the Museum of Modern Art in New York—an art exhibit which gave him the idea of how to present his work graphically. He looked at a painting, and then it suddenly dawned on him, "This was the way he could diagram the work." Ed was an "artist-alchemist." He was a very gifted thinker who gave himself unstintingly to his Art, through his many books interpreting Jung's work. Kieffer Frantz said that the best physicians were the ones who saw medicine as an art, and were artists. While others learned the science of medicine, the artists practiced the art of healing. Ed was a great healer and was one of the most generous, unpretentious men I have ever known.

MARGARET PHILLIPS JOHNSON[219]

I'm Margaret Johnson, one of the colleagues, one of the students, one of the analysands. I just want to comment—from the perspective of the C. G. Jung Institute of Los Angeles—that when Ed moved here, he was a great gift. And he continues to be a gift. He taught many seminars. The students learned from him, were encouraged to go on and do their own work in a way that very few teachers can inspire their students. And I want to thank him for his support for *Psychological Perspectives*. He was gracious enough to give us a number of his pieces. "The Vocation of Depth Psychology" in our 1997 Summer issue I think was a real gem and a real gift to all analysts—to read that and really take that in. In the com-

---

[219] Margaret Johnson, Ph.D., is a Jungian analyst practicing in Mancos, Colorado.

ing issues of *Psychological Perspectives,* we will provide a memorial for Ed in greater depth.

When I think about Dr. Edinger, an image comes to my mind. As many people have said, he was the carrier of "light," of a particularly clear and intense kind of light. Clarity and fierce intensity—those are the two qualities that I want to speak about.

First, clarity. Clarity for direction. The first hour I met with him in his study—which was a small, dark room, walls almost completely lined with books—I found myself looking around at all of those books, because there seemed to be a soft, golden, indirect light coming from all of them. I was trying to see what kind of an electrical lighting system could create that effect. When I mentioned that to Ed, he chuckled and said, "Well, perhaps the light I was seeing was coming from the objective unconscious"—that it certainly wasn't the electrical lighting system of his. But he *was* the carrier of light, a light that connected heaven and earth, the practical with the sublime. And he never lost the mystery or the immensity of his subject, down-to-earth though he could be. His clarity enabled others to be able to see, to find their own connections with the objective psyche—which would then begin to serve as their own inner guidance system, the "blessed inner star of navigation." Without that, we're lost on the sea journey.

I want to read you a short poem by David Whyte, where he writes of the "blessed inner star of navigation." He calls the poem, "Song For the Salmon":

> For too many days now I have not written of the sea,
> nor the rivers, nor the shifting currents
> we find between the islands.

> For too many nights now I have not imagined the salmon
> threading the dark streams of reflected stars,
> nor have I dreamt of his longing,
> nor the lithe swing of his tail toward dawn.

> I have not given myself to the depth to which he goes,
> to the cargoes of crystal water, cold with salt,
> nor the enormous plains of ocean swaying beneath the moon.

> I have not felt the lifted arms of the ocean

opening its white hands on the seashore,
nor the salted wind, whole and healthy,
filling the chest with living air.

I have not heard those waves,
fallen out of heaven onto earth,
nor the tumult of sound and the satisfaction
of a thousand miles of ocean,
giving up its strength on the sand.

*

But now I have spoken of that great sea,
the ocean of longing shifts through me,
the blessed inner star of navigation
moves in the dark sky above
and I am ready like the young salmon,
to leave his river, blessed with hunger,
for a great journey on the drawing tide.[220]

Next, fierce intensity, that aspect of light. Dr. Edinger was fiercely devoted to serving and illuminating the parameters of the objective unconscious. His insights often set him apart because he had to be apart—he was seeing things many of us could not see. But he never lost his focus or his devotion. He was a sea journeyer, and he often stood alone. He was not afraid to stand alone. I admire that kind of light.

One more poem by David called "Self-Portrait":[221]

It doesn't interest me if there is one God
or many gods.
I want to know if you belong or feel
abandoned,
If you can know despair or see it in others.
I want to know
if you are prepared to live in the world with its
harsh need
to change you. If you can look back
with firm eyes,

---

[220] From David Whyte, *River Flow: New and Selected Poems 1984-2007* (Langley, Washington: Many Rivers Press, 2007), p. 146.
[221] Ibid., p. 347.

saying this is where I stand. I want to know
if you know
how to melt into that fierce heat of living,
falling toward
the center of your longing. I want to know
if you are willing
to live, day by day, with the consequence of love
and the bitter
unwanted passion of your sure defeat.
I have heard, in *that* fierce embrace, even
the gods speak of God.

The Eulogy[222]

GEORGE R. ELDER

Jung once said that if Americans wished to understand him, they could read Ralph Waldo Emerson. Yet I think he would add today that we might read the works of Edward F. Edinger. The man whose death we mourn today and whose life we celebrate is the finest example of creative introversion born in America since Emerson. Indeed, I have often thought of him as "our Emerson"—a man in our time of astonishing psychological integrity with an inner authority we will not soon see again. Dr. Edinger was generous: offering us his profoundest insights for nearly half a century in dozens of lectures, scores of essays, and in sixteen book titles to date (three more books are forthcoming); in the analytic office, more privately, he was generously nonjudgmental. It would come almost as a surprise to hear, despite his visibly conservative manner, "But it's a fact"—his point being that one was not guilty of a psychological given any more than for the physical color of one's eyes.

Yet Edinger was not generous to a fault: he did not, as he put it, "pass bad checks," and make promises he could not keep. In an interview, he

---

[222] George Elder is co-editor of this book. This tribute was first published in *Quadrant* 29, no. 1 (Winter 1999), pp. 7ff.; reprinted in *Psychological Perspectives* 39 (Summer 1999), pp. 12ff.

said: "It's not virtue to sham virtue. It's much more authentically virtuous to be what one is." Have you met anyone who lived so consistently this modern morality rooted in an awareness of the shadow and responsive to the new requirements of the Self?

Ed's magical way with limits reminds me that he was not just psychologically compact but physically so. He took up very little space; and I often thought of the "Coagulatio" chapter in *Anatomy of the Psyche* when I met with him. His verbal expression was succinct—as was Emerson's—and that gave his prose power. No, he did not have his predecessor's aesthetic power but he had the modern advantage of psychological categories that lent his prose an empirical truthfulness. He did not invent Emersonian phrases like "Trust thyself" or "Envy is ignorance;" but he knew what they meant. He did say—and I choose at random— "Awareness is depressing" (laughter), "Jung is an epochal man," and (referring to paragraph 524 in Volume 5 of the *Collected Works*) "If you understand this paragraph thoroughly, you will understand Jungian psychology." Dr. Edinger boiled things down for us. He was an alchemist from his teens in Indiana. One of his dreams announced, "Here comes the Hoosier gold-maker!"

Edinger loved Jung. He had all that feeling for Jung because he saw what Jung had done. Listen to these words from the 1972 preface to *Ego and Archetype*:

> It is only beginning to dawn on the educated world what a magnificent synthesis of human knowledge has been achieved by C. G. Jung . . . . he discovered in his patients and in himself the *reality of the psyche* and the phenomenology of its manifestations at a depth never before observed systematically. . . . He has penetrated to the root source of all religion and culture and thus has discovered the basis for a new organic syncretism of human knowledge and experience. The new viewpoint thus achieved is so comprehensive and all-embracing that, once grasped, it cannot fail to have revolutionary consequences for man's view of himself and the world.

These are sublime words, hardly what one would expect of a coagulated man. Yet their writer's own psychological achievement was so "sizeable"—and Edinger liked that word—that the libido he withdrew from traditional projections onto Socrates, Buddha, and Christ, simply opened his eyes to marvel at the size of Jung. That is why he commented on entire volumes form the *Collected Works*. And so now we have crisp, incisive commentaries on Volumes 5, 9ii and 14. We have, as well, Dr. Edinger's view that someday these volumes will be read and studied as scriptures have been, that Jung's letter to the American Jungian analyst Elined Kotschnig in 1956 will someday have the status that Paul's Letter to the Romans has had for two millennia. How could he say such things?

I must tell you that these statements thrill me, that I feel like Alcibiades in *The Symposium* who confessed that Socrates' words "turned his soul upside down." He was a little drunk with wine and love but said: "If you open up his arguments, and really get into the skin of them, you'll find that they're the only arguments in the world that have any sense at all . . . ."

As many of you know, Dr. Edinger loved the Zen story of the fish who could not see water because they were in it; and then he'd extol the virtues of some lung-fish with legs leaving its watery container and able to turn around and observe. Well, this man we have known—and whom I confess, like Alcibiades, to love—was an evolved lung-fish who crawled up on the bank right behind Jung and saw the psyche objectively. I can't do that; few can. But that's why I have often thought of him as not only "our Emerson" but "our Jung."

In one of my last conversations with Dr. Edinger, we talked of death, his death that he did not expect so soon but for which he was psychologically prepared. He said he would not resist Nature's demand and would go as quickly and as peaceably as she required. That night I dreamed a dream that I do not consider mine alone. Ed has said that the event of death opens us up to levels of the psyche that are otherwise closed. (We have already heard people say they had significant dreams surrounding the death of Dr. Edinger. I do not think these are necessarily personal dreams, but they belong to all of us.)

In this dream, I was with Dr. Edinger in a mausoleum that was also a library—but there were no books, all was a beautiful cool white-pink marble, and I had the impression that we were in ancient Greece. Ed sat at a little wooden table with a stack of large pages, some of them pink, and again I had the impression these were documents containing his last will and testament. It was a big stack—he's left us a lot! I sat at a distance at another little table going over some of the pages myself, trying to get a handle on them, taking notes. When I felt stuck, I asked Dr. Edinger if I could photocopy them—and he said that I could if that would help. Fortunately, there was an "ancient Greek" photocopy machine nearby (laughter): a means to duplicate what this man has done. My pages included an image of a Goddess, the French word *maitre* (which the dream translated not as "master" but as "marriage"), and a sort of cartoon version of "The Adventures of Oedipus."

I spoke briefly to Ed about this dream. He said, "Well, there seems to be a marriage going on, and marriage does have to do with death as the Ultimate Coniunctio." And I resolved to re-read his many chapters on *coniunctio* symbolism: in *Anatomy*, in *The Mystery of the Coniunctio* and *The Mysterium Lectures*, in his commentary on "The Song of Songs" in *The Bible and the Psyche*. He added that "The Adventures of Oedipus" in the dream reminded him that he had written about Oedipus in an essay on the "Hero archetype." And it was there I found gold from the Hoosier gold-maker.

In that essay, Dr. Edinger explains that Freud discovered empirically the first archetype in Sophocles' play, "Oedipus Rex," but had not read on from that tragic view of life to the next play, "Oedipus at Colonus"— where a Jungian point of view is required. In that drama, the humiliated king (or the defeated ego) is redeemed as a "sacred object" in touch with wisdom. All who touch this older Oedipus are blessed; even his corpse and tomb—his "mausoleum"—will bless the land. But why did I dream contents with these associations?

In *The Creation of Consciousness*, in his commentary *Goethe's "Faust"*, in his lectures on "Gnosticism and Early Christianity"—and in several other places—Edinger addressed the psycho-religious imagery of "life after death." He hypothesized that the imagery of going to Heaven, of becoming a star, of having one's merits deposited into some eternal treasury, had to do with the fact that authentic psychological achievements are never lost. We can understand this to mean that what Dr. Edinger achieved professionally in his writing and other forms of expression, in the healing effects he had upon so many patients—indeed, what he achieved personally by the impression his higher level of consciousness had upon those close to him—that cannot die. These fruits of his life have already been experienced and are a significant part of the collective *consciousness*. The books, after all, go into libraries.

But this is not what Edinger had in mind with his hypothesis concerning the "afterlife." He pointed to a deeper transpersonal meaning that we can now add to the new myth of meaning outlined by Jung. And it is this: When someone achieves a level of consciousness beyond the current collective level (regardless of its appearance in the world), that essentially private, invisible achievement does not die. That is the immortal "Resurrection Body" of traditional religion that "goes to Heaven" in the sense that it drops into the archetypal psyche as an increment of "light."

In this way, the collective *unconscious* evolves into a more ethical, more creative psychological force within us all. Or, as Dr. Edinger put it mythologically, "God is transformed into a more conscious Being." And so in this new sense, the extraordinary man whose death we mourn and whose life we celebrate has passed into "immortality," and we are already beneficiaries of his "last will and testament." His psychological achievement has just now contributed to an eternal "library" without books.

Yet my dream—our dream, if you will—suggests that we need not be passive heirs, that we can more actively make "copies" of Edinger's achievement. And I think that happens when we go to the psychological "spot" where he stood, the vantage point from which he saw so much, and try to see what he saw in Greek myth, in the Bible, in alchemy, in Blake and Melville, and saw in Jung—and felt about him. In fact, for me, Edward F. Edinger's perspective is his "tomb" in our midst that also blesses the land.

I close with lines from Sophocles' play, "Oedipus at Colonus," lines which Dr. Edinger quotes in his essay. The old king has been initiated by his wanderings, with his daughter, into sacred truths. And it becomes clear that the "spot" where his dead body rests will become a source of blessing for all who visit there. The tragic hero who has become a sacred object speaks:

> There is a place where I must die,
> and I myself, unhelped, shall walk before you there.
> That place you must not tell to any human being:
> . . . .
> No chart of words, shall mark that mystery.
> Alone you'll go: alone your memory
> shall frame it in that spot.
> . . . .
> But all of this you know without my telling you.
> And now to that spot—God signals me.

Poetry on the Four Stages of Life

READ BY PATRICK ROTH[223]

Edward Edinger asked for four poems to be read at his funeral, four poems he selected and inscribed, "Stages of my life." In his directions, the following note was penciled in: "This sequence is a kind of outline summary of my inner soul-life's biography – the Child, the Youth, the Man, the Old Man."

Childhood.

Excerpts from William Wordsworth's "Ode: Intimations of Immortality from Recollections of Early Childhood":

> There was a time when meadow, grove, and stream,
> The earth, and every common sight,
>   To me did seem
>   Appareled in celestial light,
> The glory and the freshness of a dream.
> It is not now as it hath been of yore –
>   Turn whereso'er I may,

---

[223] See "Letter to Dr. Edinger," below.

By night or day,
The things which I have seen I now can see no more.

. . . .

Our birth is but a sleep and a forgetting:
The Soul that rises with us, our life's Star,
   Hath had elsewhere its setting,
    And cometh from afar:
   Not in entire forgetfulness,
   And not in utter nakedness,
But trailing clouds of glory do we come
   From God, who is our home;
Heaven lies about us in our infancy!
Shades of the prison-house begin to close
   Upon the growing Boy
   But he
Beholds the light, and whence it flows,
   He sees it in his joy;
The Youth, who daily farther from the east
   Must travel, still is Nature's Priest,
   And by the vision splendid
   Is on his way attended;
At length the Man perceives it die away,
And fade into the light of common day.

Young Manhood.

"Dover Beach," by Matthew Arnold:

The sea is calm tonight.
The tide is full, the moon lies fair
Upon the straits – on the French coast the light
Gleams and is gone; the cliffs of England stand,
Glimmering and vast, out in the tranquil bay.
Come to the window, sweet is the night air!
Only, from the long line of spray
Where the sea meets the moon-blanched land,
Listen! you hear the grating roar
Of pebble which the waves draw back, and fling,

At their return, up the high strand,
Begin, and cease, and then again begin,
With tremulous cadence slow, and bring
The eternal note of sadness in.

Sophocles long ago
Heard it on the Aegean, and it brought
Into his mind the turbid ebb and flow
Of human misery; we
Find also in the sound a thought,
Hearing it by this distant northern sea.

The Sea of Faith
Was once, too, at the full, and round earth's shore
Lay like the folds of a bright girdle furled.
But now I only hear
Its melancholy, long, withdrawing roar,
Retreating, to the breath
Of the night wind, down the vast edges drear
And naked shingles of the world.

Ah, love, let us be true
To one another! for the world, which seems
To lie before us like a land of dreams,
So various, so beautiful, so new,
Hath really neither joy, nor love, nor light,
Nor certitude, nor peace, nor help for pain;
And we are here as on a darkling plain
Swept with confused alarms of struggle and flight,
Where ignorant armies clash by night.

Maturity.

Francis Thompson, "In No Strange Land" – and Ed wrote in the margin, "Also called, 'The Kingdom of God is Within Us.'"

O world invisible, we view thee,
O world intangible, we touch thee,
O world unknowable, we know thee,
Inapprehensible, we clutch thee!

Does the fish soar to find the ocean,
The eagle plunge to find the air --
That we ask of the stars in motion
If they have rumor of thee there?

Not where the wheeling systems darken,
And our benumbed conceiving soars! –
The drift of pinions would we hearken,
Beats at our own clay-shuttered doors.

The angels keep their ancient place –
Turn but a stone and start a wing!
'Tis ye, 'tis your estrangéd faces,
That miss the many-splendored thing.

But (when so sad thou canst not sadder)
Cry—and upon thy so sore loss
Shall shine the traffic of Jacob's ladder
Pitched betwixt Heaven and Charing Cross.

Yea, in the night, my Soul, my daughter,
Cry—clinging Heaven by the hems;
And lo, Christ walking on the water,
Not of Genesareth, But Thames!

Old Age.

Alfred Tennyson, "Crossing the Bar":

Sunset and evening star,
   And one clear call for me!
And may there be no moaning of the bar,
   When I put out to sea,

But such a tide as moving seems asleep,
   Too full for sound and foam,
When that which drew from out the boundless deep
   Turns again home.

Twilight and evening bell,
   And after that the dark!
And may there be no sadness of farewell,

When I embark;

For though from out our bourne of Time and Place
    The flood may bear me far,
I hope to see my Pilot face to face
    When I have crossed the bar.

To Ed from Dianne: Music (recorded)

"The Party's Over," performed by Wynton Marsalis

Ed's Final Message

TAPED COMMENT AND MUSIC, RECORDED JUNE 1, 1997.

I want to thank you all for coming. I appreciate it very much. And now, to take us out, I'd like to play a song sung by an anima figure of mine in my youth—Helen O'Connell. Here it is:

Music: "Please, Don't Talk About Me When I'm Gone." (laughter) Goodbye. (applause)

PART VIII

MORE TRIBUTES

Edward F. Edinger: December 13, 1922—July 17, 1998[224]
Janet O. Dallett

Edward Edinger is said to have done his writing entirely by hand, standing up, rarely changing a word—remarkable in view of the clarity, clinical acumen, psychological depth, and vast scope of the sixteen books and countless lectures and papers he produced. On my bookshelf and in my heart, his works sit side by side with Jung's. Together, the two sets of volumes comprise an entire training program in the theory and practice of Jungian analysis.

Moreover, Edinger was a brilliant psychotherapist. He worked methodically and with exceptional precision. "I have no intuition," he told me once, in his self-depeciatory way, "so I have to squeeze what I can out of every little image." Although he was careful not to impose his personal opinions, he would not compromise with psychological reality as he saw it.

I do not share Edinger's assessment that he was only an interpreter of Jung and not a creative thinker in his own right. His writings are a gold mine of original observations. He had a genius for making elusive concepts comprehensible, his outstanding sensation function providing a crucial corrective to the one-sidedly intuitive collective Jungian consciousness.

A shy, private, unassuming, and physically small man, Edinger carried the gift and the cross of a monumental psyche. He spoke, however, of Jung as the giant and himself as "one of the little ones." Perhaps he was protecting himself from an inner stature that he may not have felt he

---

[224] This tribute was first published in *The San Francisco Jung Institute Library Journal* 17, no. 2 (1998), pp. 79f. Janet O. Dallett, Ph.D., is a Jungian analyst with a practice in Port Townsend, Washington.

could carry outwardly. Nevertheless, the direct impact of his psyche, especially during the last decade of his life, could be overwhelming.

As Jung was numinous to Edinger, so Edinger was numinous to me. It annoyed him to hear me talk like that, and when I protested that he sometimes appeared to deify Jung, he retorted, "If you're going to project a God-image on a human being, a dead man is a safer place for it."

A preverbal tactile memory of beautiful, wonderful smoothness contrasting with ugly, disagreeable roughness prefigured Edinger's lifelong involvement with the problem of opposites. Gentle and supportive and at the same time almost unbearably fierce, provocative and contentious, he was a carrier of the paradoxical God-image of which he often spoke. In some of those who knew him he inspired passionate loyalty; in others, intense opposition.

One of Edinger's heroes was Abraham Lincoln, of whom he said in a videotaped interview,

> Lincoln arrived on the scene, and the nation did not split. . . . I've often reflected on the question of what gave Lincoln the strength—the endurance—through those terrible years of defeat and retreat. What kept him going? All he had to do was to agree to the splitting of the country. That's all. But the notion of union was the supreme image to him. I see the *coniunctio* archetype as operating there. That's the only thing that could have enabled him to endure.

Given the factionalism that so often splits Jungian training centers, his interest in these questions hardly seems academic.

Last spring, Edinger learned that tumors on his bladder, for which he went through eight surgeries in twenty-five years, had metastasized to his lungs. He refused treatment and died at home, cared for by his partner Dianne Cordic. It would have made him happy to know that the small, private funeral was set for July 26, the hundred and twenty-third anniversary of Jung's birth.

In Memoriam: Tributes to Edward Edinger (1922-1998)[225]
from England

ANDREW BURNISTON[226]

No one would deny that Dr. Edinger merits a substantial obituary, but it seems that no one in the British Jungian community either knew him personally or had an ongoing correspondence with him. To overcome this difficulty we have taken the unusual step of publishing a number of short pieces. Each one comments on his contribution to depth psychology or to theology from a different angle. I hope the cumulative effect will achieve what could not be done by way of a single memorial.

EAN BEGG[227]

To my regret, I never met Edward Edinger or heard him speak, but I have his video course on Analytical psychology, "Science of the Soul," in which he appears as a man of deep introversion, rare wisdom and integrity. It is, thus, unsurprising that, despite his reputation as the foremost exponent and exegete of Jung's teaching, he should have avoided the limelight and hurly-burly of international conferences. Furthermore, as the standard bearer of real Jung in the English-speaking world during a period of revisionism and denigration, he would have inevitably been forced to waste his time in the disputatious wrangling that has characterized the last quarter of a century.

I first became aware of Edinger's importance as a writer in 1972 when I was asked to review *Ego and Archetype*. I have found his doctrine of the ego-Self axis to be a sure guide to the balance essential to the individuation process. His chapter, "Christ as Paradigm of the Individuating Ego," remains a key text for the enlightenment that psychology can shed

---

[225] These tributes were first published in *Harvest Journal for Jungian Studies* 46, no. 1 (2000).

[226] Andrew Burniston is an independent scholar of world religions with a special interest in Jung. He is based in Oxford, England.

[227] Ean Begg is a Jungian analyst with a practice in London, England.

on theology. The rest of Edinger's remarkable work amplifies the various themes he introduces in the work. If I had to single out one other volume of Edinger to take with me on a desert island it would be *Anatomy of the Psyche*, the finest illustration of the practical uses of alchemy.

A few lines from his obituary to his teacher, Esther Harding, from *Spring* 1973 demonstrates—better than anything I could say—his conviction of the significance of Jung for our age:

> With the advent of Jung something truly new has appeared. Through his discovery of the reality of the psyche and of individuation as the process by which the individual realizes that reality, Jung has brought to birth a wholly new view of man and his world. This new view seems nothing less than the inauguration of a new aeon.

ANDREW BURNISTON[228]

In 1996, Richard Noll's polemical war against Jung and his psychology was at a crescendo, aided by an unquestioning media. Exasperated by the lack of any coherent response from the analytic community, I decided to write to Dr. Edinger. Here is his reply, handwritten and dated 4th of December:

> In response to your letter I must confess that I am not interested in an ongoing correspondence concerning how to respond to Noll and his ilk. I try to limit myself to worthwhile pursuits. "Malice is prowling the world." (1 Peter 5:8) It cannot be met in honest intellectual terms because it is cunningly fraudulent and does not seek the truth. Attention only feeds the beast.

I felt my initiative had placed me in the position of the young fool in the fourth hexagram of the *I Ching* (Wilhelm translation):

> It is not I who seek the young fool;
> The young fool seeks me . . .
> If he importunes I give no information

---

[228] See above, note 226.

Fortunately, Edinger did not react in the same way to my importunity and went on to ask:

> Why does Jung evoke such hatred? The inferior (especially when inflated) cannot stand the superior because the latter's mere existence discredits it. As Jung puts it, "He who is truly and hopelessly little will always drag the revelation of the greater down to the level of his littleness."

This quotation is from Jung's essay, "Concerning Rebirth," and it merits a full citation:

> When the summit of life is reached, when the bud unfolds and from the lesser the greater emerges, then as Nietzsche says, "One becomes Two," and the greater figure which one always was but which remained invisible appears to the lesser personality with the force of a revelation. He who is truly and hopelessly little will always drag the revelation of the greater down to the level of his littleness, and will never understand that the day of judgment for his littleness has dawned. But the man who is inwardly great will know that the long expected friend of his soul, the immortal one, has now really come to lead captivity captive, that is to seize hold of him by whom this immortal has always been confined and held prisoner, and to make his life flow into the greater life – a moment of deadliest peril. (*CW* 9i. par. 217)

This remarkable statement puts Edinger's controversial claim that Jung's psychology has revelatory status into perspective. The kind of revelation he has in mind was not like one of the great revelations directed to a large religious collectivity. Rather it entailed an individual revelation, the return of the long-expected friend of the soul. In the new "Psychological Dispensation" that Edinger anticipated, religious life will be centered on a one to one relationship with the Angel. As Henry Corbin put it, "The Angel is the face that God assumes for each one of us, and you find your God only when you recognize your face."

Edinger's letter concludes with:

> I trust that truth and consciousness will ultimately prevail. In my view, Jung is the most intellectually honest person ever to live. His honesty is a function of his supreme self-knowledge. If there is talk of fraudulence, one must seek it in the psychology of the accuser.

These words are echoed in the 26th hexagram, "The Taming Power of the Great." The "Commentary on the Decision" says:

> The Taming Power of the Great. Firmness and strength. Genuineness and truth. Brilliance and light. Daily he renews his virtue.

Around the time of drafting my letter to Dr. Edinger, the 26th hexagram proved to be applicable in an altogether unexpected way. I was returning home from work on the bus, and during the journey I had the distinct sense of a highway opening in the sky above me. I did not know what to make of it but later discovered this line of text in "The Taming Power of the Great":

> What could take place here on the Highway of Heaven other than moving in all grandeur in the Tao? (9 at the top, Wang Bi's I Ching, trans. R. J. Lynn)

My glimpse of Heaven's highway anticipated the reply I would receive from Dr. Edinger. I had allowed myself to be sidetracked by Noll's ridiculous propaganda war and needed a corrective. This was provided by Cheng Yi's commentary on the top line of the 26th hexagram: "The highway of Heaven is wide open and unobstructed. . . change and you get through."

THE REV. MICHAEL ANDERTON[229]

Edinger was one of the last great disciples of Jung. But he was also the interpreter who expanded Jung's thought, made it available to the non-specialist and increased it beyond the historical personality of the author. If to be a Jungian is to be one's own true self, then Edinger in coming to himself and to Jung had the courage to affirm beyond the fashionable iconoclasm, the greatness and lasting nature of Jung's psychology. Jung and Edinger stand together in the dialogue of spiritual wisdom that continues to be filtered down to our world.

---

[229] Michael Anderton is a Jungian analyst with a practice in Winchester, Hampshire, England.

It is generally accepted that the great man often has more influence after his life than during it, for he is ahead of his times which are not ready for the prophetic word. With Jung this is very much so, because his work is of a revelatory nature. It is for those who have eyes to see and ears to hear. For many it is a moment of truth when the veil of surface Jung is lifted and the numinous value of the soul is revealed. Edinger's genius lay in his ability to do this for Jung's work as a living and ongoing tradition.

Where then does Edinger reveal the truth of our times? Firstly, there is his interpretation of the spiritual dimensions of Jung's psychology. While Jung, in the massive nature of his intellect, seems abrasive, even violent of temper, Edinger brings a gentler, warmer spirit to the raw seminal Jung. This allays the primary encounter with Jung that can alienate sympathy and transform it into a spiritual gift of goodness, faith, and love. When I was in Zürich I noticed that the men had in their lockers Neumann's *Origins and History of Consciousness,* but in the lockers of the women was Edinger's *Ego and Archetype.*

There are three types of Jungians: 1) those who have not experienced the collective unconscious and therefore say it does not exist; 2) those who have read Jung from cover to cover intellectually without really entering into the experience with the whole person; 3) and those who have genuinely experienced Jung's insights into the soul in depth and are really living them. These latter are the great Jungians. They cannot be bothered with the shadow politics of the analytical world and seem to be almost hermits in comparison, wise men and women which the discerning student will almost smell out as the real analysts. Edward Edinger was such a one, and those who did not know him personally knew him through his books. These books are able to mediate the true symbolic wholeness of the marriage of the soul to God. To do this is to become one of the Friends of God through whom in the corpus of faith the believers enter into discipleship.

Jung and Edinger facilitate a divine marriage, for out of the greater comes the lesser, the bud of a new tree. Here is the humility of a great soul who had the courage to acknowledge and integrate a truly evolving vision beyond the enmity that attacks those who are rising to the heights.

One of the great Jungians was working at Bollingen by the lake at Zürich on the *Collected Works*, when she had a vision of the Knight of Bayonne, a warrior of peace, who was looking around the ruins of a holocaust in Rome. He retrieved a charred fragment of Jung's writing and said that it was something essential for our day and age. But a man's writings are only the fragments of his journey through conflict into wholeness. Edinger leads us to the core of Jung, and unites us to the spirit that brings wholeness to our divided and perplexed world soul.

JOCELYNE QUENNELL[230]

The Yoruba people of North Africa believe that when a person dies they become an ancestor. They then take on a "God-like" status in the living memory of the tribe and can be called upon in times of difficulty. So many cultures and societies throughout the world take time to pay homage to the ancestors; from the healing dances of the Xhosa people in South Africa, in which they stamp a circle dance to the ancestral spirits living beneath the ground, to the annual celebration of Ching Ming in Hong Kong, where the skies fill with smoke as paper money is burnt in the streets to honor them.

I was surprised that no tribute to Edward Edinger had taken place in Britain since his death. It is appropriate that *Harvest* has given this opportunity to acknowledge Edward Edinger's contribution to Analytical psychology, and I would like to express my personal appreciation of his work. His many books reveal a man who worked with deep dedication and devotion throughout his life to transmit the ideas, philosophy and symbolic richness of the Jungian tradition.

As a follow up to the Grass Roots Seminars in 1998, the Analytical Psychology Club showed the Edward Edinger videos: *The Science of the Soul: A Jungian Perspective*. These were filmed not long before he died, and I was fortunate enough to attend this viewing. He spoke with re-

---

[230] Jocelyne Quennell is a psychotherapist practicing in London, England.

markable clarity and conviction about the fundamental concepts and principles of depth psychology. Edinger began by affirming that "for an individual to be psychologically healthy they must have a living connection to the collective unconscious." Historically this has been accomplished through organized religion, mediated through mythology, ritual and dogma. He suggested that the decline of religion witnessed towards the end of this last millennium is indicative of a "catastrophic transformation from one age to the next." Edinger maintained that the agent of this transformation was human consciousness, and that individuation, as defined by Jung, was one vital means of this transition.

He went on to explore the relationships between politics, religion, and psychology. He discussed the concept of the shadow which tends to constellate many of the issues that surround these complex relationships. He commented on the dark side of the divine within the Jewish/Christian tradition; the image of Behemoth and Leviathan opposing Yahweh in the Old Testament and the image of Satan opposing Christ in the New Testament. He spoke of the "paradoxical God-image with its dual nature" in Jung's *Answer to Job*, and suggests that during analysis the individual is required to experience and observe this divine ambiguity in depth, and therefore "penetrate the paradoxical Self with human consciousness." Jung suggested that the reality of the shadow is something to be suffered, and it is a profound challenge to experience the truth of what he meant.

He concludes the series describing the rise of National Socialism in the twentieth century and underlines that World War II was due to a "psychological" rather than a "natural" disaster. He warns of the consequences of collective shadow projections during times of apocalyptic expectations. It is this "tremendous change in the God-image"— involving extremes of tension between the opposites in the collective psyche—which occurs during the assimilation of unconscious contents or the "integration of the shadow."

This is detailed by Edinger in *The Creation of Consciousness: Jung's Myth for Modern Man*. He suggests that "the hallmark of individuation is the differentiation of the individual psyche from its containment in the collective psyche." He claims this is a lonely task, accomplished one by one. Edinger saw his own purpose as contributing to the development of a "world view that relates man (ego) to God (archetypal psyche) and promotes the smooth transfer of energy from one realm to another."

Someone described the videos as Dr. Edinger's "final testimony," and they are important viewing. Another person described him as being at the "blue end of the spectrum" in Analytical psychology, by which I think they meant "on the spiritual or intellectual side." I hope that this "blue" dimension in Jung's psychology will continue to weave its way amongst the whole spectrum of colors in our contemporary understanding of Jungian and post-Jungian thought. It is this "blue" dimension of Edinger's work that I am celebrating here, in both the character of the man and the project he made his life's work.

I am sure we need as much help as possible from the "ancestors" during the times in which we live. Therefore, today, like the Xhosa people in South Africa, I am stamping for him. I hope that the rhythm and flow of the life blood of Analytical Psychology will continue to dance on, enriched by the spirit of his significant contribution to it.

JULIAN DAVID[231]

Edinger was for many years the main mediator of the deeper levels of Jung's thought, that stratum where psychology, religion, sociology, education and politics become different facets of one brilliantly illuminating way of seeing the world. Very few Jungians have taken a text like *Mysterium Coniunctionis* or *Aion* head on and guided a class through it. Edinger was a teacher who construed these texts as teachers used to construe a passage from Homer or Virgil. In that sense, "classical" is the right term for him. The classics are those things that are not for today or yesterday but all time. It is generally time that sorts them out. Edinger was, after von Franz, foremost among those who consider Jung a classic ahead of his time—one who intuited the new collective consciousness that will form and the new myth that will give it meaning.

---

[231] Julian David is a Jungian analyst practicing in Buckfastleigh, Devon, England.

Edinger's later works were seldom published deliberately, as is the case with many of von Franz's writings. He worked quietly away at his analytic work and teaching, and it was his pupils who thought the work was important, gathered the notes together and made them into such books as *The Aion Lectures*, *The Mystery of the Coniunctio*, *Transformation of the God-Image*, and so on. The books, therefore, do not come from anxious ego striving, as is usual with books, but from a long service to the psyche. I believe he thought that this was the only way the new myth could emerge—not from the ego but from the Self. His only personal importance, he believed, was that he was able to see the greatness of Jung.

The proof of such a pudding is very much in the eating. We do not know for sure whether Jung was an "epochal" man, as Edinger thought, or not. Time will tell. What we can say is that because he made those depths available to so many people, the grief for Edinger has something of the intensity of the loss of Jung himself. It is not the men themselves, but the places they opened up to us—and the gap that their deaths leave.

LETTER TO DR. EDINGER[232]
Patrick Roth

Dear Dr. Edinger,
I don't think you can imagine how much you have meant to me over the last several years. How much you—in your books and your tapes—have given me.

You have been my steady "Begleiter," my inspirer.

A few weeks ago, I finished your book on *Moby-Dick*—the only one of your books I had not read so far. For a writer like me, it is a house of treasures to contemplate and reflect on, a furnace-fire bright enough to make me conscious of the stakes, the ultimate stakes.

---

[232] Patrick Roth is a prize-winning German-American writer living in Los Angeles. The letter was sent May 22, 1998, shortly before Dr. Edinger's death.—Eds.

You have written a book for the hunter. For all those who hunt for the One-and-Only.

I've been re-reading *Anatomy of the Psyche*. Your work manages to filter out the reader's ambient neurotic noise; it peels away the layers of distraction, guides us down, brutally honest, admirably plain, to a level of encounter, prepares us for the necessary, the truly "not-wendige" dialogue with the shadow.

You have given yourself *and* Jung to a new generation of readers— and *listeners*. Do you know how important your audio and video tapes are? Your matter-of-fact voice has just the right degree of calming influence to let one open up to these images without getting too excited about their content. I think you have made Jung accessible by reaffirming the sensation-dimension of his work, a point of view bound to the objective Psyche by the facts of individual experience.

What an immense body of work you have supplied us with! Goethe's motto "Fertigmachen!" came to mind: "Finish it!" Sounds like the clarion call to individuation, doesn't it? Goethe would whisper it to himself whenever something was in danger of being procrastinated, left undone, left incomplete.

In the sense of Goethe's "Fertigmachen!", then, you have finished something here. Your books are clarion calls to individuation, one great "Fertigmachen!" for all who have eyes to see, ears to hear.

Thank you again!

EDITOR'S FOREWORD[233]
Daryl Sharp

The world is full of unconscious people—those who don't know why they do what they do. Edward F. Edinger did as much as anyone I know to correct this situation. To my mind, he was as true to Jung as one can be. Like Marie-Louise von Franz, he was a classic Jungian: he took

---

[233] Daryl Sharp is a Jungian analyst in Toronto and publisher of Inner City Books. This foreword appeared in Edinger's *Science of the Soul: A Jungian Perspective.*—Eds.

Jung's message to heart and amplified it according to his own talents.

For those who find Jung himself tough going, Edinger has been the preeminent interpreter for more than thirty years. In lectures, books, tapes, and videos, he masterfully presented the distilled essence of Jung's work, illuminating its relevance to both collective and individual psychology. Thus, for instance, his *Mysterium Lectures* and *Aion Lectures* are not only brilliant scholarly studies of Jung's major works, they are also a practical guide to what is going on in the laboratory of the unconscious.

Since Inner City published his book, *The Creation of Consciousness*, in 1984, Ed and I had more than a good publisher-author working relationship. I visited him a couple of times at his home in Los Angeles and routinely sent him complimentary copies of each new Inner City title as it was published. He always responded quickly with a hand-written letter giving his considered opinion of its merit or failings.

Every year or two, he offered Inner City Books a new manuscript. We took every one because they were always good meaty stuff. Clean, crisp writing, no padding, no blather. Never mind that they would never appear on the *New York Times* list of best sellers; they fit perfectly with our professed mandate "to promote the understanding and practical application" of Jung's work. We are proud now to have fifteen full-length Edinger books under our wing—and this one.

Personally, I loved the man. I feel privileged and fortunate indeed to be in a position to keep his work and spirit alive, to the benefit of everyone who strives to become psychologically conscious.

A MAN FULL OF GRACE[234]
Dianne D. Cordic

Ed's life, as I knew it for the past twenty years, was motivated almost entirely by his love of Jung and his wish to articulate the "great man's work." He spoke of himself as "an ordinary man in most respects except for my ability to see Jung's size." It was his perception of Jung's consciousness that informed and guided his writing and his life.

It was inspiring to observe Ed's creative process. He would get "an assignment" to write on a certain subject, do all the homework, then wait until new insight came. He did this paragraph by paragraph; and if it took an hour or a month, he would hold the topic with intensity and at the same time be completely vulnerable to the unconscious. When the psyche sent the insight, he wrote it down.

Ed spoke of what "belonged" to him to do. The subjects he mulled over and wrote about gave him access to the depths of the unconscious. When the news came of his terminal illness, he accepted it unconditionally as simply the last "assignment," to which he brought to bear the powerful force of his psyche. He lived the mystery of the unconscious and all its ramifications with complete devotion. For me, he was a man full of grace.

---

[234] Dianne Cordic is co-editor of this book. This tribute was first published in *Quadrant* 29, no. 1 (Winter 1999): 11; reprinted in *Psychological Perspectives* 39 (Summer 1999), p. 10.

Figure 15. Dianne D. Cordic with Edinger (1995).

Figure 16. George R. Elder with Edinger (1995).

ACKNOWLEDGMENTS AND PERMISSIONS

The tributes in this volume by George R. Elder and Dianne D. Cordic first appeared in *Quadrant: The Journal of the C. G. Jung Foundation for Analytical Psychology,* published by the C. G. Jung Foundation of New York, © copyright, The C. G. Jung Foundation for Analytical Psychology, Inc., 1999. Reprinted by permission.

Grateful acknowledgment is made to the following individuals for permission to print unpublished comments: Gilda Frantz, Clara Jendrowski, Margaret Phillips Johnson, Maurice Krasnow, Pamela Power, Patrick Roth, Donald Sloggy, and Deborah Wesley.

Grateful acknowledgment is also made to the following:

American Journal of Psychiatry

Edward F. Edinger, "Review of C. G. Jung, *Psychology and Alchemy, CW* 12." This review originally appeared in the November, 1954, issue of the *American Journal of Psychiatry.* Copyright © American Psychiatric Association. Reprinted by Permission.

Edward F. Edinger, "Archetypal Patterns in Schizophrenia." Reprinted with permission from the *American Journal of Psychiatry*, American Psychiatric Association (Copyright 1955).

American Journal of Psychotherapy

Edward F. Edinger, "The Collective Unconscious as Manifested in Psychosis" (1955).

Analytical Psychology Club of Los Angeles Bulletin

"Edward F. Edinger in Conversation with David Serbin" (1983) Reprinted with permission.

In Touch

Edward F. Edinger, "The Psyche and Global Unrest: An Interview" (1993). Reprinted with permission.

Harvest

"In Memoriam: Tributes to Edward Edinger" (2000) by Michael Anderton, Ean Begg, Andrew Burniston, Julian David, and Jocelyn Quennell. Used with permission.

Journal of Analytical Psychology

Edward F. Edinger, "Review of C. G. Jung, *Mysterium Coniunctionis*, *CW* 14" (1965). Reprinted with permission.

Edward F. Edinger, "In Memory of Marie-Louise von Franz (1915-1998)" (1998). Reprinted with permission.

Psychological Perspectives

Edward F. Edinger, "Review of C. G. Jung, *Nietzsche's 'Zarathustra'*: Notes of the Seminar" (1969). Reprinted with permission.

Edward F. Edinger, "Consciousness without Peer: A Review of Marie-Louise von Franz, *C. G. Jung: His Myth in Our Time"* (1976). Reprinted with permission.

Edward F. Edinger, "Paracelsus and the Age of Aquarius" (1996). Reprinted with permission.

Edward F. Edinger, "Individuation: A Myth for Modern Man" (1999). Reprinted with permission.

Edward F. Edinger, "The Question of a Jungian Community" (2005). Reprinted with permission.

Robin Robertson, "A Guide to the Writings of Edward F. Edinger" (1999). Reprinted with permission.

Quadrant

Dianne D. Cordic, "In Memoriam" (1999). Reprinted here as "A Man Full of Grace," with permission.

Edward F. Edinger, "An Outline of Analytical Psychology" (1968). Reprinted with permission.

George R. Elder, "Edward F. Edinger" (1999). Reprinted with permission.

The San Francisco Jung Institute Library Journal (now *Jung Journal: Culture and Psyche*)

Janet O. Dallett, "Edward F. Edinger: December 13, 1922—July 17, 1998" (1998). Reprinted with permission.

Spring Journal

Edward F. Edinger, "Ralph Waldo Emerson: Naturalist of the Soul" (1965).

Edward F. Edinger, "Eleanor Bertine: A Memorial" (1968).

Edward F. Edinger, "M. Esther Harding, 1888-1971" (1972)

Poetry

David Whyte (Many Rivers Company)
   "Song For the Salmon"
   "Self-Portrait"

Anthony Hecht (Alfred A. Knopf)
   "Dover Bitch"

An American Jungian

"Edward F. Edinger in Conversation with Lawrence W. Jaffe" (1990)

The editors have made every effort to secure permissions from holders of copyrighted material. They regret that some were not received by the time of printing.

INDEX
For Edinger essays, etc., refer to Contents pages

son's, 145; Jung's patient's, 50; Harding's, 177; Socrates', 145; *see* Edinger (his dreams); Jung (his dreams)

earth, 82, 89, 123-126, 241, 256; *see also* "Paracelsus and the Age of Aquarius"
ecclesia spiritualis, 156, 173, 204
Edinger, Edward F.
   autobiography/biography, 10, 33, 118, 208-212, 221-222; his religion, 39, 41, 219; his typology, 210-211, 242, 252, 261, 263; *see* "An American Jungian," Part 1 (Personal Life and Development)" 34-46; "The Memorial Service;" "More Tributes"; cluster chart method 26-27, 29, 121, 208, 248; *see* figs. 3, 11; chemistry as "object of fascination," 11, 40-41, 45-46, 218; *see* alchemy, science. His dreams: "pre-memory" of rough and smooth, 34, 262; Hoosier gold maker, 37, 252; grandfather 37; driving, unable to see, 42; heating fish blood, 45; flaming iris, 45-46; fallen tree, 46; one-celled organism, 132-135. Reference to his works: *Aion Lectures,* 27, 229, 246, 270, 273; "An American Jungian," 232; *Anatomy of the Psyche,* 26, 231, 252, 264, 272; *Bible and the Psyche,* 29, 254; *Christian Archetype,* 30, 75; *Creation of Consciousness,* 23-25, 226, 235, 245, 254, 269, 273; *Ego and Archetype,* 20, 26, 252, 267; *Encounter with the Self,* 24; *Eternal Drama,* 22; *Goethe's "Faust,"* 22, 58, 254; *Living Psyche,* 29; *Melville's "Moby-Dick,"* 21-22, 59, 271; *Mystery of the Coniunctio,* 27, 254, 271; *Mysterium Lectures,* 27, 229, 254, 270, 273; *New God-Image,* 19, 31, 229; "Romeo and Juliet," 62-63; *Science of the Soul,* 245, 263, 268; "Tragic Hero," 62; *Transformation of Libido,* 27, *Transformation of the God-Image,* 25, 40, 229, 271; "Vocation of Depth Psychotherapy," 248
ego, 20-21, 30, 65, 72-73, 76, 90-94, 98, 101, 103, 106, 110, 112, 114-115, 120, 123-126, 132, 134, 141, 145, 147, 155, 162, 167, 170, 173, 191-192, 195, 204-205, 218, 254; defined, 83-85; *see* consciousness and Self/collective unconscious 20, 30, 33, 61, 67, 95 132, 134, 154, 160-165, 192-193, 211, 235, 244-245, 269-274 (fig. 2); -Self axis 20, 68, 263 (fig. 2); ambivalent/devilish, 58, 183, 218; *see* inflation, sin; archetypalizing/ divinizing of, 62, 71, 125; *see* incarnation (continuing)
Elder, George, 14, 33, 251, 275
Eliot, T. S., 34
Emerson, Ralph Waldo, 11, 55, 57-58, 197, 208, 251-254; *see also* "Ralph Waldo Emerson: Naturalist of the Soul"
enantiodromia, 80, 184, 186; defined, 58
Eros, 86, 241; *see* love
ethics/morality, 25, 54-55, 157, 198, 251, 255
Europe, 10, 13, 34, 177; *see* "In Memoriam: Tributes," from England
evil, 25, 85, 214-215, 264-265; good and evil, 25, 54, 75, 91, 112-113, 194-195, 246; *privatio boni,* 152; *see* God (paradoxical); Satan, shadow, sin
extraversion, *see* typology

faith, 39, 57, 130, 167-168, 176, 182, 223, 245, 258, 267
father/grandfather, 36-37, 125; *see* archetype (Spiritual Father)
Faust, 129, 185-186, 190, 192-193, 230
   Goethe/*Faust* 57-60, 129, 159-160, 185, 193, 272, 272; *see* Edinger (*Goethe's Faust*); *see also* "Paracelsus and the Age of Aquarius."
fire, 25, 46, 91, 271
fish image, 45, 58, 184, 200-201, 223, 249-250, 253, 259; *see* Melville
Frantz, Gilda and Kieffer, 247-248
Freud, Sigmund, 46, 62, 77, 83, 93, 100-101, 107, 182, 220, 254; *see* Oedipus/Oedipal
frog image, 222-223
fundamentalisms, 41, 75, 129, 226, 228, 230;

Books by Edward F. Edinger in this Series

SCIENCE OF THE SOUL: A Jungian Perspective
ISBN 978-1-894574-03-6. (2002) 128 pp. $25

THE PSYCHE ON STAGE: Individuation Motifs in Shakespeare and Sophocles
ISBN 978-0-919123-94-6. (2001) 96 pp. **Illustrated** $25

EGO AND SELF: The Old Testament Prophets
ISBN 978-0-919123-91-5. (2000) 160 pp. $25

THE PSYCHE IN ANTIQUITY
  Book 1: Early Greek Philosophy
  ISBN 978-0-919123-86-1. (1999) 128 pp. $25
  Book 2: Gnosticism and Early Christianity
  ISBN 978-0-919123-87-8. (1999) 160 pp. $25

THE AION LECTURES: Exploring the Self in Jung's *Aion*
ISBN 978-0-919123-72-4. (1996) 208 pp. **30 illustrations** $30

MELVILLE'S MOBY-DICK: An American Nekyia
ISBN 978-0-919123-70-0. (1995) 160 pp. $25

THE MYSTERIUM LECTURES
A Journey Through Jung's *Mysterium Coniunctionis*
ISBN 978-0-919123-66-3. (1995) 352 pp. **90 illustrations** $40

THE MYSTERY OF THE CONIUNCTIO
Alchemical Image of Individuation
ISBN 978-0-919123-67-6. (1994) 112 pp. **48 illustrations** $25

GOETHE'S FAUST: Notes for a Jungian Commentary
ISBN 978-0-919123-44-1. (1990) 112 pp. $25

THE CHRISTIAN ARCHETYPE A Jungian Commentary on the Life of Christ
ISBN 978-0-919123-27-4. (1987) 144 pp. **34 illustrations** $25

THE BIBLE AND THE PSYCHE
Individuation Symbolism in the Old Testament
ISBN 978-0-919123-23-1. (1986) 176 pp. $30

ENCOUNTER WITH THE SELF
A Jungian Commentary on William Blake's *Illustrations of the Book of Job*
ISBN 978-0-919123-21-2. (1986) 80 pp. **22 illustrations** $25

THE CREATION OF CONSCIOUSNESS: Jung's Myth for Modern Man
ISBN 978-0-919123-13-7. (1984) 128 pp. **10 illustrations** $25

Also in this Series, by Daryl Sharp

Please see next page for discounts and postage/handling.

THE SECRET RAVEN
Conflict and Transformation in the Life of Franz Kafka
ISBN 978-0-919123-00-7. (1980) 128 pp. $25

PERSONALITY TYPES: Jung's Model of Typology
ISBN 978-0-919123-30-9. (1987) 128 pp. **Diagrams** $25

THE SURVIVAL PAPERS: Anatomy of a Midlife Crisis
ISBN 978-0-919123-34-2. (1988) 160 pp. $25

DEAR GLADYS: The Survival Papers, Book 2
ISBN 978-0-919123-36-6. (1989) 144 pp. $25

JUNG LEXICON: A Primer of Terms and Concepts
ISBN 978-0-919123-48-9. (1991) 160 pp. **Diagrams** $25

GETTING TO KNOW YOU: The Inside Out of Relationship
ISBN 978-0-919123-56-4. (1992) 128 pp. $25

THE BRILLIG TRILOGY:

1. CHICKEN LITTLE: The Inside Story *(A Jungian romance)*
ISBN 978-0-919123-62-5. (1993) 128 pp. $25

2. WHO AM I, REALLY? Personality, Soul and Individuation
ISBN 978-0-919123-68-7. (1995) 144 pp. $25

3. LIVING JUNG: The Good and the Better
ISBN 978-0-919123-73-1. (1996) 128 pp. $25

JUNGIAN PSYCHOLOGY UNPLUGGED: My Life as an Elephant
ISBN 978-0-919123-81-6. (1998) 160 pp. $25

DIGESTING JUNG: Food for the Journey
ISBN 978-0-919123-96-0. (2001) 128 pp. $25

JUNG UNCORKED: Rare Vintages from the Cellar of Analytical Psychology
Four books. ISBN 978-1-894574-21-1/22-8/24-2 (2008-9) 128 pp. each. $25 each

THE SLEEPNOT TRILOGY:

1. NOT THE BIG SLEEP: On having fun, seriously *(A Jungian romance)*
ISBN 978-0-894574-13-6. (2005) 128 pp. $25

2. ON STAYING AWAKE: Getting Older and Bolder *(Another Jungian romance)*
ISBN 978-0-894574-16-7. (2006) 144 pp. $25

3. EYES WIDE OPEN: Late Thoughts *(Another Jungian romance)*
ISBN 978-0-894574-18-1.. (2007) 160 pp. $25